SIGNAL 2017

The Second International Conference on Advances in Signal, Image and Video Processing

May 21 - 25, 2017

Barcelona, Spain

SIGNAL 2017 Editors

Claus-Peter Rückemann, Leibniz Universität Hannover / WWU Münster / North-German Supercomputing Alliance (HLRN), Germany

Ramiro Sámano Robles, CISTER Research Centre, ISEP - Instituto Superior de Engenharia do Porto – Porto, Portugal

Antonio J. R. Neves, University of Aveiro, Portugal

Printed from e-media with permission by:

Curran Associates, Inc.
57 Morehouse Lane
Red Hook, NY 12571

Some format issues inherent in the e-media version may also appear in this print version.

Printed by Curran Associates, Inc. (2017)

International Academy, Research, and Industry Association (IARIA)
412 Derby Way
Wilmington, DE 19810

Phone: (408) 893-6407
Fax: (408) 527-6351

petre@iaria.org

Additional copies of this publication are available from:

Curran Associates, Inc.
57 Morehouse Lane
Red Hook, NY 12571 USA
Phone: 845-758-0400
Fax: 845-758-2633
Email: curran@proceedings.com
Web: www.proceedings.com

TABLE OF CONTENTS

SIGNAL 2017

Foreword

The Second International Conference on Advances in Signal, Image and Video Processing (SIGNAL 2017), held between May 21 - 25, 2017 - Barcelona, Spain, continued the inaugural event considering the challenges mentioned above. Having these motivations in mind, the goal of this conference was to bring together researchers and industry and form a forum for fruitful discussions, networking, and ideas.

Signal, video and image processing constitutes the basis of communications systems. With the proliferation of portable/implantable devices, embedded signal processing became widely used, despite that most of the common users are not aware of this issue. New signal, image and video processing algorithms and methods, in the context of a growing-wide range of domains (communications, medicine, finance, education, etc.) have been proposed, developed and deployed. Moreover, since the implementation platforms experience an exponential growth in terms of their performance, many signal processing techniques are reconsidered and adapted in the framework of new applications. Having these motivations in mind, the goal of this conference was to bring together researchers and industry and form a forum for fruitful discussions, networking, and ideas.

We take here the opportunity to warmly thank all the members of the SIGNAL 2017 Technical Program Committee, as well as the numerous reviewers. The creation of such a high quality conference program would not have been possible without their involvement. We also kindly thank all the authors who dedicated much of their time and efforts to contribute to SIGNAL 2017. We truly believe that, thanks to all these efforts, the final conference program consisted of top quality contributions.

Also, this event could not have been a reality without the support of many individuals, organizations, and sponsors. We are grateful to the members of the SIGNAL 2017 organizing committee for their help in handling the logistics and for their work to make this professional meeting a success.

We hope that SIGNAL 2017 was a successful international forum for the exchange of ideas and results between academia and industry and for the promotion of progress in the field of signal processing.

We are convinced that the participants found the event useful and communications very open. We also hope that Barcelona provided a pleasant environment during the conference and everyone saved some time for exploring this beautiful city.

SIGNAL 2017 Chairs:

Wilfried Uhring, Université de Strasbourg, France
G. Sahoo, BIT Mesra, Ranchi, India
Malka N. Halgamuge, University of Melbourne, Australia
Laurent Fesquet, TIMA / CNRS-Grenoble INP-UGA, France
Jérôme Gilles, San Diego State University, USA
Constantin Paleologu, Polytechnic University of Bucharest, Romania
Zhongyuan Zhao, Beijing University of Posts and Telecommunications, China
Demetrios Sampson, Curtin University, Australia
Andrea Kutics, International Christian University, Japan
Pavel Loskot, Swansea University, UK

SIGNAL 2017

Committee

SIGNAL Steering Committee

Wilfried Uhring, Université de Strasbourg, France
G. Sahoo, BIT Mesra, Ranchi, India
Malka N. Halgamuge, University of Melbourne, Australia
Laurent Fesquet, TIMA / CNRS-Grenoble INP-UGA, France
Jérôme Gilles, San Diego State University, USA
Constantin Paleologu, Polytechnic University of Bucharest, Romania
Zhongyuan Zhao, Beijing University of Posts and Telecommunications, China
Demetrios Sampson, Curtin University, Australia
Andrea Kutics, International Christian University, Japan
Pavel Loskot, Swansea University, UK

SIGNAL Industry/Research Advisory Committee

Sergey Y. Yurish, Excelera, S. L. | IFSA, Spain
Filippo Vella, National Research Council of Italy, Italy
Jai Gopal Pandey, CSIR-CEERI (Gov. of India), India
Tudor-Catalin Zorila, Toshiba Cambridge Research Laboratory, UK

SIGNAL 2017 Technical Program Committee

Afaq Ahmad, Sultan Qaboos University, Oman
Kiril Alexiev, Institute for Information and Communication Technologies -Bulgarian Academy of Sciences, Bulgaria
Hamada Alshaer, University of Edinburgh, UK
Cristian Anghel, Politehnica University of Bucharest, Romania / Pentalog, France
Vijayan K. Asari, University of Dayton, USA
Nadia Baaziz, Université du Québec en Outaouais, Canada
Junaid Baber, Asian Institute of Technology, Thailand
Vesh Raj Sharma Banjade, Intel Coporation, USA
Haithem Ben Chikha, Tunisia Polytechnic School, Tunisia
Wassim Ben Chikha, Tunisia Polytechnic School, Tunisia
Stefano Berretti, University of Florence, Italy
Silvia Biasotti, CNR - IMATI, Italy
Jacques Blanc-Talon, DGA, France
Abdel-Ouahab Boudraa, Ecole Navale/Arts & Métiers ParisTech, France
Samia Boukir, Bordeaux INP (Bordeaux Institute of Technology), France
Rafael F. S. Caldeirinha, Polytechnic Institute of Leiria, Portugal
George Caridakis, University of the Aegean, Greece
Chin-Chen Chang, Feng Chia University, Taiwan
Jocelyn Chanussot, Université Grenoble Alpes, France
Amitava Chatterjee, Jadavpur University, Kolkata, India

Copyright Information

Chan-Vese Model with Semi-Implicite AOS Scheme for Images Segmentation: Biphase and Multiphase Cases

Messaoudi Zahir*, Berki Hemza†and Younsi Arezki‡

Ecole Militaire Polytechnique, Algiers, Algeria
* Email: messaoudi_zahir06@yahoo.fr
†Email:hemza.berki@yahoo.fr
‡Email:arezki.younsi@yahoo.fr

***Abstract*—Active contour models are designed to evolve an initial curve, called level set, to extract the desired object(s) in an image. Various models are used, such as Chan-Vese (CV) model. The CV model has the global segmentation property to segment all objects in an image. The problem with this model is the high time computing. In order to reduce it, our contribution in this work is the association of a semi-implicit Additive Operator Splitting (AOS) technique with the CV model in biphase and multiphase cases. In this paper, we present the new association in biphase and multiphase cases with simulations showing the efficiency of the proposed method.**

Keywords–Image segmentation; actives contours; Chan Vese; AOS scheme.

I. Introduction

Image segmentation is the task of partitioning an image into multiple regions. The most known region based method has been proposed by Mumford Shah [1] who have introduced a general optimization framework. To determine desired curves or surfaces, this method uses an energy functional based on regional geometric properties such as the area of the region, its contour length and the variation of individual pixel intensities inside and outside the region. However, the Mumford Shah [2] model cannot be easily implemented. The CV method [2] is a special implementation of Mumford Shah using a level set function for the case of two phases with two piecewise constants. The basic idea of CV model is to minimize energy functional by solving the Euler-Lagrange equation. This minimisation takes enough time in image segmentation.

To reduce the time of segmentation, Weickert et al. [3] provide a fast algorithm using the semi-implicit AOS scheme. The basic idea behind the AOS schemes is to decompose a multi-dimensional problem into one-dimensional ones that can be solved very efficiently. Then the final multi-dimensional solution is approximated by averaging the one-dimensional solutions. In [4], the authors present a combination of the semi-implicite AOS scheme and a narrow-band technique which is associated to the geodesic active contours. This association requires re-initialization for each iteration which is the weakness of the method. As solution, Kuhne et al. [5] provide a fast algorithm using an semi-implicit AOS scheme technique which is suitable both for the geometric and the geodesic active contour model. In [6], the authors propose a new selective segmentation model, combining ideas from global segmentation, that can be reformulated in a convex way such that a global minimizer can be found independently of initialization. They present the Convex Distance Selective Segmentation (CDSS) functional (based on CV model) which is associated with the semi-implicite AOS scheme. In our work, we use a level set representation of the CV model with the semi-implicite AOS scheme in order to improve the speed of the segmentation in biphase and multiphase cases.

This paper is organized as follows. Section 2 contains a review of level set method and the CV model for biphase and multiphase cases. In Section 3, we present the semi-implicite AOS scheme. Then, we present the CV model with the semi-implicite AOS scheme in biphase and multiphase cases in Section 4. Experimental results are given in Section 5.

II. Active Contour Models

In this section, we shall first provide an overview of level set theory before we get into the details of the CV model.

A. Level set method

A level set method is a numerical technique, which helps with tracking moving fronts to interfaces and shapes. This technique was first introduced by Osher et al. in [7], where the boundaries are given by level sets of a function $\phi(\mathbf{x})$, naming it as the level set method. This method is very successful due to a very easy way of following shapes that change topology. For a given interface $\Gamma = \partial\Omega$ as shown in Figure 1, the level set is independent of the parametrisation of the contour and can be used to represent the interface evolution. The idea of the level set method is to implicitly represent an interface Γ as the level set of a function ϕ. The level set function ϕ of the closed front Γ is defined as follows:

$$\begin{cases} \phi(\mathbf{x}) > 0 \ inside\ \Gamma \\ \phi(\mathbf{x}) < 0 \ outside\ \Gamma, \\ \phi(\mathbf{x}) = 0 \ on\ \Gamma. \end{cases}$$

Where $\mathbf{x} \in R^2$.

The adjusting contour at time t is denoted by $\phi(\mathbf{x}(t);t)$

$$\begin{cases} \phi(\mathbf{x}(t);t) > 0 \ inside\ \Gamma \\ \phi(\mathbf{x}(t);t) < 0 \ outside\ \Gamma, \\ \phi(\mathbf{x}(t);t) = 0 \ on\ \Gamma. \end{cases}$$

The level set value of a point on the contour with motion must always be 0.

$$\phi(\mathbf{x}(t);t) = 0 \tag{1}$$

A derivation of (1) with respect to t and after some manipulation, yields PDE equation:

$$\frac{\partial\phi}{\partial t} + F|\nabla\phi| = 0 \tag{2}$$

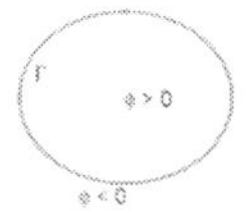

Figure 1. Representation of the interface Γ.

Where F stands for the speed in which the contour propagates in normal direction with an initial condition $\phi(\mathbf{x}, t = 0)$ (the initial drawn curve).

B. The CV model

1) biphase case: In [2], the authors present a special implementation of the CV method based on the use of the level set method to minimize the piecewise constant two phases Mumford Shah functional [1]. The advantage of this implementation is the possibility to detect objects whose boundaries are not necessarily defined by gradient and overcame the problematic tracking of Γ. For a given image u_0 in domain Ω, the CV model is formulated by minimizing the following energy functional :

$$\begin{aligned} F^{CV} = {} & \mu \int_\Omega \delta(\phi)|\nabla\phi| dxdy + \nu \int_\Omega H(\phi) dxdy + \\ & \lambda_1 \int_\Omega |u_0(x,y) - c_1|^2 H(\phi(x,y)) dxdy + \\ & \lambda_2 \int_\Omega |u_0(x,y) - c_2|^2 (1 - H(\phi(x,y))) dxdy \end{aligned} \quad (3)$$

Where μ, λ_1 and λ_2 are positive parameters, ϕ is a level set function, $H(\phi)$ is the Heaviside function and $\delta(\phi)$ is the Dirac function. Generally, the regularized versions are selected as follows:

$$\begin{cases} H_\epsilon(\phi) = \frac{1}{2}\left(1 + \frac{2}{\pi}\arctan\left(\frac{\phi}{\epsilon}\right)\right), \\ \delta_\epsilon(\phi) = \frac{1}{\pi}\frac{\epsilon}{\phi^2+\epsilon^2}. \end{cases} \quad (4)$$

The two piecewise constants c_1 and c_2 are defined as

$$c_1 = \frac{\int_\Omega u_0(x,y) H_\epsilon(\phi(x,y)) dxdy}{\int_\Omega H_\epsilon(\phi(x,y)) dxdy}, \quad (5)$$

$$c_2 = \frac{\int_\Omega u_0(x,y)(1 - H_\epsilon(\phi(x,y))) dxdy}{\int_\Omega (1 - H_\epsilon(\phi(x,y))) dxdy}, \quad (6)$$

The evolution equation is given by :

$$\frac{\partial\phi}{\partial t} = \delta_\epsilon(\phi)[\mu\nabla.(\frac{\nabla\phi}{|\nabla\phi|}) - \nu - \lambda_1(u_0 - c_1)^2 + \lambda_2(u_0 - c_2)^2] \quad (7)$$

2) multiphase case: The CV model for multiphase piecewise constant (we use two level set functions ϕ_1 and ϕ_2) is formulated by minimizing the following energy functional [8]:

$$\begin{aligned} F_{\epsilon,4} = {} & \int_\Omega (u_0 - c_{11})^2 H_\epsilon(\phi_1) H_\epsilon(\phi_2) dxdy \\ & + \int_\Omega (u_0 - c_{10})^2 H_\epsilon(\phi_1)(1 - H_\epsilon(\phi_2)) dxdy \\ & + \int_\Omega (u_0 - c_{01})^2 (1 - H_\epsilon(\phi_1)) H_\epsilon(\phi_2) dxdy \\ & + \int_\Omega (u_0 - c_{00})^2 (1 - H_\epsilon(\phi_1))(1 - H_\epsilon(\phi_2)) dxdy \\ & + \mu \int_\Omega |\nabla H_\epsilon(\phi_1)| + \mu \int_\Omega |\nabla H_\epsilon(\phi_2)| \end{aligned} \quad (8)$$

Where

$$c_{11}(\phi) = \frac{\int_\Omega u_0 H_\epsilon(\phi_1) H_\epsilon(\phi_2) dxdy}{\int_\Omega H_\epsilon(\phi_1) H_\epsilon(\phi_2) dxdy}, \quad (9)$$

$$c_{10}(\phi) = \frac{\int_\Omega u_0 H_\epsilon(\phi_1)(1 - H_\epsilon(\phi_2)) dxdy}{\int_\Omega H_\epsilon(\phi_1)(1 - H_\epsilon(\phi_2)) dxdy}, \quad (10)$$

$$c_{01}(\phi) = \frac{\int_\Omega u_0(1 - H_\epsilon(\phi_1)) H_\epsilon(\phi_2) dxdy}{\int_\Omega (1 - H_\epsilon(\phi_1)) H_\epsilon(\phi_2) dxdy}, \quad (11)$$

$$c_{00}(\phi) = \frac{\int_\Omega u_0(1 - H_\epsilon(\phi_1))(1 - H_\epsilon(\phi_2)) dxdy}{\int_\Omega (1 - H_\epsilon(\phi_1))(1 - H_\epsilon(\phi_2)) dxdy}, \quad (12)$$

Evolution equations of ϕ_1 and ϕ_2 are given by:

$$\begin{aligned} \frac{\partial\phi_1}{\partial t} = {} & \delta_\epsilon(\phi_1)\{\mu div(\frac{\nabla\phi_1}{|\nabla\phi_1|}) \\ & -[((u_0 - c_{11})^2 - (u_0 - c_{01})^2)(H_\epsilon(\phi_2)) \\ & +((u_0 - c_{10})^2 - (u_0 - c_{00})^2)(1 - H_\epsilon(\phi_2))]\} \end{aligned} \quad (13)$$

$$\begin{aligned} \frac{\partial\phi_2}{\partial t} = {} & \delta_\epsilon(\phi_2)\{\mu div(\frac{\nabla\phi_2}{|\nabla\phi_2|}) \\ & -[((u_0 - c_{11})^2 - (u_0 - c_{10})^2)(H_\epsilon(\phi_1)) \\ & +((u_0 - c_{01})^2 - (u_0 - c_{00})^2)(1 - H_\epsilon(\phi_1))]\} \end{aligned} \quad (14)$$

III. AOS SCHEME

The AOS method is proposed by Tai et al. in [9] and Weickert et al. in [3]. The AOS scheme guarantees equal treatment of all coordinate axes and is stable for big time steps. The scheme presents the semi-implicit algorithm based on a discrete non-linear diffusion scale-space framework. This scheme is applied to the m-dimensional diffusion equation and it is given in the following form:

$$\frac{\partial\phi}{\partial t} = div(g\nabla\phi) + f(\mathbf{x}, \phi). \quad (15)$$

$$\frac{\partial\phi}{\partial t} = \sum_{j=1}^{m} \frac{\partial}{\partial x_j}(g_j(\phi)\frac{\partial\phi}{\partial x_j}) + f(\mathbf{x}, \phi). \quad (16)$$

Where $[0, T] \times \Omega \subset \mathbb{R}^m$. The initial and boundary conditions are:

$$\phi(0, .) = \phi_0 \ \ and \ \ \frac{\partial\phi}{\partial n} = 0 \ \ on \ \partial\Omega,$$

We consider discrete times $t_k = k\Delta t$, where $k \in \mathbb{N}_0$ and Δt a semi-implicit discretization of the diffusion equation.

$$\phi^{k+1} = \left(I - \Delta t \sum_{l=1}^{m} A_l(\phi)\right)^{-1} \hat{\phi}^k,\ k = 1, 2, ... \quad (17)$$

Where $\hat{\phi}^k = \phi^k + \Delta t f$.

We may consider AOS variant (for m=2)

$$\phi^{k+1} = \frac{1}{2}\sum_{l=1}^{2} \left(I - 2\Delta t A_l(\phi^k)\right)^{-1} \hat{\phi}^k,\ k = 1, 2, ... \quad (18)$$

The AOS scheme offers one important advantage [10] : the operators $B_l(u^k) = I - 2\Delta t A_l(\phi^k)$ lead to strictly diagonally dominant tridiagonal linear systems, which can be solved very efficiently with Thomas algorithm. This algorithm has a linear complexity and can be implemented very easily.

To implement equation (18), we proceed in three steps [10]:

1) Evolution in x direction with step size $2\Delta t$:
   Solve the tridiagonal system $\left(I - 2\Delta t A_x(\phi^k)\right) v^{k+1} = \hat{\phi}^k$ for v^{k+1}.
2) Evolution in y direction with step size $2\Delta t$:
   Solve the tridiagonal system $\left(I - 2\Delta t A_y(\phi^k)\right) \omega^{k+1} = \hat{\phi}^k$ for ω^{k+1}.
3) Averaging:
   Compute $\phi^{k+1} := 0.5(v^{k+1} + \omega^{k+1})$.

IV. THE CV MODEL WITH THE SEMI-IMPLICITE AOS SCHEME

In this section, we present the CV model with the semi-implicite AOS scheme in biphase and multiphase cases.

A. *Biphase case*

From equation (7), we denote:

$$\begin{aligned} f &= \delta_\epsilon(\phi)\{-[\lambda_1(u_0 - c_1)^2 - \lambda_2 \\ &\quad (u_0 - c_2)^2] - \nu\}. \end{aligned} \quad (19)$$

To avoid singularities, we replace the term $|\nabla\phi|$ with $|\nabla\phi|_\beta = \sqrt{\phi_x^2 + \phi_y^2 + \beta}$ and denote $W = frac1|\nabla\phi|_\beta$.

Discretizing (7) by employing the AOS scheme, we get the following equation:

$$\phi^{n+1} = \frac{1}{2}\sum_{l=1} 2(I - 2\Delta t A_l(\phi^n))^{-1}\hat{\phi}^n \quad (20)$$

The matrices A_l, for $l = 1, 2$, are tridiagonal matrices derived using finite differences [11] and $\hat{\phi}^n = \phi^n + \Delta t f$. One modification is introduced on the AOS equation is in A_1 and A_1, where we add the term $\mu\delta_\epsilon(\phi^n)$ because we work directly with the level set function ϕ.

$$\begin{aligned} (A_1(\phi^n)\phi^{n+1})_{i,j} &= \mu\delta_\epsilon(\phi^n)\frac{E^n_{i+1,j} + E^n_{i,j}}{2h_x^2} \\ &\quad (\phi^{n+1}_{i+1,j} - \phi^{n+1}_{i,j}) \\ &\quad -\mu\delta_\epsilon(\phi^n)\frac{E^n_{i,j} + E^n_{i-1,j}}{2h_x^2} \\ &\quad (\phi^{n+1}_{i,j} - \phi^{n+1}_{i-1,j}) \end{aligned}$$

$$\begin{aligned} (A_2(\phi^n)\phi^{n+1})_{i,j} &= \mu\delta_\epsilon(\phi^n)\frac{E^n_{i,j+1} + E^n_{i,j}}{2h_y^2} \\ &\quad (\phi^{n+1}_{i,j+1} - \phi^{n+1}_{i,j}) \\ &\quad -\mu\delta_\epsilon(\phi^n)\frac{E^n_{i,j} + E^n_{i,j-1}}{2h_y^2} \\ &\quad (\phi^{n+1}_{i,j} - \phi^{n+1}_{i,j-1}) \end{aligned}$$

The algorithm of the CV model with the semi-implicit AOS in biphase case is:

1) Initialize ϕ^0 by ϕ_0, k=0.
2) compute f from equation (19),
3) Compute $c_1(\phi^k)$ and $c_2(\phi^k)$ by (5) and (6).
4) Compute $\phi^{(k)}$ using (20).
5) Check whether the solution is stationary. If not, repeat 2-5

B. *multiphase case*

From equation (13), we denote :

$$\begin{aligned} f_1 &= \delta_\epsilon(\phi_1)\{-[((u_0 - c_{11})^2 - (u_0 - c_{01})^2) \\ &\quad (H_\epsilon(\phi_2)) + ((u_0 - c_{10})^2 \\ &\quad -(u_0 - c_{00})^2)(1 - H_\epsilon(\phi_2))]\} \end{aligned} \quad (21)$$

From equation (14), we denote :

$$\begin{aligned} f_2 &= \delta_\epsilon(\phi_2)\{-[((u_0 - c_{11})^2 - (u_0 - c_{10})^2) \\ &\quad (H_\epsilon(\phi_1)) + ((u_0 - c_{01})^2 \\ &\quad -(u_0 - c_{00})^2)(1 - H_\epsilon(\phi_1))]\} \end{aligned} \quad (22)$$

To avoid singularities, we replace the term $|\nabla\phi_1|$ with $|\nabla\phi_1|_\beta = \sqrt{\phi_{1x}^2 + \phi_{1y}^2 + \beta}$ and $|\nabla\phi_2|$ with $|\nabla\phi_2|_\beta = \sqrt{\phi_{2x}^2 + \phi_{2y}^2 + \beta}$

The algorithm of the CV model with the semi-implicit AOS in multiphase case is:

1) Initialize ϕ_1^0 and ϕ_2^0 by ϕ_{1_0} and ϕ_{2_0} , k=0.
2) compute $c_{11}(\phi^k)$, $c_{10}(\phi^k)$, $c_{01}(\phi^k)$ et $c_{00}(\phi^k)$
3) compute f_1 and f_2 by equation (21) and (22).
4) Compute $\phi_1^{(k)}$ using (20) and $\phi_2^{(k)}$ using (20)
5) Check whether the solution is stationary. If not, repeat 2-5

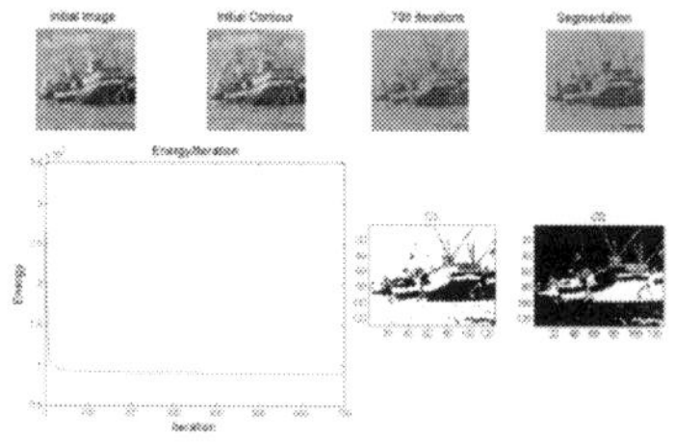

Figure 2. Segmentation by CV model (biphase case) of boat.

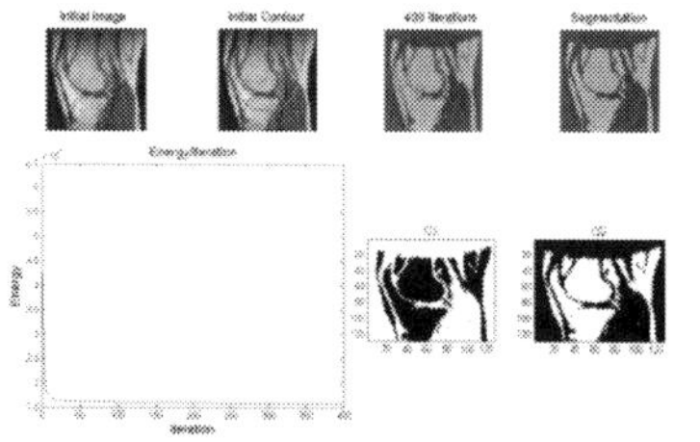

Figure 3. Segmentation by CV model (biphase case) of MR image of knee.

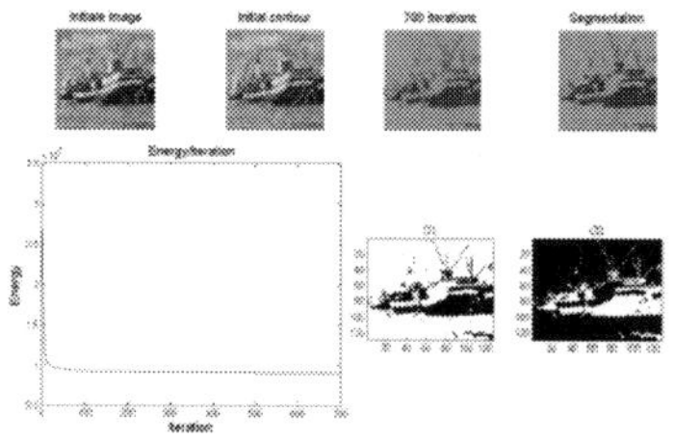

Figure 4. Segmentation by the CV model with semi-implicite AOS scheme (biphase case) of boat.

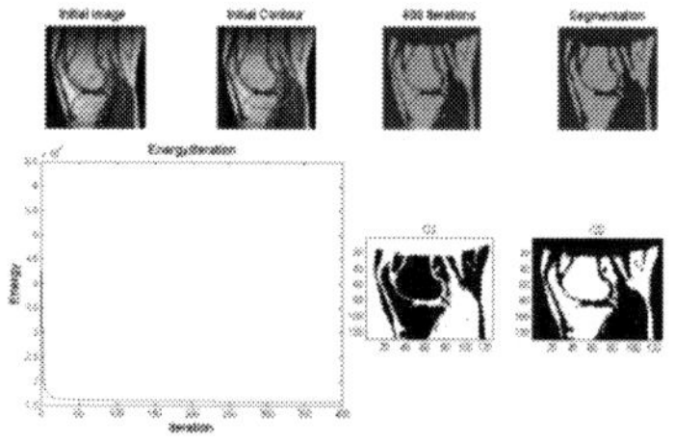

Figure 5. Segmentation by the CV model with semi-implicite AOS scheme (biphase case) of MR image of knee.

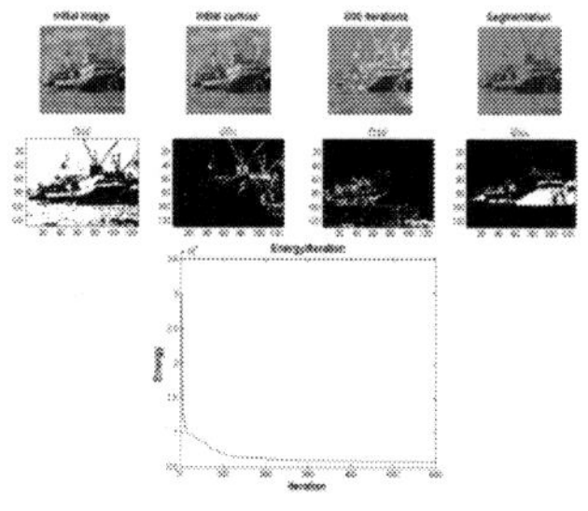

Figure 6. Segmentation by CV model (multiphase case) of boat.

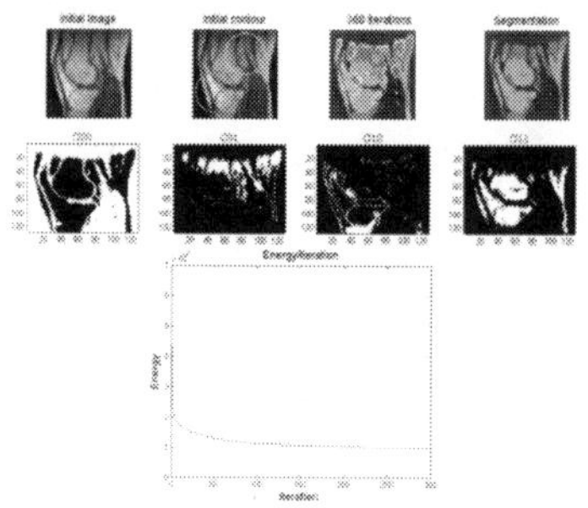

Figure 7. Segmentation by CV model (multiphase case) of MR image of knee.

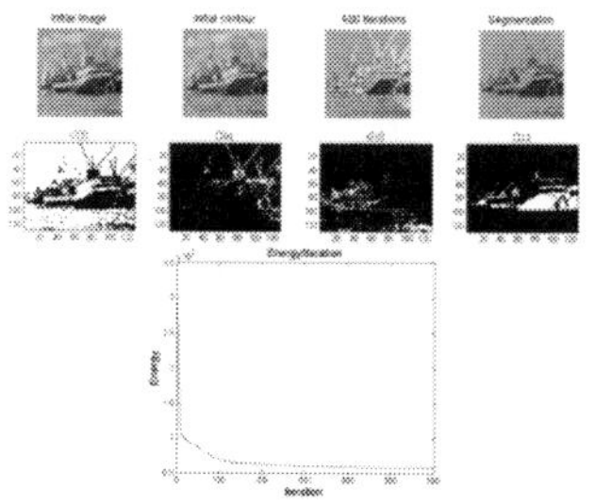

Figure 8. Segmentation by the CV model with semi-implicite AOS scheme (multiphase case) of boat.

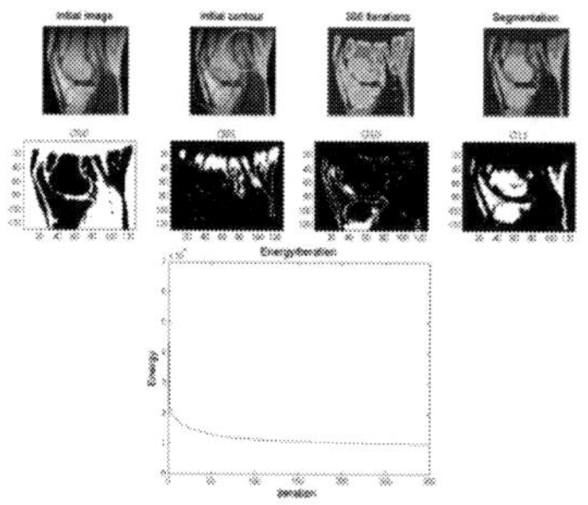

Figure 9. Segmentation by the CV model with semi-implicite AOS scheme (multiphase case) of MR image of knee.

V. EXPERIMENTAL RESULTS

In the biphase case, the constants are given as follow $\nu = 0$, $\Delta t = 1$ and $\lambda_1 = \lambda_2 = 1$. In Figures 2 and 3, we illustrate the segmentation by the CV model for boat and MR of knee images. In Figures 4 and 5, we show the segmentation by the CV model with semi-implicite AOS scheme for the same images. The segmentation illustrates the two phases and the results are almost similar for the two methods. For the multiphase case, the constants are given as follow $\nu = 0$ and $\lambda_1 = \lambda_2 = 1$. In Figures 6 and 7, we illustrate the segmentation by the CV model for boat and MR of knee images, but in Figures 8 and 9 we show the segmentation by the CV model with the semi-implicite AOS scheme for the same images. The two methods give exactly the same segmentation where we can see the four phases. The comparison study relative to time computing is summarized in Tables I and II; we deduce that the CV model with semi-implicite AOS scheme reduces the time computing of the segmentation by half.

TABLE I. COMPARISON BETWEEN THE CV MODEL AND THE CV MODEL WITH THE SEMI-IMPLICITE AOS SCHEME IN BIPHASE CASE.

Image	Boat		MR image of knee	
Method	*CV*	CV-AOS	*CV*	CV-AOS
CPU time (s)	110.6671	56.7532 s	51.9639	22.1521

TABLE II. COMPARISON BETWEEN THE CV MODEL AND THE CV MODEL WITH THE SEMI-IMPLICITE AOS SCHEME IN MULTIPHASE CASE.

Image	Boat		MR image of knee	
Method	*CV*	CV-AOS	*CV*	CV-AOS
CPU time (s)	158.2630	71.0429	70.3253 s	28.1270

VI. CONCLUSION

In this paper, we have used the advantages of the semi-implicit AOS technique in order to fast the CV model for image segmentation in biphase and multiphase cases. The experimental results show that the segmentation is done in the two cases, with the the superiority of the CV model with the semi-implicite scheme compared to the CV model concerning the time computing. As future work, we plan to associate the semi-implicit AOS technique with other active contour models.

REFERENCES

[1] D. Mumford and J. Shah, "Optimal approximations by piecewise smooth functions and associated variational problems," *Communications on pure and applied mathematics*, vol. 42, no. 5, pp. 577–685, 1989.

[2] T. F. Chan and L. A. Vese, "Active contours without edges," *Image processing, IEEE transactions on*, vol. 10, no. 2, pp. 266–277, 2001.

[3] J. Weickert, B. T. H. Romeny, and M. A. Viergever, "Efficient and reliable schemes for nonlinear diffusion filtering," *Image Processing, IEEE Transactions on*, vol. 7, no. 3, pp. 398–410, 1998.

[4] E. R. R. Goldenberg, R. Kimmel and M. Rudzsky, "Fast geodesic active contours," *IEEE Transactions on Image Processing*, vol. 10, no. 10, pp. 1467–1475, 2001.

[5] M. B. G. Kuhne, J. Weickert and W. Effelsberg, "Fast implicit active contour models," *Pattern Recognition*, vol. 2449.

[6] J. Spencer and K. Chen, "A convex and selective variational model for image segmentation," *Communications in Mathematical Sciences*, vol. 13, no. 6, 2015.

[7] S. Osher and J. A. Sethian, "Fronts propagating with curvature-dependent speed: algorithms based on hamilton-jacobi formulations," *Journal of computational physics*, vol. 79, no. 1, pp. 12–49, 1988.

[8] L. A. Vese and T. F. Chan, "A multiphase level set framework for image segmentation using the mumford and shah model," *International journal of computer vision*, vol. 50, no. 3, pp. 271–293, 2002.

[9] T. Lu, P. Neittaanmaki, and X.-C. Tai, "A parallel splitting-up method for partial differential equations and its applications to navier-stokes equations," *RAIRO-Modélisation mathématique et analyse numérique*, vol. 26, no. 6, pp. 673–708, 1992.

[10] J. Weickert and G. Kühne, "Fast methods for implicit active contour models," *Geometric Level Set Methods in Imaging, Vision, and Graphics*, pp. 43–57, 2003.

[11] L. Rada and K. Chen, "Improved selective segmentation model using one level-set," *Journal of Algorithms & Computational Technology*, vol. 7, no. 4, pp. 509–540, 2013.

Principal Fiber Bundles and Geometry of Color Spaces

Edoardo Provenzi

Laboratoire MAP5 (UMR CNRS 8145)
Université Paris Descartes
45 rue des Saints Pères, 75006, Paris, France
Email: edoardo.provenzi@parisdescartes.fr

Abstract—**In 1974, H.L.Resnkikoff published an inspiring paper about the use of differential geometry to study, among others, the intrinsic shape of the space of perceived colors and the Riemannian metrics on it. The mathematical techniques that he used is shared with modern theories of theoretical physics, which are far from being a common background for scientists in color vision and processing. Due to this, Resnikoff's paper remained unnoticed for decades. In this brief contribution, some insights about how to update Resnikoff's ideas will be given and discussed in relationship with a moder theory of color spaces and to the mathematical concept of principal fiber bundle.**

Keywords–Geometry of Color Spaces; Principal Fiber Bundles; Human Perception; Applications to Perceived Color Distances.

I. Resnikoff's framework for the space of perceived colors

In the 1974 paper [1], H.L. Resnikoff analyzed the geometrical and topological properties of the space of perceived colors $\mathcal{P}$ with a high level mathematical rigor. He decided to start from Schrödinger's axioms [2] for $\mathcal{P}$: *Axiom 1* (Newton 1704): if $x \in \mathcal{P}$ and $\alpha \in \mathbb{R}^+$, then $\alpha x \in \mathcal{P}$. *Axiom 2*: if $x \in \mathcal{P}$ then it does not exist any $y \in \mathcal{P}$ such that $x + y = 0$. *Axiom 3* (Grassmann 1853, Helmholtz 1866): for every $x, y \in \mathcal{P}$ and for every $\alpha \in [0, 1]$, $\alpha x + (1 - \alpha)y \in \mathcal{P}$. *Axiom 4* (Grassmann 1853): every collection of more than three perceived colors is a linear dependent family in the vector space V spanned by the elements of $\mathcal{P}$. Note, in particular, that Axiom 3 implies that $\mathcal{P}$ is closed under convex linear combinations, i.e., every two colors in $\mathcal{P}$ can be joined by a line segment, i.e., $\mathcal{P}$ is *convex*.

Resnikoff added another axiom, that of *local homogeneity* of $\mathcal{P}$ with respect to changes of background illumination of the visual scene. If X is a topological space and G is a group of transformations that acts on X, then X is called a *homogeneous space with respect to* G if, for any two points $x, y \in X$, there exists a transformation $g \in G$ such that $g(x) = y$, i.e., any two points of X can be joined by an opportune transformation g induced by G. X is only *locally homogeneous with respect to* G if this property holds only locally, i.e., if for every $x \in X$ there is an open neighborhood U_x containing it and such that every $x' \in U_x$ can be written as $x' = g(x)$ for a certain $g \in G$. The reason for introducing this further axiom is that it is possible to modify a color to reach a 'very similar' color with a change of illumination and this means that $\mathcal{P}$ should be locally homogeneous with respect to the group of transformations of illuminations.

Resnikoff claimed that this group can be assumed as the following:

$$GL(\mathcal{P}) := \{g \in GL(V) \mid g(x) \in \mathcal{P} \ \forall x \in \mathcal{P}\},$$

where $GL(V)$ is the group of orientation-preserving invertible linear operators on V, or, equivalently, the group of real $n \times n$ matrices with determinant greater than zero, where $n = dim(V) \leq 3$ thanks to Axiom 4. He justifies this choice from the consideration that Axiom 1 implies that $\mathcal{P}$ is a cone embedded in V and so a general transformation of illumination must preserve the orientation of the cone and it must also be invertible, since it is possible to turn back to the initial conditions of illuminations. The condition $g(x) \in \mathcal{P}$ is perfectly natural because after the change of illumination we can still perceive the colors.

The observation that a change of illumination slightly modifies the perception of colors of a visual scene can thus be stated in this mathematical formalism by saying that $\mathcal{P}$ is locally homogeneous with respect to $GL(\mathcal{P})$. But, thanks to Axiom 3, for every couple of perceived colors $x, y \in \mathcal{P}$ there exists the line segment that join x to y. This segment is compact, hence it can be covered by a finite partition of open neighborhoods $U_1, \ldots, U_n$ and the color x can be moved along this line segment passing from a neighborhood to the next one with the transformations $g_1, \ldots, g_n$. Thus, the global transformation that enables us to pass from x to y is the composition of the single transformations, i.e., $y = g(x)$, $g = g_n \circ \cdots \circ g_1$ and so local homogeneity for the convex $\mathcal{P}$ implies its global homogeneity.

For this reason, Resnikoff postulates a fifth axiom on the structure of the color space: *Axiom 5* (Resnikoff 1974): $\mathcal{P}$ is globally homogeneous with respect to the group of transformations of illumination $GL(\mathcal{P})$.

Starting from the set of axioms 1-5 and by using Lie groups and algebras representation theory [3], Resnikoff managed showed that the only two geometrical structures compatible with these axioms are:

$$\mathcal{P} \simeq \mathbb{R}^+ \times \mathbb{R}^+ \times \mathbb{R}^+,$$

or

$$\mathcal{P} \simeq \mathbb{R}^+ \times SL(2, \mathbb{R})/SO(2),$$

where $SL(2, \mathbb{R})$ is the group of 2×2 matrices with real entries and determinant $+1$ and $SO(2)$ is the group of matrices that perform rotations in the plane $\mathbb{R}^2$.

The first geometrical structure agrees with the usual trichromatic space, such as RGB, XYZ, and so on. The Cartesian product, which represents the second one, is totally new.

Moreover, he found out that the only color constancy metric compatible with the homogeneous structure of the RGB-like model is precisely the metric found by Stiles, i.e.,

$$ds^2 = \alpha_1 \left(\frac{dx_1}{x_1}\right)^2 + \alpha_2 \left(\frac{dx_2}{x_2}\right)^2 + \alpha_3 \left(\frac{dx_3}{x_3}\right)^2,$$

where $x_j \in \mathbb{R}^+$ and α_j are positive real constants for $j = 1, 2, 3$. This metric agrees with the one found by Stiles with totally different methods.

The distinction of perception between the color x and the color y is calculated with the integral

$$d(x, y) = \int_\gamma ds \qquad \gamma(0) = x, \gamma(1) = y,$$

where γ is the unique geodesic arc (i.e the arc of minimal length) between x and y. For more information, the interested reader is referred to [4].

II. Updating Resnikoff's model: Principal fiber bundles

Resnikoff's model is one of the most elegant treatises on color perception and it paved the road to the introduction of some advanced mathematical techniques used in theoretical physics, e.g., differential geometry, Lie groups and algebras representation theory and Jordan algebras, to the theory of color perception. In this section, it is discussed the idea that another fundamental mathematical object commonly used in classical and quantum field theory of mathematical physics, the principal fiber bundle, can be a fundamental (missing) piece in the Resnikoff framework.

First of all, note that Axiom 1 fails for $\alpha \simeq 0$ and $\alpha \gg 1$. In fact, as α approaches zero, the retinal cones responsible for color vision do not work anymore and retinal rods are activated, allowing only black and white vision, which can be identified with achromatic colors in $\mathcal{P}$. However, rods sensitivity is finite, so that under a certain threshold $\bar{\alpha}$, vision ceases and with it the geometric structure of $\mathcal{P}$. The same can be said when α overcomes an upper limit, after which retinal cones saturate and sight is lost.

A second issue is that, in Resnikoff's model, only independent light stimuli over a uniform background are considered; however, color vision in real world conditions is much more complex. In fact, color perception of natural scenes is intrinsically local: hue, saturation and brightness of a patch strongly depend on the surrounding patches, a phenomenon called 'induction'. This is the reason why one must distinguish between spectral colors of light sources isolated from the rest of the visual field, and *color in context*. Induction analysis is an active research field both in image processing and cognitive psychology, see e.g., [5]–[9].

When induction phenomena are taken into account, it is clear that if we want to represent color differences a spatially variant Riemannian metric on $\mathcal{P}$ must be considered, instead of a global one. This is where the framework of principal fiber bundles [10] [11] can be helpful.

Without entering in the very complicated matter of field theory, it is nevertheless possible to give an idea of what fiber bundles are by considering a *field* as an entity which assigns to every point x of a manifold M a point f of another manifold F, representing the value taken by the field in x. A *configuration* of a field on an open subset U of M is a map $\varphi : U \subset M \to F$ completely defined by its graph, i.e., by the set $\mathrm{Graph}(\varphi) := \{(x, f) \in U \times F \mid f = \varphi(x)\}$.

It is quite natural to think at $U \times F$ as the local model of a more complicated geometric structure obtained by 'gluing together' these Cartesian products (in a suitable way). This structure is precisely what is called a fiber bundle over M with standard fiber F. Hence, naively, a fiber bundle can be seen as a generalization of the concept of a manifold, now modeled on a Cartesian product instead of an Euclidean space. A fiber bundle is a *principal bundle* if the standard fiber is a Lie group G.

The importance of considering Lie groups has been discussed in the previous section, thus it seems necessary to consider, among all fiber bundles, principal fiber bundles as the candidates to provide the rich geometrical structure needed to introduce in Resnikoff's framework the phenomenon of local induction. A formalization of this idea can lead to new, context-dependent, color metrics rigorously obtained from first principles and not by ad-hoc procedures.

III. Conclusion

The Resnikoff's model of perceived color space has been recalled and some critics about its assumptions have been pointed out. These observations can be the staring point for a new analysis of color spaces, based on the mathematical concept of principal fiber bundles, which it has been motivated to seem the most adequate framework to further develop Resnikoff's analysis.

References

[1] H. Resnikoff, "Differential geometry and color perception," Journal of Mathematical Biology, vol. 1, 1974, pp. 97–131.

[2] E. Schrödinger, "Grundlinien einer theorie der farbenmetrik im tagessehen (outline of a theory of colour measurement for daylight vision). available in english in sources of colour science, ed. david l. macadam, the mit press (1970), 13482." Annalen der Physik, vol. 63, no. 4, 1920, pp. 397–456; 481–520.

[3] A. W. Knapp, Representation Theory of Semisimple Groups: An Overview Based on Examples (PMS-36). Princeton university press, 2016.

[4] E. Provenzi, "A differential geometry model for the perceived colors space," International Journal of Geometric Methods in Modern Physics, vol. 13, no. 08, 2016, p. 1630008.

[5] H. Wallach, "Brightness constancy and the nature of achromatic colors," Journal of Experimental Psychology, vol. 38, no. 3, 1948, pp. 310–324.

[6] M. Rudd and I. Zemach, "Quantitive properties of achromatic color induction: An edge integration analysis," Vision Research, vol. 44, 2004, pp. 971–981.

[7] E. Provenzi, L. De Carli, A. Rizzi, and D. Marini, "Mathematical definition and analysis of the retinex algorithm," Journal of the Optical Society of America A, vol. 22, no. 12, December 2005, pp. 2613–2621.

[8] R. Palma-Amestoy, E. Provenzi, M. Bertalmío, and V. Caselles, "A perceptually inspired variational framework for color enhancement," IEEE Transactions on Pattern Analysis and Machine Intelligence, vol. 31, no. 3, 2009, pp. 458–474.

[9] G. Gronchi and E. Provenzi, "A variational model for context-driven effects in perception and cognition," Journal of Mathematical Psychology, vol. 77, 2017, pp. 124–141.

[10] J. Baez and J. Muniain, Gauge fields, knots and gravity. World Scientific Publishing Co Inc, 1994, vol. 4.

[11] L. Fatibene and M. Francaviglia, Natural and gauge natural formalism for classical field theorie: a geometric perspective including spinors and gauge theories. Springer Science & Business Media, 2003.

A Low Cost Technology-based Device for Breath Analysis and Self-monitoring

Danila Germanese

Institute of Information Science and Technology,
ISTI-CNR, Pisa, Italy
mail: danila.germanese@isti.cnr.it

Mario D'Acunto

Institute of Matter Science
ISM-CNR, Rome, Italy
mail: mario.dacunto@ism.cnr.it

Massimo Magrini
and Marco Righi

Institute of Information Science and Technology,
ISTI-CNR, Pisa, Italy
mail: name.surname@isti.cnr.it

Ovidio Salvetti

Institute of Information Science and Technology,
ISTI-CNR, Pisa, Italy
mail: ovidio.salvetti@isti.cnr.it

***Abstract*—Here, we describe the development of a portable device, based on low cost technology, able to collect and analyze in real time the composition of the breath. Despite its great potential, breath analysis is not widely used in clinical practice: high costs for standard analytical instrumentation (i.e., gas chromatograph-mass spectrometer), the need for specialized personnel able to read the results and the lack of standardized protocols to collect breath samples, set limits to its exploitation. The presented device, named *Wize Sniffer*, is based on commercial gas sensors and a widely employed open-source controller; in addition, it is very easy to use also for non-specialized personnel. The *Wize Sniffer* is composed of three modules: signal measurement, signal conditioning and signal processing. The idea was born in the framework of the European SEMEiotic Oriented Technology for Individual's CardiOmetabolic risk self-assessmeNt and Self-monitoring (SEMEOTICONS) Project, in order to monitor individual's lifestyle by detecting in the breath those molecules related to the noxious habits for cardio-metabolic risk. Nonetheless, the modular configuration of the *Wize Sniffer* makes it usable also for other applications by changing the type of the gas sensors according to the molecules to be detected.**

Keywords–Bio-signals; Breath analysis; Signal processing; E-noses; Semiconductor gas sensors.

I. INTRODUCTION

Breath analysis is a technique as new as promising. On one hand, it enables the monitoring of biochemical processes: the volatile organic compounds (VOCs) from the metabolic processes are generated within the body, travel via the blood, participate to the alveolar exchanges and appear in exhaled breath; on the other hand, breath is easily and non-invasively accessible [1], [2], [3]. Many studies aim for assessing the clinical potential of breath analysis: exhaled pentane and ethane were investigated as lipid per-oxygenation product in case of oxidative stress [4]; breath ammonia can be a useful biomarkers both for the evaluation of clinical treatments in case of renal diseases [5], [6] and for monitoring the level of severity in case of liver diseases [7]. Nonetheless, despite its great potential, the use of breath analysis in clinical diagnostic is limited because of the high costs of the specific, high accurate instrumentation (i.e., gas chromatograph, mass spectrometer) and the need of expert personnel to perform the analysis, which also are very time consuming [5].
Recently, e-noses are gaining the attention of the scientific community. Formerly designed for broader applications (environmental gases monitoring, for instance), in recent years the idea of exploiting e-noses also for clinical applications has been arisen [8]. E-noses allow for performing breath analysis in a very short time, being quicker than a gas chromatograph. Since they are able to follow the trend in time of breath molecules, in many studies they have been employed in different fields of medicine: in oncology, for instance, to monitor volatile biomarkers related to cancer [9], in infectiology [10], in respiratory medicine to evaluate asthma [11]. Nevertheless, the majority of such e-noses exploit very expensive technology [12], [13] or requires complex circuitry [14], [15]. By developing the *Wize Sniffer* (WS), presented in this paper, we aimed to overcome this limitations:

- it is a portable device for the monitoring of a number of breath molecules in real time;
- it is entirely based on low cost technology: the employed gas sensors are commercial, semiconductor-based and easily embeddable in the circuitry; breath signals are analyzed by a widely employed open source controller: Arduino Mega2560;
- the WS is very easy to use, also for non-specialized personnel. However, it is programmed in order to send breath analysis results also to a remote care center.

The WS was conceived in the framework of SEMEOTICONS European Project [16]. It aimed to develop the *Wize Mirror*, a multi-sensory platform having the appearance of a mirror, able to assess individual's well-being state by detecting in the human face all those signs related to cardio-metabolic risk [17]. The WS was designed to be integrated in *Wize Mirror*'s hardware platform in order to detect in human breath the molecules related to those noxious habits for cardio-metabolic risk: alcohol intake, wrong diet,

smoke. Not only: we aimed to develop a device, which could be also used in a stand-alone configuration and for broader applications, thanks to its modular configuration [18], [19].
In the paper, Section II lists the molecules detected by the WS and describes the device's general architecture; Section III explains the WS functionality tests and the experimental results, later discussed in Section IV.

II. The Wize Sniffer, how it works

A. *Breath compounds detected by the WS*

The WS is composed of an array of semiconductor-based gas sensors able to detect those breath VOCs considered as indices of noxious habits for cardio-metabolic risk:

- **Carbon monoxide** (CO): it is the major compound of cigarette smoke and it is very dangerous, even in minimal part. Its baseline value for a non-smoker subject is round about 3.5ppm, and it reaches 14-30ppm in smokers;
- **Oxygen and carbon dioxide** (O_2 and CO_2): their variations can be considered as a measure of the metabolism, that means, how much O_2 is retained in the body, and how much CO_2 is produced as a by-product of cellular metabolism. Their baseline values are respectively 40000ppm and 13-15%;
- **Hydrogen** (H_2): it is related to the carbohydrates breakdown in the intestine and in the oral cavity by anaerobic bacteria. Its baseline value is round about 9.1ppm, but it may vary from an individual to another, especially in case of lactose intolerance;
- **Ethanol** (C_2H_6O): it derives from alcoholic drinks. Ethanol breakdown leads to an accumulation of free radicals into the cells, causing oxidative stress. Its baseline value is round about 0.62ppm;
- **Hydrogen sulfide** (H_2S): it is a vascular relax agent; for instance, it has a therapeutic effect in hypertension. Its baseline value is round about 0.33ppm.

B. *Wize Sniffer, hardware and software*

In Figure 1, WS' hardware is shown. The user blows once into a disposable mouthpiece, placed at the beginning of a corrugated tube. A flowmeter allows for assessing the exhaled gases volume. A heat and moisture exchanger (HME) filter absorbs the water vapor present in exhaled breath, reducing the humidity which affects gas sensors' behavior. The gases reach the sampling box (whose capacity is 600ml according to the tidal volume [20]), which can be considered as the signal measurement module. Indeed, within the sampling box, made up of ABS and Delrin, six semiconductor-based gas sensors are placed. Other two gas sensors work in *flowing regime* by means of a sampling pump, which inject the gases from the sampling box at a fixed rate (120ml/sec). Within the gas sampling box also a sensor for temperature and humidity (Sensirion SHT11) is placed. Sensors' output are pre-processed by a signal conditioning module. A series of voltage buffer amplifiers is used to transfer sensors' signal from the measurement module to the micro-controller board: an Arduino Mega2560 with Ethernet module (which is low cost, widely employed and has an open source integrated development environment). At the end of a breath test, a flushing pump "purges" the sampling box to

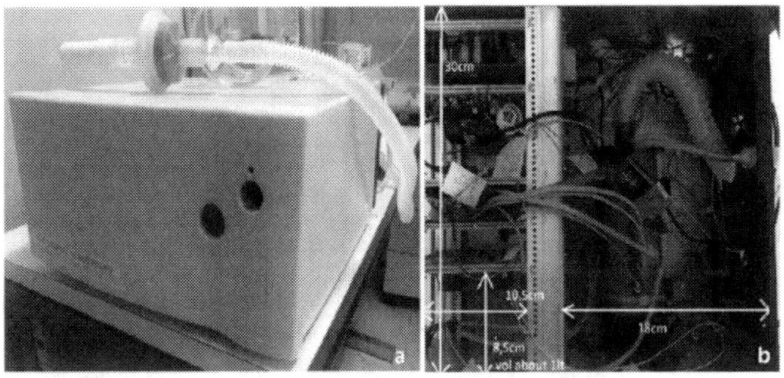

Figure 1. Wize Sniffer's hardware. *a*) external configuration; *b*) internal configuration.

recovery the sensors' steady state.
In Table I, all the gas sensors are listed. Our choice was to employ MOS-based gas sensors, manufactured by Figaro Engineering, because of their long life, strong sensitivity, rapid recovery; in addition, they are low cost (20-30Euro on average) and easy to be integrated in the circuitry. As mentioned before, humidity strongly affects their behavior, as well as cross-sensitivity [21], which makes these sensors be non-selective.

TABLE I. MOS-based gas sensors integrated in the Wize Sniffer's measurement module.

Detected molecule	*Sensor*	*Best detection range*
Carbon monoxide	TGS2442	50-1000ppm
	MQ7	20-200ppm
	TGS2620	50-5000ppm
Ethanol	TGS2602	1-10ppm
	TGS2620	50-5000ppm
Carbon dioxide	TGS4161	0-40000ppm
Oxygen	MOX20	0-16%
Hydrogen sulfide	TGS2602	1-10ppm
Hydrogen	TGS821	10-5000ppm
	TGS2602	1-10ppm
	TGS2620	50-5000ppm
	MQ7	20-200ppm
Ammonia	TGS2444	1-100ppm
	TGS2602	1-50ppm

The aim of developing a device which could be used also in a stand-alone configuration, and which could be useful for user self-monitoring and self-surveillance, also in home environment, is evident about software implementation. We implemented a client-server architecture (Figure 2) in order to send breath data also to a remote personal computer. It means that, after performing a test and processing the results, the device, thanks to an internet connection and a communication protocol, can send the results to the family doctor, for instance. For this purpose, Arduino is programmed to process sensors' raw data and to execute a daemon on port 23. By implementing a Telnet server, it waits a command line from the remote personal computer and provides the data.
Finally, in Figure 3, WS' operation modes are shown. In the smaller picture, the WS is working as a *Wize Mirror*'s tool. In the other picture, the WS is working as a stand-alone device.

III. Wize Sniffer functionality tests and data analysis

Breath analysis performed by low-cost technology based gas sensors is a great challenge. If, on one hand, semiconductor-based gas sensors are low cost, robust and very

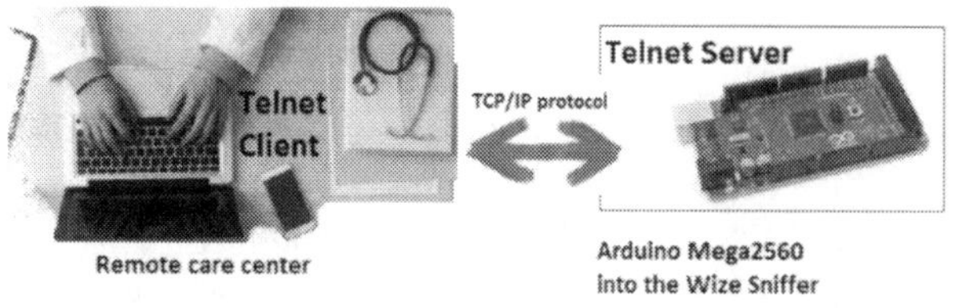

Figure 2. Wize Sniffer's client-server architecture including Arduino Mega2560 with Ethernet module

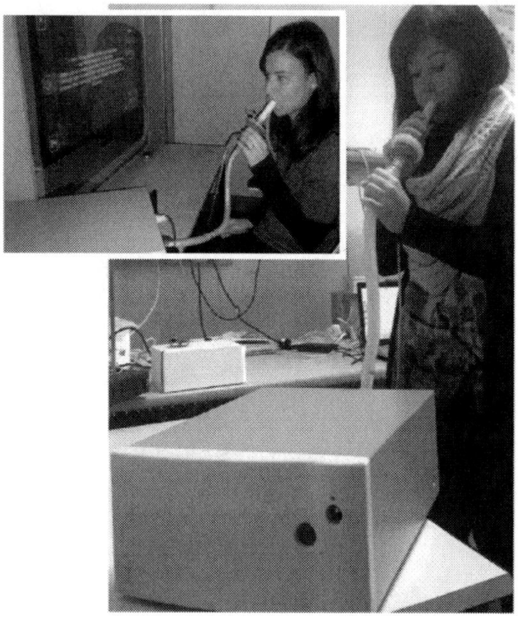

Figure 3. The two Wize Sniffer's configurations.

simple to integrate in the circuitry, on the other hand, their behavior is strongly affected by humidity and cross-sensitivity. It means that there is not a single sensor for each compound, but each sensor may be sensitive to many VOCs. As a consequence, the estimation of the breath molecules' concentration is an arduous challenge. Nevertheless, we tried to do a step toward this direction: we investigated gas sensors' sensitivity in our measurement conditions (30C+/-7%, 70%RH+/-5%, that are the ones that occur in the sampling box during a breath test). Not only, we also investigated how the several breath molecules influence each other in the chemical interaction with the sensors' sensing element.
Moreover, breath gases are something extremely variable: breath composition may vary according to heart rate, breath flow rate [22], posture [23], ambient air [24], lung volume [25], breath sampling mode [26]. Exhaled breath is affected by a strong inter-variability (among different subjects), and also by a marked intra-variability (relative to the same subject). As summarized in Figure 4, we have to face first with an uncertainty of measure relative to those factors that affect the gas sensors' behavior; then, we have also un uncertainty due to all the physiological conditions that influence breath composition. For instance, in our case, also factors such as BMI [27], sex, age may influence ethanol's concentration in breath.

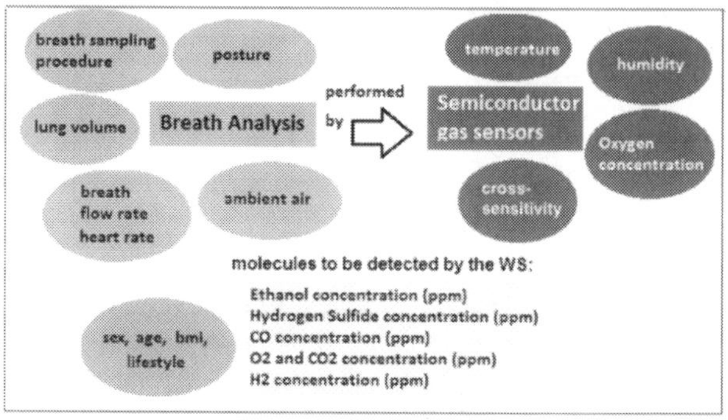

Figure 4. All the influencing factor (in the circles) related to breath analysis performed by semiconductor-based gas sensors.

A. Sensitivity tests on gas sensors with well-known gases concentrations

These experimental tests aimed to reproduce our measurement conditions when a breath analysis is performed: in particular, the temperature in the gas sampling box increases up to 30C+/-7% and the humidity reaches 70%RH+/-5%. We investigated sensors' response to a well-known gases concentrations, as well as their cross sensitivity.
Figure 5 shows how the humidity strongly affects such type of gas sensors (in this case, MQ7 sensor, sensitive to CO). The relationship between humidity and sensors' output generally can be modeled by means of a power law:

$$V_{out} = f(hum) = a * (hum^b) + c \tag{1}$$

where a and c are constant. Understanding such a behavior is useful to calculate humidity sensors' drift and then compensate it. We considered the entire range of humidity variation (for instance, 50%-55%RH in the case of MQ7, as shown in Figure 5) and then we calculated the slope of the curves. Based on the slope, drift coefficients were assessed as the decrease in sensors' output (Volt) per unit decrease in humidity (eq. 2):

$$S_d = \Delta V / \Delta hum \tag{2}$$

Also the gas flow rate indirectly influences gas sensors' behavior: a high flow-rate leads to a decrease in humidity, which causes (as shown in Figure 5), a decrease in sensor's output. By keeping the humidity constant, sensor's output will depend on the gas concentration only. Indeed, by means of the experimental set-up that is shown in Figure 6, we kept the humidity at 70%RH+/-5% by means of a saturated solution of NaCl placed on the bottom of the vial; then, we injected in the vial well-known gases concentrations. In Figure 7, we can see TGS2620 output when well-known concentrations of carbon monoxide, ethanol and hydrogen were separately injected into the vial. Also in this case, the relationship between sensor's output and gases contraction can be modeled by means of an equation similar to eq.1.

In order to assess TGS2620 cross sensitivity, well-known mixed concentrations of the three gases were injected into the vial at the same time. In this way, how the different VOCs add together and influence gas sensors' output can be understood. In Figure 8, the results are shown. Each gas

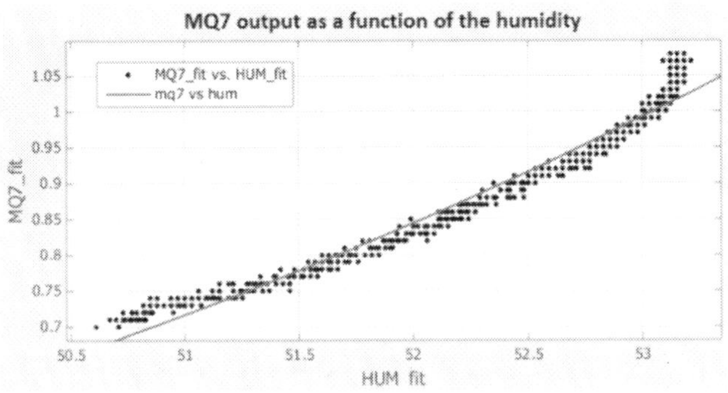

Figure 5. The relationship between MQ7 sensor and humidity is plotted. A power model is used for fitting curve.

Figure 6. a) and b) Experimental setup. c) The data stream from sensors is read by an Arduino Mega2560 board via serial port.

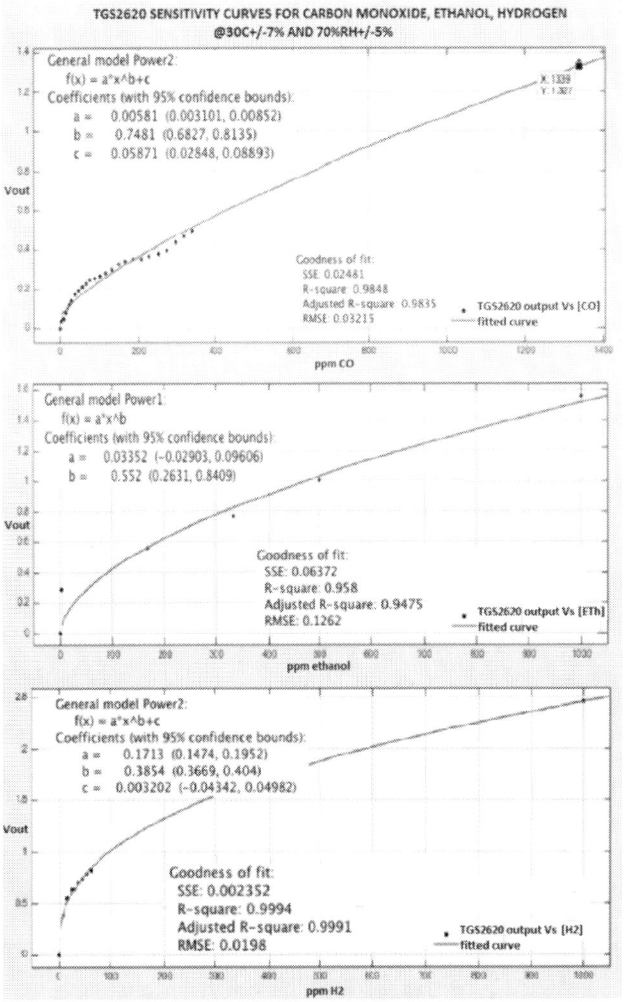

Figure 7. The curves show the relationship between TGS2620 output and well-known concentrations of CO, (first plot), C_2H_6O (second plot) and H_2 (third plot).

contribution can be modeled by a power law (see eq. 1). By investigating such behavior of semiconductor gas sensors, the "weight" of each compound on the output can be addressed. A simple model to describe this phenomenon can be based on a linear regression.

B. *WS functionality test: the clinical validation*

The WS underwent a clinical validation in three research centers: CNR in Pisa and Milan, CRNH (Centre de Recherche en Nutrition Humaine) in Lyon. The validation campaign involved 77 volunteers overall. The population was composed of individuals with different habits and lifestyle, as shown in Figure 9. People had to answer some questionnaires about their lifestyle, among which Audit test and Fagerstrom test, which respectively assess the alcohol and smoke dependence. 35% of them was no-risk subjects (that means, subject which never smoke, and with no-or-very low risk drinking); 6% of them was light smokers (low nicotine dependence); 19% of them was heavy smokers (high nicotine dependence); 17% of them was social drinker (low risk drinking); there were not people with high or increasing risk drinking (heavy drinkers); 23% of them was a combination of the previous classes.

A measuring protocol was draft, which took into account the methodological issues about breath sampling procedure [26] that, as shown in Figure 4, may strongly influence the breath composition. Actually, there is no standardized procedures to sample the breath. The most common methods of sampling are three: "alveolar sampling" (that is used if only the VOCs participating to the alveolar exchanges are to be assessed), "mixed expiratory air sampling" (which corresponds to a whole breath sample), "time-controlled sampling" (which corresponds to the exhaled air sampled after the start of expiration). For our purposes, mixed expiratory air sampling method was chosen, since our interest was focused on both endogenous and exogenous biomarkers. The subjects took a deep breath in, held the breath for 10sec., and then exhaled once into the corrugated tube trying to keep the expiratory flow constant and to completely empty their

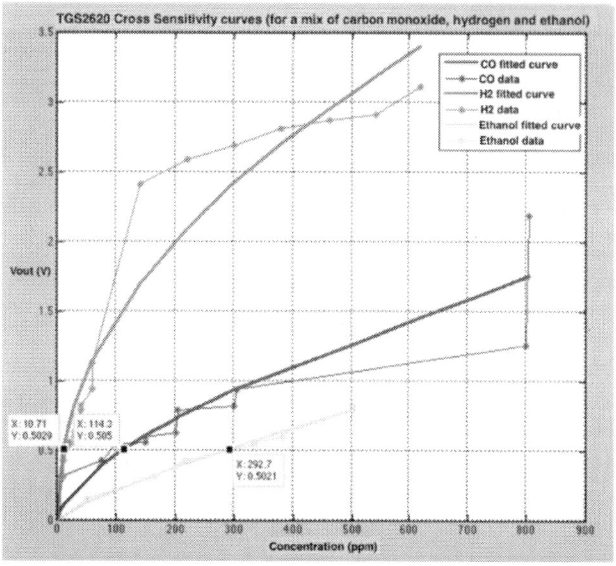

Figure 8. The curves show the relationship between TGS2620 output and well-known concentrations of CO, (blu plot), C_2H_6O (green plot) and H_2 (red plot).

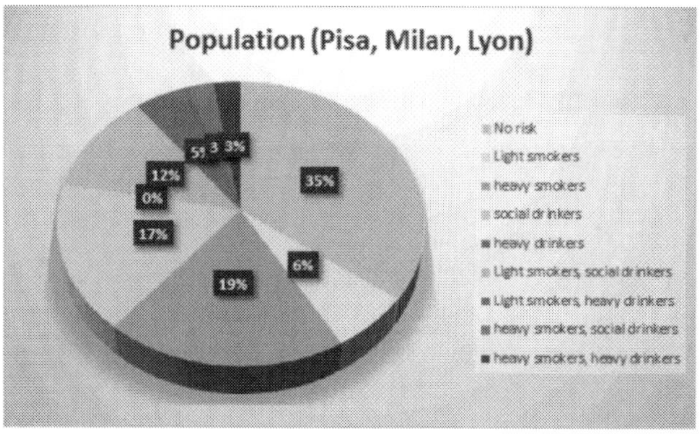

Figure 9. The population involved in SEMEOTICONS clinical validation.

lungs. The study was approved by the Ethical Committee of the Azienda Ospedaliera Universitaria Pisana, protocol n.213/2014 approved on September 25th, 2014; all patients provided a signed informed consent before enrollment.

The aim was to assess if the WS was able to monitor and evaluate the individuals' noxious habits for cardio-metabolic risk (smoke and alcohol intake in particular). In Subsection III-A we have confirmed, by means of experimental tests, the cross-selectivity of the sensors, which make their responses ambiguous. As a consequence, because of the difficulty of making an accurate quantitative analysis of VOCs' concentrations, we exploited another approach for data analysis, more classical, based on multivariate methods of pattern recognition. Pattern recognition, by exploiting the cross-correlation, extracts informations contained in sensors' outputs ensemble.

Sensors' raw data first were zero-centered and normalized, thus putting in evidence the qualitative aspects of the data. Then, Principal Component Analysis (PCA) was performed, in order to provide a representation of the data in a space of dimensions lower than the original sensors space. In particular, the first two components were extracted, exploiting 89% of variance. By the PCA we also removed the noise of the sensors. In Figure 10 and 11 the biplots of PCA scores are shown. In the 3D-plot, in particular, several cluster can be identified. Furthermore, in 2D-plot, we can see that the two first principal components seem to arrange according to the two first noxious habits for cardio-metabolic risk: Component 1 seems to be representative of smoking (MQ7 vector is aligned with it), as well as Component 2 seems to be representative of alcohol intake and wrong diet (TGS2602, TGS2620, TGS821 vectors are aligned with it).

After assessing the presence of clusters, the data were

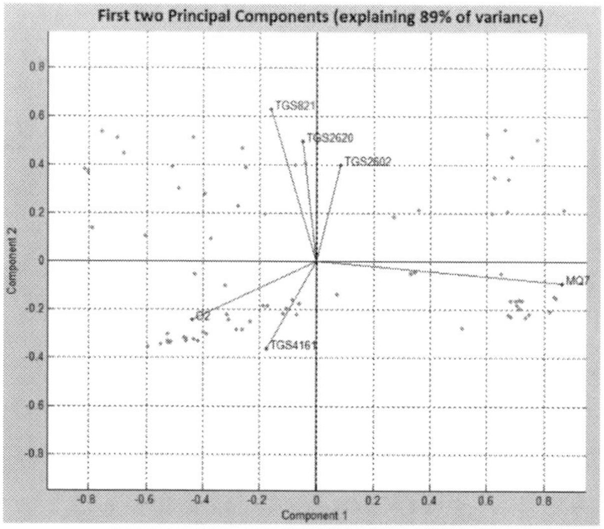

Figure 10. First two Principal Components.

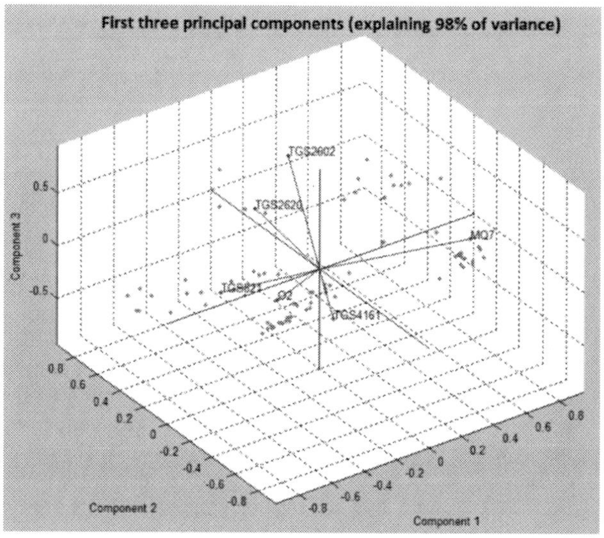

Figure 11. First three Principal Components.

processed with a K-nearest neighbor (KNN) classification

algorithm, previously trained with the data coming from another acquisition campaign. The aim was to classify the subjects according to their habits: "Healthy" (that means, no cardio-metabolic risk), "Light Smoker", "Heavy Smoker", "Social Drinker", "Heavy Drinker", "LsSd" (Light smokers, Social drinker), "LsHd" (tLight smokers, Heavy drinkers), "HsSd" (Heavy smokers, Social drinker), "HsHd" (Heavy smokers, Heavy drinker). The Audit and Fagerstrom questionnaires were our ground truth. It is important to highlight that while an alcohol consumption up to 1-2 Alcohol unit/ day is often considered not dangerous (in healthy subjects), smoking is considered very noxious in any case. The KNN classifier was able to correctly classify in 89,61% of cases. Errors are due to TGS2602 and TGS2620 cross-sensitivity for hydrogen. In fact, for instance, three "no-risk" subjects were classified as "social drinker" because of high hydrogen contribution which caused a rise in these sensors voltage output.

IV. Conclusion

In this paper, we described the development of a portable, very easy-to-use, low cost technology-based device for real-time breath analysis. The Wize Sniffer is based on an array of low cost, semiconductor-based gas sensors. Such type of gas sensors are, of course, very sensitive and easy to be integrated in the circuitry. On the other hand, they require a very robust data post-processing because of the difficulty of discriminating the molecules' contribution due to sensors' cross sensitivity. Pattern recognition algorithms turn out the best way to overcome such problem. Nevertheless, our aim will be to develop a model in order to calculate, as accurately as possible, the concentration of breath molecules to be detected by the WS, in order to compare such concentrations with the reference ones (see Subsection II-A). This model should be based on the data regarding the gas sensors' behavior (see Subsection III-A), but it also has to take into account other parameters (Figure 4) that can influence breath composition.
In addition, the fact that the WS is able to detect a large number of VOCs, allows for using such device in broader applications: for instance, TGS2444, selective to ammonia, could be exploited to monitor patients with acute liver diseases. In addition, its modular configuration allows for changing the type of the sensors according to the molecules to be detected. Therefore, we retain that a big effort should be devoted in order to foster breath analysis in clinical practice. Not only, having a portable device for real-time breath analysis, easy to use, affordable to maintain, may allow for a daily self-monitoring also in home environment.

Acknowledgment

This work was funded in the framework of the Collaborative European Project SEMEOTICONS (SEMEiotic Oriented Technology for Individuals CardiOmetabolic risk selfassessmeNt and Self- monitoring), grant N. 611516.
Paolo Paradisi, Massimo Martinelli, Massimo Guidi and COSMED s.r.l. are warmly acknowledged for useful support.

References

[1] C. Lourenco and C. Turner, "Breath analysis in disease diagnosis: methodological considerations and applications," Metabolites, vol. 4, 2014, pp. 465–498.

[2] F. DiFrancesco, R. Fuoco, M. Trivella, and A. Ceccarini, "Breath analysis: trends in techniques and clinical applications," Microchemical Journal, vol. 79, 2005, pp. 405–10.

[3] W. Miekisch, J. Schubert, and G. Noeldge-Schomburg, "Diagnostic potential of breath analysis- focus on volatile organic compounds," Clinica Chimica Acta, vol. 347, 2004, pp. 25–39.

[4] M. Phillips, R. Cataneo, J. Greenberg, R. Grodman, and M. Salasar, "Breath markers in oxidative stress in patients with unstable angina," Heart Disease, vol. 5, 2003, pp. 95–99.

[5] D. Guo, a. L. Z. D. Zhang, N. Li, and J. Yang, "A novel breath analysis system based on electronic olfaction," IEEE Transaction on Biomedical Engineering, 2010, pp. 2753 – 2763.

[6] I. Essiet, "Diagnosis of kidney failure by analysis of the concentration of ammonia in exhaled breath," Jo. of Emerg. Trends Eng. Appl., Science, vol. 6, 2013, pp. 859–862.

[7] R. Adrover and al., "Breath-Ammonia Testing of Healthy Subjects and Patients with Cirrhosis," Digestive Diseases and Sciences, vol. 57, 2012, pp. 189–195.

[8] A. Wilson, "Recent progress in the design and clinical development of electronic-nose technologies," Nanobiosensors in Disease Diagnosis, 2016, pp. 15–27.

[9] T. de Meij and al., "Electronic nose can discriminate colorectal carcinoma and advanced adenomas by fecal volatile biomarker analysis: proof of principle study," Int. J. Cancer, 2014, pp. 1132–1138.

[10] N. Yusuf and al., "In-vitro diagnosis of single and poly microbial species targeted for diabetic foot infection using e-nose technology," BMC Bionformatics, 2015, pp. 158–169.

[11] P. Montuschi, N. Mores, A. Trov, C. Mondino, and P. Barnes, "The electronic nose in respiratory medicine," Respiration, 2013, pp. 72–84.

[12] URL: http://www.bedfont.com/.

[13] D. Walt and al., "Optical sensor array for odor recognition," Biosens. Bioelectron., 1998, pp. 697–699.

[14] F. Lai and H. Huang, "Fabrication of high frequency and low-cost surface-acustic wave filters using near field phase shift photolitography," Microelectronic Engineering, 2006, pp. 1407–1409.

[15] L. Fan, H. Ge, S. Zhang, H. Zhang, and J. Zhu, "Optimization of sensitivity induced by surface conductivity and adsorbed mass in surface acoustic wave gas sensors," Sensor Act. B-Chem, 2012, pp. 114–123.

[16] URL: http://www.semeoticons.eu/.

[17] S. Colantonio and al., "A smart mirror to promote a healthy lifestyle," Biosystems Engineering,Special Issue: Innovations in Medicine and Healthcare, Elsevier, vol. 138, 2015, pp. 33–43.

[18] D. Germanese and al., A low cost, portable device for breath analysis and self-monitoring, the Wize Sniffer. Springer International Publishing, 2017, pp. 51–57.

[19] M. D'Acunto and al., "Wize sniffer - a new portable device designed for selective olfaction," in International Conference on Health Informatics, 2014, pp. 577–582.

[20] D. Shier, J. Butler, and R. Lewis, Hole's Human Anatomy and Physiology. McGraw-Hill 11th Ed, 2007.

[21] P. Clifford and D. Tuma, "Characteristics of semiconductors gas sensors i. steady state gas response," Sensors and Actuators, vol. 3, 1983, pp. 233–254.

[22] J. Jones and S. Clarke, "Effect of expiratory flow rate on regional lung emptying," Clin. Sci., 1969, pp. 343–56.

[23] N. Anthonisen, P. Robertson, and W. Ross, "Gravity-dependent sequential emptying of lung regions," J. of Appl. Physiol., 1970, pp. 589–95.

[24] F. DiFrancesco and al., "Implementation of fowler's method for end-tidal air sampling," Journal of Breath Research, 2008, p. 037009 (10pp).

[25] J. Jones, "The effect of pre-inspiratory lung volumes on the result of the single breath o_2 test," Respiratory Physiology, 1967, pp. 375–85.

[26] W. Miekisch and al., "Impact of sampling procedures on the result of breath analysis," 2008, p. 026007 (7pp).

[27] K. E. Maudens, L. Patteet, A. L. N. van Nuijs, C. V. Broekhoven, A. Covaci, and H. Neels, "The influence of the body mass index (bmi) on the volume of distribution of ethanol," Forensic Science International, Elsevier, 2014, pp. 74–78.

A Novel Location and Neighborhood Adaptive Method for Binary Image Interpolation

Pullat Joy Prabhakaran, Palanganda Ganapathy Poonacha
International Institute of Information Technology – Bangalore,
Electronic city, Bangalore, India 560100
Email: joy@iiitb.ac.in, poonacha.pg@iiitb.ac.in

Abstract—**In this paper, we propose a new zooming technique for binary images using location and neighborhood adaptive non-linear interpolation rules. These rules are inspired by the way an artist would draw an enlarged image. We have shown that our method overcomes a number of problems associated with known interpolation techniques, such as blurring and thickening of edges. Our method uses a set of sixteen rules in five categories. Each pixel in the interpolated image is computed by a chosen rule. The choice depends on the location of the pixel and the content in the neighborhood. The size of the neighborhood is a variable. Some rules can be influenced by and influence distant pixels. We present examples showing the effectiveness of our method. The results are visually appealing. Lines and dots, with single pixel thickness, retain their thickness. Inclined lines and solids don't develop as much jaggedness as happens with bicubic interpolation. Similarly, curves are also relatively smoother.**

Keywords-Interpolation; binary-image; thinness; corner; slope.

I. Introduction

When High Resolution (HR) images are created by interpolating Low Resolution (LR) images using popular methods like nearest neighbor, bilinear and bicubic interpolation, unpleasant artifacts are seen. Two commonly noticed artifacts are smoothing of edges and pixelation. These are most likely to arise at object edges, on lines and curves that are one pixel thick, on inclined and curved solids or object intersections. Such methods cause more unwanted artifacts in the case of binary image zooming.

A large number of interpolation methods are available in the literature [1]–[14]. Some of these, like Nearest Neighbor, Bilinear and Bicubic [1] methods, use surface fitting techniques with pre-defined constraints. These methods often create undesirable artifacts in the output. Many methods have been proposed to minimize such artifacts. In [2], an orientation constraint is computed for each pixel to be generated. The pixel value is computed as a function of this constraint and the four surrounding neighbors. In an earlier work [3], we proposed an interpolation method called Average of Nearest Neighbors (ANN). This was based on the idea that each pixel in the interpolated image should be generated by using all the available nearest neighbors in the original image and none of the other pixels.

In [4], curvature of the low resolution image is evaluated and this curvature information is interpolated using bilinear interpolation. The interpolated curvature information is used as a driving constraint to interpolate the complete image. In [5], the image is first interpolated using bilinear interpolation. As a second step, the quality is improved using a fourth order Partial Differential Equation (PDE) based method. A directional bicubic scheme is proposed in [6]. Here, the strongest edge in each 7x7 neighborhood is detected. If the edge strength is greater than a threshold, a one-dimensional bicubic interpolation is done along the edge. Our method shares some similarities with [6] because it also tries to find and preserves local edges.

In [7] and [8], a two-step super resolution process is studied. In the first step, the low resolution image is interpolated using Bicubic interpolation. In the second step, the interpolated image is further processed to improve the quality at the edges. In [7], the gradient profile of the low resolution image is used as a driving gradient prior to change the gradient profile of the interpolated image. This process makes the edges sharper. In [8], this idea is extended by splitting the feature space into multiple subspaces and generating multiple priors.

In some scenarios, a frame from a video sequence needs to be interpolated. In [9] and [10], techniques to use information from adjacent frames to improve quality are discussed. The former uses an adaptive Wiener filter while the later uses Delaunay triangulation.

A training based approach is discussed in [11]. Unknown pixels in the interpolated image are generated using the training data set that best matches. The patch around the unknown pixel is matched with patches in the training set. Using the best matched stored patch, the pixel is assigned a value. A training based method, to expand binary text images, with an explicit noise model is discussed in [12].

In [13], edges are found as a first step. The edges are used to compute unknown pixels using cubic spline. In [14], unknown pixels are assigned the value of the neighbor that is closest to the value got by bilinear interpolation.

In this paper, we have developed interesting rules, based on location and nature of content in the neighborhood, for the interpolation of binary images by a scale factor of 2. These rules derive inspiration from the way an artist might zoom an image. We present a method of obtaining interpolated image pixels using sixteen rules, grouped into five categories. The rules are of widely varying complexities.

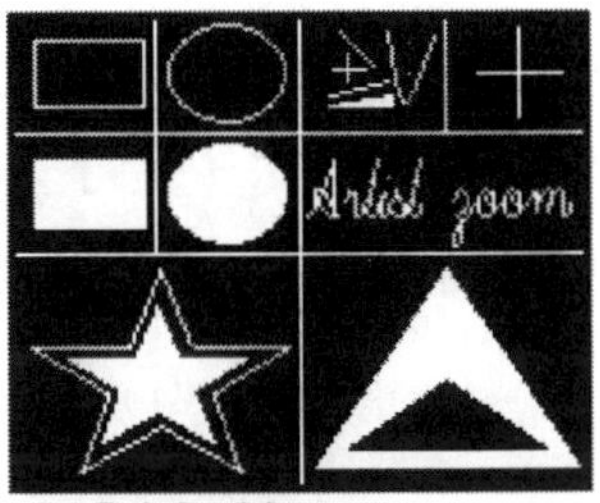

A. Original Image

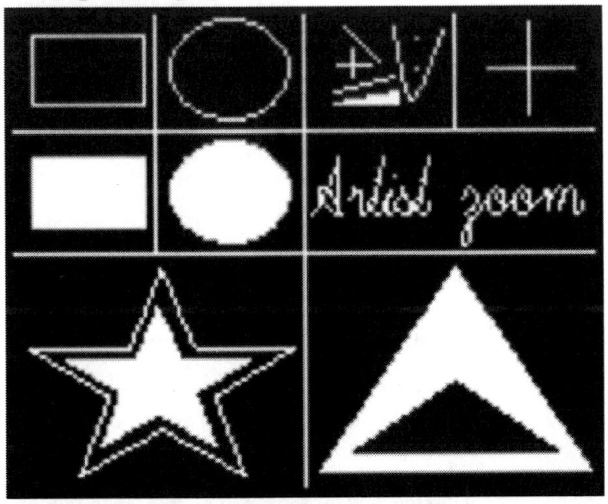

B. Interpolated using Bicubic interpolation.

C. Interpolated using our method.

Figure 1. Comparison of our method with bicubic interpolation.

The choice of the rule to assign value to a particular pixel depends on its location and the content in the neighborhood. The size of the neighborhood is dynamic and depends on the content. Some rules can be influenced by distant pixels in the input. Similarly, some rules can influence distant pixels in the output.

If the neighborhood meets certain conditions, our method tries to detect if an unknown pixel is part of an edge, a line or a corner. Based on this, it applies appropriate rules. To maintain smoothness of lines and edges, it both adds and deletes pixels in the foreground color when compared with simple pixel replication. The deletion ensures that smoothing does not cause extra thickening.

Figure 1A shows the image we have used to explain our method. Figure 1B shows the image, interpolated using bicubic interpolation. The bicubic interpolation is done using Matlab. Figure 1C shows the same image, magnified using our method. As can be seen, the bicubic interpolation introduces more distortion than our method. The region in Figure 1C, shown in the red box, will be used to explain our method.

The rest of this paper is organized as follows. Section 2 describes the interpolation process and five categories of rules. Sub sections A to E, in Section 2, describe the categories and associated rules. Experimental results are given in Section 3. Conclusions and suggestions for further extensions are given in Section 4.

II. The Interpolation Process

For each unknown pixel, the method does four things. Based on the location, it gets the neighbors and decides the applicable category of rules. The neighbors are from the LR image. Based on the content, it determines the neighborhood to be considered. The neighborhood can extend well beyond immediate neighbors. Based on the neighborhood, the method chooses the rule to be applied. The rule sets the unknown pixel and may also assign values to other pixels.

The interpolation process starts with an empty canvas that is double the height and width of the input image. We use blue color to represent pixels in the empty canvas. These will be assigned values by applying appropriate rules. We refer to these blue pixels as unknown pixels. At the start of the process, all the pixel values are unknown.

We assume that the row and column numbering start at the top left corner of the image. The first row and first column are referred to as row zero and column zero respectively.

In all the examples, we have used a white foreground and black background.

In order to handle the boundary pixels in a uniform way, we assume a two pixel wide background region on all four boundaries.

In the interpolation process, we say that a pixel in the LR image is horizontally (vertically) thin if its immediate horizontal (vertical) neighbors, on the left (above) and right (below) are of different magnitude from it.

The method categorizes unknown pixels in the HR canvas based on their locations. This is shown in Figure 2. The circles in the image represent individual pixels. At the start of the interpolation process, all these pixels are unknown. We categorize the pixels as O, H, V and D. Pixels on the even rows and even columns are of type O. Pixels on even rows and odd columns are of type H. Pixels on the odd rows and even columns are of type V. Pixels on odd rows and odd columns are of type D. Every pixel in the image falls into one of these categories.

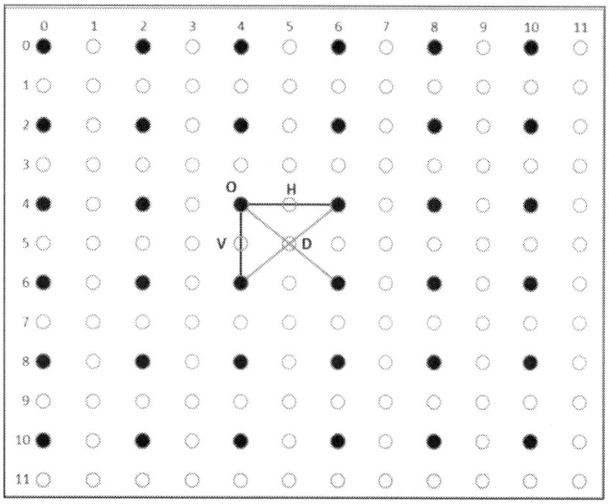

Figure 2. A representation of the HR image showing the types of pixels that need to be generated through interpolation.

The pixels of type O, H, V and D are assigned values using Category 1 to 4 rules respectively. The rules to assign value to pixels, in each category, are discussed in sub-sections A to D.

Some rules can override or pre-empt other rules, depending on the neighborhood conditions.

Different rules use data from neighborhoods of different sizes. In some cases, the size of the neighborhood is adaptive and it depends on the content in the neighborhood.

Depending on the neighborhood of the pixel, one of the rules in the chosen category is invoked. The rules, in each category, have an order of precedence. If one rule is applied, the rules with lower precedence are not applied even if their invocation conditions are met. In the following sub-sections, the rules are described in the order of their decreasing precedence.

Category 5 has one rule and it can change values assigned by other rules.

The method is implemented as a single pass. It starts at the top left corner and scans through the image, row by row. For each pixel, it chooses the appropriate rule and applies it.

We describe the method as a set of rules. Corresponding to each rule or a group of rules, we have a figure showing impact of the rule or group of rules. For example, Figure 3A represents the output if only Category 1 rules are applied and Figure 3B shows the output if both Category 1 and Category 2 rules are applied. The change from Figure 3A to Figure 3B is the impact of the Category 2 rules.

A. *Category 1 rule*

This category has one rule and applies to all pixels of the type O. In Figure 2, these pixels are shown as filled, black circles. The rule maps all pixels in the LR image to the HR image.

1) Rule 1: Assign the value of the pixel at location (x, y) in the original image (LR) to the pixel at location (2x,2y) in the interpolated (HR) image.

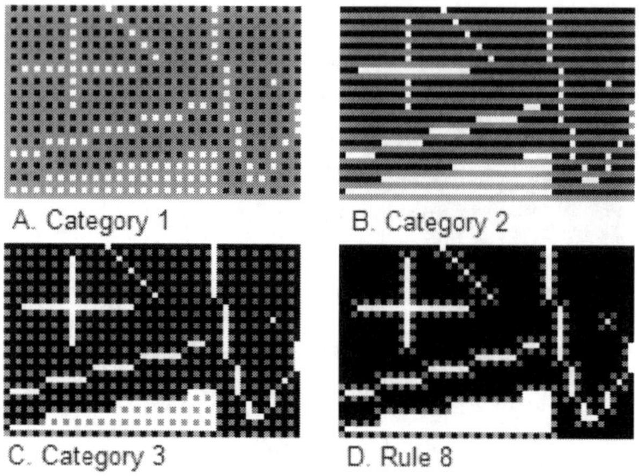

Figure 3. Impact of different rules. The captions show the additional category of rules or specific rule applied.

For example, pixels at locations (4,4) and (6,4) in the HR image are assigned values of pixels at locations (2,2) and (3,2) respectively in the LR image. Figure 3A shows the enlarged portion of the destination canvas and it depicts how the empty destination canvas gets partially populated.

B. *Category 2 rules*

The three rules in this category apply to unknown pixels of the type H. H pixels have a known horizontal neighbor each on the left and right. In Figure 2, the neighbors of pixel H are shown connected to it by black lines. The values of these neighbors are known because they are the values in the LR image.

1) Rule 2: If the neighbors on the left and right are equal, assign the value of the neighbors to the unknown pixel.

2) Rule 3: If the neighbors on the left and right differ and if only one of them is horizontally thin, assign the value of the pixel that is not thin to the unknown pixel.

3) Rule 4: If none of the preceding rules assigned a value to the unknown pixel, set it to the background color.

Figure 3B is generated by applying Rules 1 to 4. The changes from Figure 3A are caused by the category 2 rules. We see that the horizontal lines, in both colors, have become better formed. We also see that unknown pixels on either side of known pixels, in a vertical line in the foreground color, have been set to the background color.

C. *Category 3 rules*

These rules are similar to the category 2 rules but apply to unknown pixels of the type V. Such pixels have vertical neighbors with known magnitudes. In Figure 2, the neighbors of pixel V are shown connected to it by black lines. Here we will use the concept of vertical thinness that was defined earlier.

1) Rule 5: If the neighbors above and below are equal, assign their value to the unknown pixel.

2) Rule 6: If the neighbors above and below differ and if only one of them is vertically thin, assign the value of the pixel that is not thin to the unknown pixel.

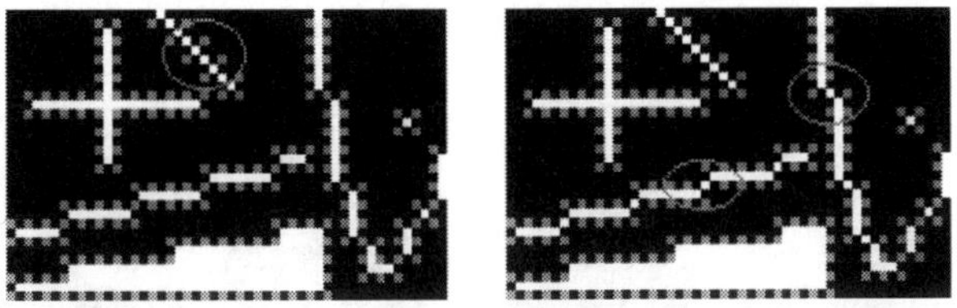
A. Rule 9 B. Rule 10 C. Rule 11 D. Rule 12

Figure 4. Impact of Rules 9-12. The captions show the additional rule and the red call outs show its impact.

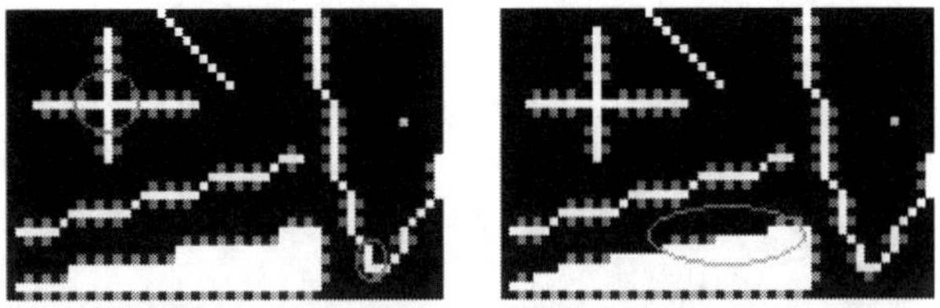
A. Rule 13 B. Rule 14 C. Rule 15 D. Rule 16

Figure 5. Impact of applying Rules 13-16. The captions show the additional rule and the red call outs show its impact.

3) Rule 7: If none of the preceding rules assigned a value to the unknown pixel, set it to the background color.

Figure 3C shows the impact of these rules. The changes from Figure 3B to Figure 3C are caused by the category 3 rules. We see that the vertical lines have become well-formed and more unknown pixels near horizontal lines have been assigned values.

D. Category 4 rules

The eight rules in this category apply to the unknown pixels of the type D. Such pixels have four diagonal neighbors whose magnitudes are known. In Figure 2, the four neighbors of pixel D are shown connected to it by red lines. Unlike the rules in the preceding categories, some of the rules here impact more than one pixel. However, they do not change any pixel that was assigned value by Rule 1.

1) Rule 8: If all four diagonal neighbors are equal, assign the value of the neighbors to the unknown pixel.

Figure 3D is generated by applying Rules 1 to 8. The change from Figure 3C to Figure 3D is caused by Rule 8. We see that most of the unknown pixels have been resolved and solids are well-formed. Most of the unknown pixels that remain are at the edges.

2) Rule 9: If all four neighbors are not equal and diagonally opposite neighbors are equal, then attempt to resolve as follows. If one and only one diagonal pair is both horizontally and vertically thin, then assign its value to the unknown pixel. Else, if all neighbors are horizontally and vertically thin, then assign it the foreground color.

Figure 4A shows the impact of this rule. We see that the diagonal lines are better formed. Unknown pixels adjacent to the diagonal line and also at its end remain unresolved.

3) Rule 10: If all four neighbors are not equal but the diagonally opposite neighbors are equal and the two diagonally opposite pixels in the foreground color are end points of two horizontal or two vertical line segments, assign the foreground color to the unknown pixel. After doing this, apply Rule 16.

Figure 4B shows the impact of this rule. This rule connects line segments forming longer lines or curves.

4) Rule 11: If diagonally opposite neighbors are equal and the preceding rules did not resolve the unknown pixel, assign it the foreground color.

Figure 4C shows the impact is similar to that of Rule 10.

5) Rule 12: If the unknown pixel has three diagonal neighbors of the background color, set it to the background color.

This rule makes corners of solids and dots better formed. The impact can be seen in Figure 4D.

The next three rules use the following definitions. These are applicable when only three neighbors are equal to the foreground color. These pixels form two perpendicular segments. Each of these has a length two pixels or is part of a longer segment. The lengths are with reference to the LR image.

Corner: If both the perpendicular arms have a length of two or if both of them are parts of longer segments.

Slope: If one perpendicular arm is of length two and the other is part of a longer segment.

Well-formed slope: If the longer arm of a slope does not have any adjacent pixel, on the same side as the shorter arm, having the foreground color.

6) Rule 13: If the unknown pixel has three neighbors that are a part of a corner, set it to the background color.

Figure 5A shows the impact of this rule. The corners formed by intersecting segments become better formed.

7) Rule 14: If three neighbors are part of a slope, set the unknown pixel to the foreground color. If the slope is well-formed, extend the unknown pixel in the direction of the longer arm by the length of the longer arm in the original image. Flag the extension to prevent overwriting.

Figure 5B shows the impact of the rule. Rule 14 differs from the preceding rules as it can impact pixels far removed from the unknown pixel. It makes inclines smoother, as seen on the inclined edge of the solid element in the figure.

Figure 6. Comparison of zooming. The first image is the input; the second is generated by our method and the third by bicubic interpolation.

This smoothness in the feature is achieved by converting each step like feature into two steps. This makes transitions smaller. This rule can impact pixels about half way across in the image, in either horizontal or vertical directions. The new step drawn is always on an odd numbered row or column. So it does not change any pixel that was assigned a value from the original image by Rule 1.

8) Rule 15: If none of the preceding rules assigned a value to the unknown pixel, set it to the background color.

Figure 5C shows the impact of this rule. After Rule 15 is applied, no pixel remains unknown.

E. Category 5 rule

Category 5 has one rule. It is categorized separately because of its unique behavior. It is invoked whenever Rule 10 is applied. If Rule 10 assigns a value to the unknown pixel, two of the diagonal neighbors of the pixel are end points of two horizontal or two vertical segments in the foreground color.

1) Rule 16: Draw two segments from the unknown pixel, parallel to the two segments whose endpoints are diagonal neighbors. The length of the new segments should be half the lengths of the corresponding segments in the original image. Set the pixels corresponding to the two original segments that are now adjacent to the new segments, to the background color. Flag all the impacted pixels so that they are not changed later when subsequent pixels are considered.

Figure 5D shows the impact of Rule 16. It is the only rule that changes pixels that were assigned values by Rule 1. Rule 16 helps better interpolate inclined lines where the inclination is not 45 degrees. The impact is seen on curves also because curves are formed using segments and points.

Figure 6 shows another comparison of our method with bicubic interpolation. The differences are clearly visible and the output of our method is more pleasing.

III. EXPERIMENTAL RESULTS

In this section, we evaluate our method using geometric shapes. This allows us to specify the desired result of interpolation and generate reference images in HR for comparison.

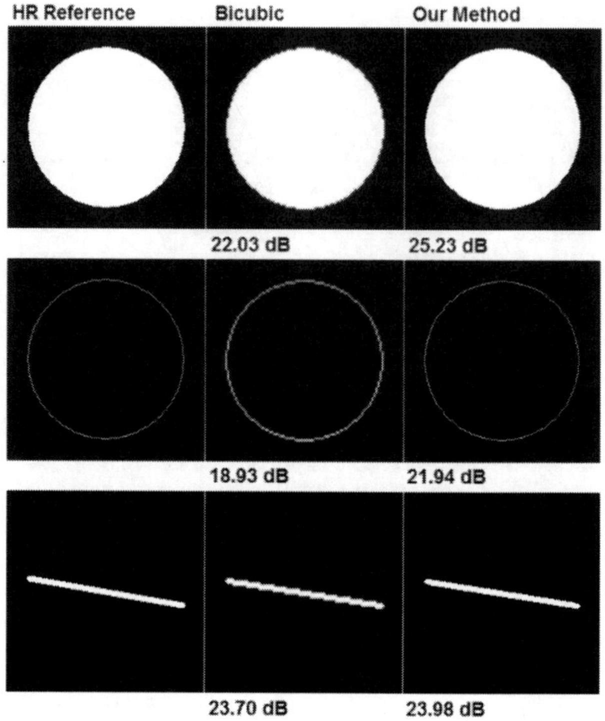

Figure 7. PSNR comparison of Bicubic interpolation and our method.

TABLE I. COMPARISON OF PSNR AND MPSNR

	Thickness		PSNR in dB		MPSNR in dB	
	LR	*HR*	*Our method*	*Bicubic*	*Our method*	*Bicubic*
Rectangle	1	1	match	22.98	Match	27.33
Circle	1	1	21.94	18.93	36	24.33
Line - 45 degree	1	1	46.02	26.54	56.16	31.92
Line - 10 degree	1	1	24.35	23.11	35.43	27.98
Rectangle	3	6	22.37	21.10	27.57	25.13
Circle	3	6	21.46	19.96	29.19	25.27
Line - 45 degree	3	6	25.19	27.40	32.14	34.68
Line - 10 degree	3	6	23.98	23.70	30.09	28.12
Filled Rectangle	NA	NA	match	26.49	Match	30.85
Filled Circle	NA	NA	25.23	22.03	33	26.76

The reference HR images, for a scale factor of two, are defined as follows. For a line thickness of one, a line of length l in LR should produce a line length 2l in HR, a circle of radius r should produce a circle of radius 2r and a rectangle of dimension h x w should produce a rectangle of size 2h x 2w. Each of the interpolated images should retain a line thickness of one pixel.

If the source image has thickness, then the thickness is also to be doubled. A line of n pixel thickness and length l, should produce a line of thickness 2n and length 2l, if n > 1.

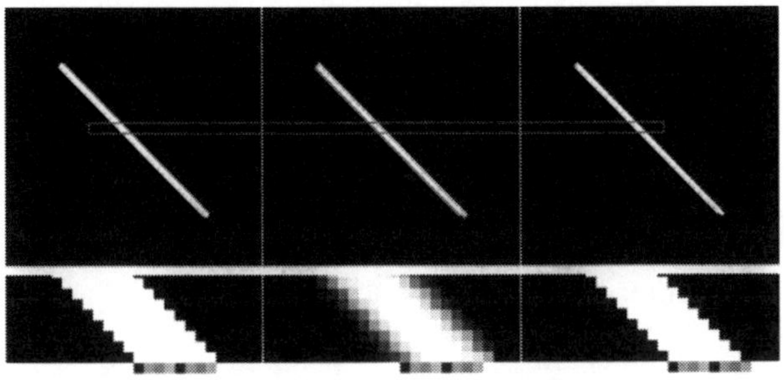

Figure 8. Magnified comparison of the outputs of interpolation.

TABLE II. COMPARISON OF OUR METHOD WITH OTHER METHODS.

	Percentage of PSNR improvement over Bicubic				
	Our Method		***CIM [4]***	***Gradient Orientation [13]***	***NNV [14]***
	PSNR	MPSNR			
Lena	2.59	12.90	2.35	0.92	
Peppers	2.50	14.12	1.09		1.71

The input images and reference images were drawn using Visual C++. Lines, rectangles and circles were drawn using the LineTo, Ellipse and Rectangle functions in the CDC class. Line thickness was set using the CreatePen function in the CPen class.

Figure 7 shows the comparison of our method with Bicubic interpolation. In the figure, the first test case is a filled circle. The reference image was drawn as a filled circle of radius 80. The input to Bicubic interpolation and to our method was a filled circle of radius 40. The same approach was used to generate reference images for other shapes also. The Bicubic interpolation was done using Matlab.

Table I shows the comparison for more images using both PSNR and Modified PSNR (MPSNR). MPSNR is generated by passing the images being compared through a low pass filter and then finding the PSNR of the filtered images. We have used a nine point mean filter. We see good PSNR improvement by both measures. Table I also shows a PSNR decrease for a three pixel thick line at 45 degrees. In Figure 8, this image is analyzed. The figure shows a portion of the image, marked in red, magnified 8 times. In the magnified region, a set of colored squares with the same size as a pixel, have been shown just below the line. Using these pixels to help count, we see that the reference line is 8 pixels wide along the x axis, while our method has generated a line of width 7 pixels. This happens because, in many situations, our method assigns the background color when other rules don't resolve an unknown pixel. This biases images towards thinness and the bias is of one pixel. This helps the image look sharp but the difference in thickness is reflected in the lower PSNR.

A direct comparison of our method with results available in [1]-[14] is difficult because our method is only formulated for binary images. To do a comparison, we converted two of the commonly used images, Lena and Peppers, to binary and used these as the reference images. We decimated these images by a factor of 2 and then interpolated them back to original size. We compared the interpolated images with the reference. The results are shown in Table II. The results have to be viewed keeping in mind the fact that the input for our experiments is binary while the input to the other methods is a grayscale image.

In [12], a text super-resolution is considered. Here the input is binary. It uses text images for training. It achieves an improvement between 0% and 19% in Mean Square Error (MSE), when compared with pixel replication. The results are for different text symbols. Our method improved MSE by 5.7% for Lena and 2.1% for Peppers.

We compared the execution times of our method with bicubic (on a computer with Intel i5-3210M CPU @ 2.50GHz, 4.00 GB RAM and running 64 bit Windows 8) by running ten iterations. The minimum time taken for bicubic interpolation of Lena and Peppers was 37.98 and 36.16 milliseconds respectively. The corresponding values for our method were 28.56 and 27.68 milliseconds.

IV. CONCLUSIONS

We have developed a new method of zooming binary images using rules inspired to some extent by what an artist may do. All images shown in this paper are generated by a computer program that implements the rules discussed. The results from our method are visually appealing. Lines and dots, with single pixel thickness, retain their thickness. Inclined lines and solids don't develop as much jaggedness as happens with bicubic interpolation. Similarly, curves are also relatively smoother. Also, corners retain sharpness.

From the results, we observe that one pixel thin lines remain thin while thick lines become thicker in our method. This is a desirable feature and one of the goals of our method. However, this might not lead to visually appealing results for fonts. This aspect requires more study.

More work is needed to extend this method to grayscale and color images. A useful solution could probably be built by working with ranges of color values and using functions to specify values for unknown pixels. This can lead to better image zooming techniques due to its location and content based adaptive nature.

REFERENCES

[1] W. H. Press, S. A. Teukolsky, W. T. Vetterling, and B. P. Flannery, Numerical Recipes in C, 2nd ed. Cambridge University Press, pp. 125-127, 1992.

[2] H. Jiang and C. Moloney, "A new direction adaptive scheme for image interpolation," International Conference on Image Processing, Vol. 3, pp. 369-372, 2002.

[3] P. J. Prabhakaran and P. G. Poonacha, "A new decimation and interpolation algorithm and an efficient lossless compression technique for images," Communications (NCC), 2015 Twenty First National Conference on, pp. 1-6, 2015.

[4] H. Kim, Y. Cha, and S. Kim, "Curvature Interpolation Method for Image Zooming," IEEE Transactions on Image Processing, Vol. 20, No. 7, pp. 1895-1903, July 2011.

[5] R. Gao, J. P. Song, and X. C. Tai, "Image zooming algorithm based on partial differential equations technique," International Journal of Numerical Analysis and Modelling, Vol. 6, No. 2, pp. 284-292, 2009.

[6] L. Jing, Z. Gan, and X. Zhu, "Directional Bicubic Interpolation-A New Method of Image Super-Resolution," 3rd International Conference on Multimedia Technology (ICMT-13). Atlantis Press, pp 470-477, November 2013.

[7] J. Sun, Z. Xu, and H. Y. Shum, "Image super-resolution using gradient profile prior," 2008 IEEE Conference on Computer Vision and Pattern Recognition, Anchorage, AK, pp. 1-8, 2008.

[8] C. Y. Yang and M. H. Yang, "Fast Direct Super-Resolution by Simple Functions," 2013 IEEE International Conference on Computer Vision, Sydney, NSW, pp. 561-568, 2013.

[9] R. Hardie, "A fast image super-resolution algorithm using an adaptive Wiener filter," IEEE Transactions on Image Processing, Vol. 16, No. 12, pp. 2953-2964, 2007.

[10] S. Lerttrattanapanich and N. K. Bost, "High resolution image formation from low resolution frames using delaunay triangulation," IEEE Transaction on Image Processing, Vol. 11, No. 12, pp. 1427-1441, 2002.

[11] W. T. Freeman, T. R. Jones, and E. C. Pasztor, "Example-Based Super-Resolution," IEEE Comput. Graph. Appl. 22, 2, pp. 56-65, 2002.

[12] G. Dalley, B. Freeman, and J. Marks, "Single-frame text super-resolution: a Bayesian approach," Image Processing, 2004. ICIP '04. 2004 International Conference on, 2004, Vol. 5, pp. 3295-3298, 2004.

[13] S. Ousguine, F. Essannouni, L. Essannouni, and D. Aboutajdine, "A new image interpolation using gradient-orientation and cubic spline interpolation," ISSR-Journals, vol. 5, no. 3, 2014.

[14] O. Rukundo and C. Hanqiang, "Nearest Neighbor Value Interpolation," in 2014 International Conference on Computer Vision Theory and Applications (VISAPP), 2012.

Robust Object Tracking Using Unreliable Object Recognizers

Li Li
Shannon Cognitive Computing Lab
Huawei
Bridgewater, New Jersey, USA
email: li.nj.li@huawei.com

Masood Mortazavi
Shannon Cognitive Computing Lab
Huawei
Santa Clara, California, USA
email: masood.mortazavi@huawei.com

Abstract—**This paper presents a method for video surveillance systems to correct noisy observations from distributed object recognizers that are unreliable. An unreliable recognizer consists of a hardware sensor (e.g., a camera) and a recognition program (e.g., facial recognition) that may produce random errors including false positives, false negatives, or failures. To address this issue, we use a Bayesian Network (BN) to connect multiple factors that can cause the noisy observations with random errors. We then incorporate the BN into an extended Hidden Markov Model (HMM) to infer optimal object paths from noisy observations. A prototype system is implemented and the simulation tests show that the Forward-Backward algorithm can achieve 77.3% accuracy on average with 47.9% relative improvement over the Viterbi algorithm. Both algorithms are robust to increasing noises and errors in the observations, even when 100% observations have over 66% errors.**

Keywords-video surveillance; object tracking; camera network; baysian network; hidden markov model; forward-backward algorithm; Viterbi algorithm.

I. INTRODUCTION

A video surveillance system consists of distributed cameras that cover the critical areas or even an entire city. These cameras are connected by wireless and wired networks to a regional control center, where the video streams are processed, stored, analyzed and searched by various algorithms to assist the authorities in controlling and preventing hazardous and criminal activities.

A main challenge in video surveillance systems is to automatically track moving objects, such as a person or a vehicle. Traditional approaches focus on monolithic algorithms that integrate three distinct functions: 1) extract features from video frames; 2) recognize the objects across video frames based on the features; and 3) determine object trajectories based on object recognitions and extracted features. While the monolithic approaches allow a tracking system to jointly optimize these functions, they make it difficult to combine different object recognition algorithms and tracking algorithms on the market. To achieve such flexibility, we propose to divide a tracking system into two layers: object recognition and object tracking that can change independently as blackboxes through a well-defined interface. A layered tracking system can easily include additional sensors and recognizers, such as radar, sonar, LIDAR, Infrared, etc. without changing the tracking model. On the other hand, we can easily port a tracking model to different domains with different sensors and recognizers.

Facial recognition can match an unknown human face in image or video to one of the known faces in a database (face identification), or determine if two human faces are the same (face verification). Despite 98% accuracy in some datasets, facial recognition in uncontrolled environment only achieves 74.7% classification accuracy [1]. Gait recognition can identify a person at a distance based on how he or she walks as recorded by camera or motion sensors. A recent survey [2] shows the gait recognition accuracies of different approaches vary from 60% to 90%.

Automatic License Plate Recognition can extract and recognize license plate from images and videos of vehicles. A 2013 survey [3] shows that the accuracies of different methods vary from 80% to 90%. Recent researches in computer vision [4][5] can recognize vehicle make and model, as well as distinct marks, with accuracy in the range of 70% to 84%.

Visual recognizers are unreliable due to constraints imposed by physical environment, such as variations in visibility, reflection, scale, view point, occlusion and motion. An unreliable object recognizer can produce noisy observations with 3 types of random errors: 1) *false positive*: when it recognizes an object that is actually not in its field of view; 3) *false negative:* when it does not recognize an object that is actually in its field of view; and 4) *failure*: when the camera breaks, the network fails or the recognition program crashes. When a tracking system receives an observation from an object recognizer, it should not completely trust the observation. Instead, the tracking system should identify and correct the random errors in the observation.

For this purpose, we introduce three probabilistic models: 1) competence model; 2) intention model; and 3) motion model, to describe the uncertain behaviors of the objects and recognizers. We then use a Bayesian Network (BN) to connect the factors in these models based on how they cause noisy observations. The BN is then incorporated into an extended Hidden Markov Model (HMM) that can correct the noisy observations using the well-known inference algorithms, such as the Forward-Backward and Viterbi algorithms. Simulated tests show that the approach can correct 77.3% noisy observations on average and is robust to increasing noises and errors in the observations, even when 100% observations have over 66.66% errors.

The rest of the paper is organized as follows. Section II reviews the related work. Section III describes the BN and extended HMM for object tracking. Section IV shows the experimental results and we conclude with Section V.

II. Related Work

Taj et al. [6] surveys the two main types of distributed camera network architectures and well-known tracking methods, including Graph matching, HMM, Particle filtering and Kalman filters. The decentralized recognizers send their results to the fusion centers which combine the results into a global trajectory. In contrast, distributed recognizers act as peers that exchange and combine results from their neighbors. In both cases, recognizers in a camera network can form dynamic clusters that move along with the object, in order to reduce search space, save energy and mitigate video traffic.

Within such camera networks, various methods [7]-[10] have been proposed to track objects across different cameras. These methods tightly integrate feature extraction, object recognition and object tracking as each method develops its own set of features.

Our approach is motivated by Fleuret et al. [10] who describes a probabilistic generative model that combines a motion model, an appearance model and a color model to infer the locations of objects from video streams. The method can track up to six people across two to four synchronized video streams taken at eye level and from different angles. In addition, the model can derive accurate trajectories of each individual using a grid map that divides an area into cells, each of which can only be occupied by one person at a time. The motion model calculates the conditional probability that an individual at cell a will travel to cell b at time k based on the distance between the cells, while the appearance and color models estimate the likelihood that a video stream is observed when an individual is at a cell.

However, our approach differs from [10] in some significant ways. First, our approach decouples object recognition from object tracking whereas [10] integrates them tightly. Second, our approach runs parallel HMM inferences for multiple objects whereas [10] is sequential by inferring the most likely object trajectory first and uses it to constrain the next object trajectory. Third, our motion model considers travel modes whereas [10] does not. Fourth, our approach can correct noisy observations, whereas [10] does not.

III. Tracking System Based on BN and HMM

The logic architecture of our tracking system is illustrated in **Figure 1**, where N recognizers receive video streams from distributed cameras, perform object recognitions and send the observations to the tracker. The tracker estimates object paths based on extended HMM.

The architecture is independent of camera resolutions and frame rates as well as video compression and transmission technologies. This allows the tracking system to reduce network bandwidth without losing tracking accuracy by matching the camera operations with the speed ranges of the target objects. The tracking system provides sufficient computing power to run the recognizers and trackers in real-time on the video streams.

Each recognizer R is treated as a blackbox function $R(C,O)=(t,S_t)$ that maps a video stream from camera C and an object O to observation S_t at time t. For convenience, $S_t=M>0$ denotes that R observes O at some mode M, $S_t=0$ denotes that R does not observe O, and $S_t=-1$ denotes that R fails. Travel mode M includes various means of mobility, such as walking, running, bicycle, car, boat, airplanes.

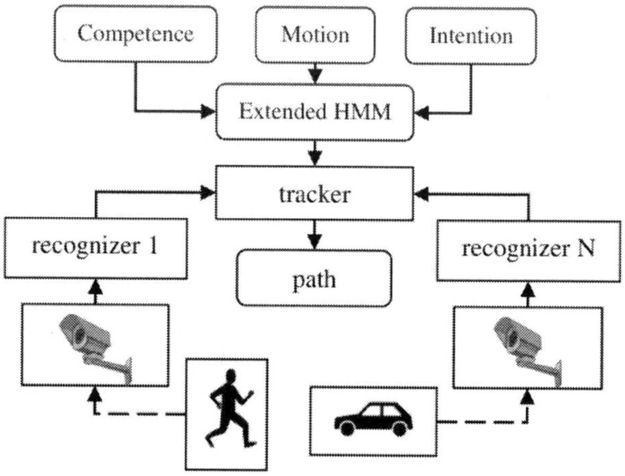

Figure 1. Logic architecture of tracking system

When object O moves within a camera network, the cameras it visits form an *object path*. When the recognizers are unreliable, the observed cameras may differ from the actual object path due to random errors:

- Type 0 false negative: $S_t=0$ but the correct values is $S_t>0$ since O was at C;
- Type 1 failure: $S_t=-1$ but the correct value is $S_t>0$ since O was at C;
- Type 2 false positive: $S_t>0$, but the correct value is $S_t=0$ since O was not at C.

To correct these random errors, we model the object path as the hidden states of an extended HMM that generates noisy observations according to some probabilistic distributions. The probabilistic distributions are derived from a BN that connects three probabilistic behavioral models: intention, motion and competence, to define the causes of noisy observations. With these probabilistic distributions, efficient inference algorithms are used to estimate the object paths as the optimal states of the HMM given the noisy observations.

A. Probablistic Behavioral Models

The **intention model** captures the uncertainty of object paths with three conditional probabilities. $P_I(C_i|O)$ is the probability that object O will enter the camera network at camera C_i. $P_I(C_j|C_i,O)$ is the probability that object O selects a place covered by camera C_j to visit from a place covered by camera C_i. $P_I(M|C_i,C_j,O)$ is the probability that object O will travel from camera C_i to C_j in transportation mode M. For simplicity, this model assumes that where an object travels and what mode it uses only depend on the current and next places.

The **motion model** captures the uncertainty of travel time Δt in mode M from camera C_i to camera C_j with conditional probability $P_M(\Delta t|C_i,C_j,M)$. For simplicity, we assume that $P_M(\Delta t|C_i,C_j,M)$ is a Gaussian (Normal) distribution $N(\mu,\sigma)$ with mean μ and standard deviation σ. The motion model is independent of objects and abstracts complex indoor and outdoor physical environments as a 3 dimensional matrix.

The **competence model** captures the uncertainty of recognizers with three probability distributions:

- $true\_pos(C)=P_C(S_t>0|O \text{ at } C \text{ at } t)$ is the conditional probability that recognizer R observes object O when it is at C at time t;
- $false\_neg(C)=P_C(S_t=0|O \text{ at } C \text{ at } t)$ is the conditional probability that recognizer R misses object O when it is at C at time t, where $false\_neg(C) = 1-true\_pos(C)$;
- $failure(C)=P_C(S_t=-1|O \text{ at } C \text{ at } t)$ is the probability that recognizer R fails at time t.

B. Bayesian Network

The BN [11] in **Figure 2** connects the 3 probabilistic models according to the causal processes that produce the random observations when object O transitions between cameras. The BN is represented as a directed factor graph [11], where the circles represent random events and the rectangle, called *factors*, represent the conditional probability distributions between the random events. O is omitted from the factors for clarity.

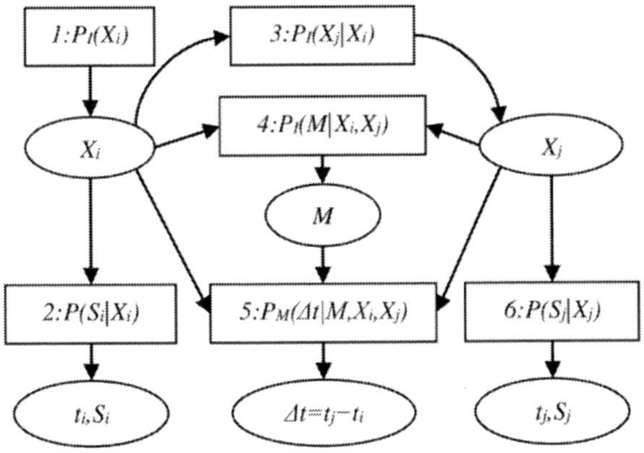

Figure 2: BN represented as a directed factor graph

Object O enters the places covered by the cameras according to factor 1. While at camera X_i at time t_i, object O selects a place to go next according to factor 3, while the place is covered by camera X_j. Then object O chooses mode M according to factor 4. Finally, object O transitions to the selected place during interval Δt according to factor 5. We can combine factors 3, 4 and 5 into one that defines the joint probability distribution of next place, mode and interval given the current place:

$$P(X_j,M,\Delta t|X_i)= P_I(X_j|X_i)P_I(M|X_i,X_j)P_M(\Delta t|X_i,X_j,M) \quad (1)$$

When object O is at camera X_i or X_j, the recognizer will produce observations according to factors 2 and 6, which are defined below:

$$P(S_i|X_i)=(1-falure(X_i))true\_pos(X_i) \text{ if } S_i>0 \quad (2)$$

$$P(S_i|X_i)=(1-falure(X_i))false\_neg(X_i) \text{ if } S_i=0 \quad (3)$$

$$P(S_i|X_i)=falure(X_i) \text{ if } S_i=-1 \quad (4)$$

C. Extended HMM

As object O moves across N cameras in $T\text{-}1$ transitions, the causal processes in the BN (**Figure 2**) are repeated $T\text{-}1$ times to produce T observations. The repetitions of $T\text{-}1$ copies of the BN forms an extended HMM for O in **Figure 3**, which has $N\times T$ states that represent all possible object paths of O that could have produced the T observations.

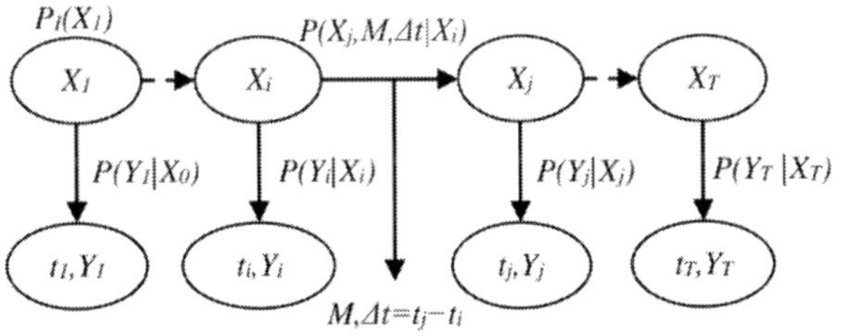

Figure 3: Extended HMM

Since any recognizers can generate false positive observations, concurrent observations of object O at multiple states can occur at the same time, although only one may be true. However, conventional HMM [12] does not permit concurrent observations. To address this problem, we use vector Y_i to represent concurrent observations of N recognizers at time t_i, where $Y_i[j]=S_i$ of the j-th recognizer. For example, $Y_i=[1, 0, 2, -1]$ indicates that at time t_i, recognizer R_1 observes object O in mode 1 and R_3 observes O in mode 2, while R_2 does not observe O and R_4 fails. Furthermore, we assume that each recognizer R observes object O independently at any time. Under this assumption, (5) reduces the probability of concurrent observations to the probability of individual observations.

$$P(Y_i|X_i)=P(Y_i[X_i]|X_i)=P(S_i|X_i) \quad (5)$$

Equations (6)-(8) define the parameters of the extended HMM using the notations in [12], where:

1. a_{ij} is the state transition probability from X_i to X_j;
2. $b_j(k)$ is the probability of observation k at state X_j;
3. π_i is the initial state distribution.

$$a_{ij}=P(X_j,M,\Delta t|X_i) \quad (6)$$

$$b_j(k)=P(Y_j[k]|X_j) \quad (7)$$

$$\pi_i=P_I(X_i) \quad (8)$$

Equation (6) is tied to the intention and motion models by (1), while (7) is tied to the competence model by (2)-(5).

Two well-known algorithms can be used to infer the optimal state sequence with $O(N^2T)$ operations for N states and T observations. The Forward-Backward (FB) algorithm

[12] selects T optimal states X_i that independently maximize $P(X_i|Y_1...Y_T)$ as follows:

$$q_t = \underset{1\le i\le N}{\operatorname{argmax}}[\gamma_t(i)], \gamma_t(i) = \frac{\alpha_t(i)\beta_t(i)}{\sum_{i=1}^{N}\alpha_t(i)\beta_t(i)} \quad (9)$$

The right-hand side of (9) is computed using the forward pass (10) and the backward pass (11) based on (6)-(8).

$$1)\ \alpha_1(i) = \pi_i b_i(Y_1), 1 \le i \le N$$
$$2)\ \alpha_{t+1}(j) = [\sum_{i=1}^{N}\alpha_t(i)a_{ij}]b_j(Y_{t+1}), 1 \le t < T, 1 \le j \le N \quad (10)$$

$$1)\ \beta_T(i) = 1, 1 \le i \le N$$
$$2)\ \beta_t(i) = \sum_{j=1}^{N} a_{ij}b_j(Y_{t+1})\beta_{t+1}(j), 1 \le t < T, 1 \le i \le N \quad (11)$$

The Viterbi (VI) algorithm [12] selects T optimal states that jointly maximize $P(X_1... X_T|Y_1...Y_T)$ as follows:

$$1)\ \delta_1(i) = \pi_i b_i(Y_1), \psi_1(i) = 0, 1 \le i \le N$$
$$2a)\ \delta_t(j) = \max_{1\le i\le N}[\delta_{t-1}(j)a_{ij}]b_j(Y_t)$$
$$2b)\ \psi_t(i) = \underset{1\le i\le N}{\operatorname{argmax}}[\delta_{t-1}(j)a_{ij}], 2 \le t \le T, 1 \le j \le N \quad (12)$$
$$3)\ p^* = \max_{1\le i\le N}[\delta_T(i)],\ q_T^* = \underset{1\le i\le N}{\operatorname{argmax}}[\delta_T(i)]$$
$$4)\ q_t^* = \psi_{t+1}(q_{t+1}^*), 1 \le t < T$$

We extend the FB and VI algorithms to return N-best optimal states at each timestamp, called *N-best path* to be distinguished from object path. A N-best path contains T N-best ranks, and each rank is a sequence of triples (t_i, X_i, P_i) sorted by descending order of P_i, where X_i is the optimal state (camera), and P_i is the probability of the object in state X_i at timestamp t_i given T observations.

IV. EXPERIMENTAL RESULTS

A prototype tracking system was implemented in Python 3.4.3 based on the extended HMM and tested on simulated data. The test procedures are illustrated in **Figure 4**, where the rectangle boxes represent the procedures and the curved boxes represent data. Based on a US city distance map, we bootstrapped the intention, motion and competence models. We then generated object paths and noisy observations from these models. The noisy observations are fed to the extended HMM to infer the N-best paths. Finally, we compare the N-best paths against the object paths to measure the accuracy and performance of the HMM.

The US city map was downloaded from a website [13], which includes distance d_{ij} between 31 cities, where $d_{ij}=d_{ji}$ and $d_{ii}=0$. We simulate a situation where an object (a vehicle) is driving across the cities, while the cameras in the cities may produce noisy observations about the object. The tracker must decide which cities the object has actually visited based on the noisy observations.

A. *Probablistic Model Generations*

The intention model of the object is derived from the distances by setting $P_I(C_j|C_i,O)=d_{ij}^{-1}/Z_1$ if $d_{ij}\neq 0$, and $P_I(C_j|C_i,O)=0.0$ if $d_{ij}=0$, where $Z_1=\sum_j d_{ij}^{-1}$ normalizes the numbers into a probability distribution. These assignments make the object more likely to travel to closer cities. The initial state distribution is obtained by setting $P_I(C_i|O)=1/Z_2\sum_j P_I(C_j|C_i,O)$, where Z_2 normalizes the sum into a probability distribution, such that the object is more likely to be in a city which has a more close neighbors.

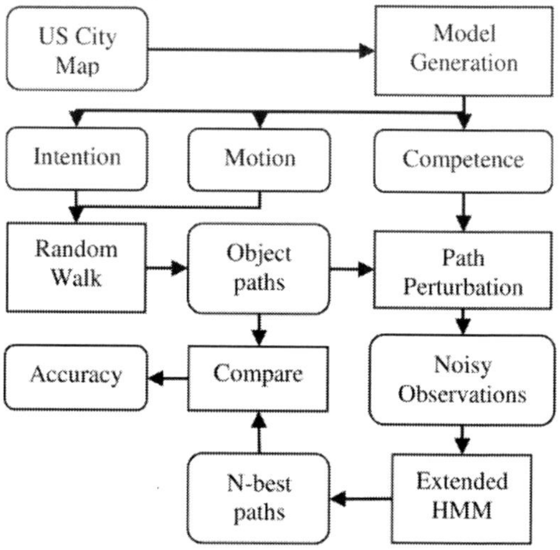

Figure 4: Test procedures

The motion model is derived from distances d_{ij} by setting $\mu=d_{ij}/65$ and $\sigma=d_{ij}/(4\times 65)$, based on the average US highway speed limit of 65 miles/hour, and the fact that travel time tends to vary more as the distance increases. As the result, $P_M(\Delta t|C_i,C_j,M)\sim N(d_{ij}/65, d_{ij}/260)$ for driving mode M.

The competence model is derived from a range of random choices. For each camera C_i, we randomly selected $true\_pos(C_i)$ from $\{1.0, 0.90, 0.80, 0.70\}$, $false\_neg(C_i)$ from $\{0.1, 0.01, 0.001\}$, and $failure(C_i)$ from $\{0.01, 0.001, 0.0001\}$, all with uniform distributions, to simulate a tracking system with mixed high-end and low-end recognizers.

B. *Object Path and Noisy Observation Generations*

We first generated the object paths from the models using a *Random Walk* procedure and then perturbed the paths to obtain the noisy observations using a *Path Perturbation* procedure. An object path is a sequence of (t_i, Z_i, M_i) triples, where t_i is the timestamp, Z_i the camera, and M_i the mode. A noisy observation $Y=[Y_0,..,Y_L]$ is a sequence of observation vectors Y_i as described in Section III, where each Y_i may contain random errors.

The *Random Walk* procedure accepts three arguments: start time t_0, a list of modes ML and step count L and it produces an object path, which is a random sample of the HMM states. The procedure first randomly selects the initial camera Z_0 according to distribution $P_I(C_i|O)$ and then randomly selects a mode M_0 from ML. These selections constitute the first triple (t_0, Z_0, M_0) of the object path. To construct the next triple, the procedure randomly selects the next camera Z_1 according to distribution $P_I(C_j|Z_0,O)$ and mode M_1 from ML. It then generates a random interval t_1 from Gaussian distribution $P_M(\Delta t|Z_0,Z_1,M_1)$ to construct the second triple (t_1, Z_1, M_1). These steps are repeated L times to produce a path of $L+1$ triples.

The *Path Perturbation* procedure accepts an object path of L+1 triples and produces a noisy observation Y of $L+1$ N-dim vectors Y_i. For each triple (t_i, Z_i, M_i) in the object path, the procedure sets the timestamp of Y_i to t_i, $Y_i[Z_i]=M_i$ and $Y_i[k]=0$ for $k \neq Z_i$. It then randomly selects an error type from set $\{0, 1, 2\}$ to modify Y_i as follows:

- If $type=0$, set $Y_i[Z_i]=0$ with probability $false\_neg(Z_i)$ to simulate false negative errors;
- If $type=1$, set $Y_i[Z_i]=-1$ with probability $failure(Z_i)$ to simulate failures;
- If $type=2$, randomly select two indexes m, n not equal to Z_i and set $Y_i[m]=Y_i[n]=M_i$ to simulate *false positive* errors by cameras C_m and C_n.

For each vector Y_i, there is $false\_neg(Z_i)/3$ chance of 1 type *0* error, $failure(Z_i)/3$ chance of 1 type *1* error, and *1/3* chance of 2 type *2* errors. Type 0 and 1 errors create observation gaps in the object path, while type 3 errors introduce distractions into the object path. These errors significantly deviate a noisy observation from the true object path at multiple timestamps.

We use two measures, *error count* and *noise ratio*, to quantify the deviation of noisy observations from the object paths. The *error count* of Y is the total number of errors in Y. The *noise ratio* of N observations Y is M/N, where M is the number of observations Y whose error count is greater than 0. Since the error count is proportional to L and the noise ratio is proportional to the error count, both measures will increase as L increases. The plot in **Figure 5** illustrates these relations when L increases from 1 to 20.

C. Accuracy Measurement

After a tracking system produces an N-best path S_b (described in Section III) from noisy observation Y perturbed from an object path S_o, we can measure its accuracy by three metrics: *recall*, *precision* and *F-measure*. Recall measures how many triples in S_o are in S_b, while precision measure how many triples in S_b belong to S_o. If S_b is a perfect match of S_o, then both recall and precision will be 1. If they have no common triple, then both recall and precision will be 0. Higher recall and precision yield higher F-measure. The metrics are calculated by (13), where $NB>0$ decides the size of the N-best ranks in S_b. Since $length(S_b) \geq length(S_o)$, these metrics are in range $[0,1]$.

The *rank* function determines if a triple $R_i=(t_i, Z_i, M_i)$ in S_o can be found in S_b which consists of ranked triples (t_i, X_i, P_i). A match is found if both triples have the same t_i and $Z_i=X_i$. When a match is found, the rank position $0 \leq k < NB$ of the N-best triple is returned. The *hit* function weights and accumulates the results of rank functions, such that a higher rank receives more weight up to 1. Since S_0 and S_b have the same length in our case, the recall, precision and F-measure metrics become equal. For this reason, we only include F-measure in our test results.

$$rank(R_i) = \begin{cases} NB \text{ if } R_i \notin S_b \\ k \text{ if } R_i \in S_b \end{cases} \in [0, NB]$$

$$hit(S_o, S_b) = \sum_{R_i \in S_o} \frac{NB - rank(R_i)}{NB} \in [0, length(S_o)]$$

$$recall(S_o, S_b) = \frac{hit(S_o, S_b)}{length(S_o)} \in [0,1] \quad (13)$$

$$precision(S_o, S_b) = \frac{hit(S_o, S_b)}{length(S_b)} \in [0,1]$$

$$F(S_o, S_b) = \frac{2recall(S_o, S_b)precision(S_o, S_b)}{recall(S_o, S_b) + precision(S_o, S_b)} \in [0,1]$$

D. Test data and Results

To simulate object tracking with small amount of observations, we selected path lengths L=1, 2, 3, 4, 5, 10, 15 and 20 to generate 8 sets of 500 object paths and noisy observations. **Figure 5** plots the *error count* and *noise ratio* of the noisy observations. The noisy observations deviate significantly from the object paths and the deviation increases monotonically with path length. At path length 1, 60% observations have over 2 errors. At path length 20, 100% observations have over 14 errors, which means that 66.66% vectors in an observation have some errors.

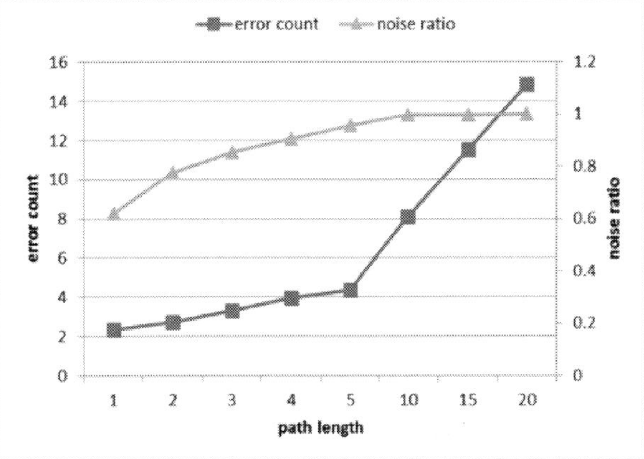

Figure 5. Error counts and noise ratios of 8 datasets

For each of the 8 datasets, we ran 6 configurations (Table I) of the tracking system, by activating different models and inference algorithms. We then averaged the F-measures of the 500 N-best paths as the F-measure of each configuration. The results are shown in Figure 6, where the FB family of configurations 1, 3, 5 clearly outperforms the VI family of configurations 2, 4, 6. The average F-measure of the FB family is 77.3%, with 47.9% relative improvement over the 52.2% of the VI family.

One possible reason that the VI family is more prone to the observation errors than the FB family is because the Viterbi algorithm selects the next optimal state based on the previous one such that one early mistake can derail the entire selections.

TABLE I. 6 CONFIGURATIONS OF TRACKING SYSTEM

	intention	motion	algorithm
1	used	not used	Forward-Backward (FB)
2			Viterbi (VI)
3	used	used	FB
4			VI
5	not used	used	FB
6			VI

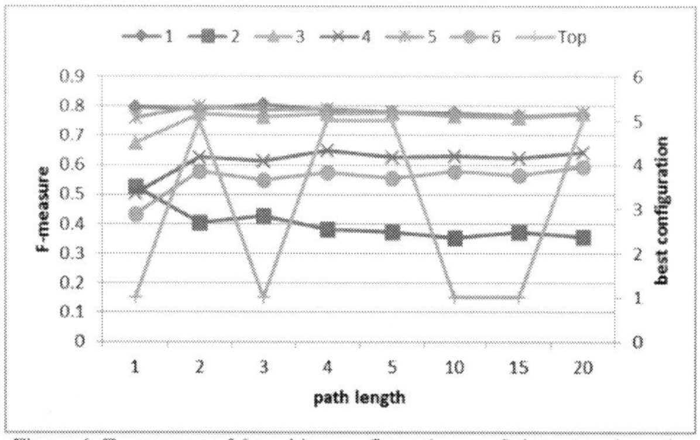

Figure 6. F-measures of 6 tracking configurations on 8 datasets, where the Top line connects the best configurations for each dataset

The top configurations for the 8 tests alternate between configurations 1 and 5, indicating that using the intention and motion models alone is better than combining them. We suspect that using both models may have over-fitted the HMM to the object paths that deviate significantly from the noisy observations.

The F-measures of the FB and VI algorithms are quite stable as the path length increases, with standard deviations of 0.010 and 0.017 respectively. This shows that the algorithms are robust to the increasing noises and errors in the observations shown in **Figure 5**.

All the tests were run on a 32-bit Windows 7 Lenovo T410 notebook computer with 2.67Ghz Dual Core CPU and 3GB RAM. The average tracking time is 26.6 milliseconds with a standard deviation of 0.68.

V. CONCLUSIONS

This paper described a probabilistic method to correct concurrent noisy observations about moving objects from unreliable recognizers (cameras). Our main contributions are:

- A BN to connect 3 probabilistic models of object behaviors and recognizer competence into causal relations to explain the noisy observations;
- An extension to HMM to support inference on concurrent observations from multiple cameras;
- An extension to FB and VI algorithms to return N-best optimal states.

As the simulated tests demonstrated that it is feasible to build a robust tracking system from unreliable recognizers, future work is needed to improve the accuracy. One important direction for future research is to learn the probabilistic models from noisy observations using statistical machine learning techniques [11][12]. It is also interesting to extend the tracking model to deal with more challenging errors in more realistic datasets.

REFERENCES

[1] M. Gunther, L. E. Shafey, and S. Marcel, "Face Recognition in Challenging Environments: An Experimental and Reproducible Research Survey," Face Recognition Across the Imaging Spectrum, Springer, pp 247-280, 2016.

[2] A. P. Patel, V. C. Gandhi, "Survey on Human Gait Recognition," IJCST Vol. 5, Issue 4, Oct - Dec 2014, pp 275-277, 2014.

[3] S. Du, M. Ibrahim, M. Shehata, and W. Badawy, "Automatic license plate recognition (ALPR): A state-of-the-art review," Circuits and Systems for Video Technology, IEEE Transactions on, 23(2), 311-325, 2013.

[4] J. Sochor, A. Herout, J. Havel, "BoxCars: 3D Boxes as CNN Input for Improved Fine-Grained Vehicle Recognition," The IEEE Conference on Computer Vision and Pattern Recognition (CVPR), pp. 3006-3015, 2016.

[5] H. Liu, Y. Tian, Y. Wang, L. Pang, and T. Huang, "Deep Relative Distance Learning: Tell the Difference Between Similar Vehicles," The IEEE Conference on Computer Vision and Pattern Recognition (CVPR), pp. 2167-2175, 2016.

[6] M. Taj and A. Cavallaro, "Distributed and decentralized multi-camera tracking," IEEE Signal Processing Magazine, Volume 28, Issue 3, pp. 46-58, May 2011.

[7] P. Climent-Perez, D. N. Monekosso, and P. Remagnino, "Multi-view event detection in crowded scenes using tracklet plots," The 22nd International Conference on Pattern Recognition (ICPR), pp. 4370-4375, 2014.

[8] Y. Xu, X. Liu, Y. Liu and S.-C. Zhu, "Multi-view People Tracking via Hierarchical Trajectory Composition," The IEEE Conference on Computer Vision and Pattern Recognition (CVPR), pp. 4256-4265, 2016.

[9] D.-T. Lin and K.-Y. Huang, "Collaborative Pedestrian Tracking and Data Fusion With Multiple Cameras," IEEE Transactions on Information Forensics and Security, Vol. 6, No. 4, pp. 1432-1444, December 2011.

[10] F. Fleuret, J. Berclaz, R. Lengagne, and P. Fua, "Multicamera People Tracking with a Probabilistic Occupancy Map," IEEE Transactions on Pattern Analysis and Machine Intelligence, Vol. 30, No. 2, pp. 267-282, February 2008.

[11] C. M. Bishop, Pattern Recognition and Machine Learning, Springer, 2006.

[12] L. R. Rabiner, "A Tutorial on Hidden Markov Models and Selected Applications in Speech Recognition," Proceedings of IEEE, Vol. 77, No. 2, pp. 257-286, February 1989.

[13] MapCrow, Cities in United States, http://www.mapcrow.info/united_states.html, last accessed: April 3, 2017.

InVideo: An Automatic Video Index and Search Engine for Large Video Collections

Shuangbao Paul Wang
Metonymy Corporation
Fairfax, Virginia 22030
Email: paul.wang@computer.org

Xiaolong Cheng
Department of Computer Science
George Washington University
Washington, DC 20052
Email: xiaolongcheng@gwu.edu

Carolyn Maher
Department of Psychology
Rutgers University
New Brunswick, New Jersey 08901
Email: carolyn.maher@csu.rutgers.edu

William Kelly
Metonymy Corporation
Fairfax, Virginia
Email: william.kelly@metonymylabs.com

***Abstract*—In this paper, we present a novel system, inVideo, for automatically indexing and searching videos based on the keywords spoken in the videos and the content of the video frames. Using the highly efficient video indexing engine we developed, InVideo is able to analyze videos using machine learning and pattern recognition without the need for initial viewing by a human. The time-stamped commenting and tagging features refine the accuracy of search results. The cloud-based implementation makes it possible to conduct elastic search, augmented search, and data analytics. Our research shows that inVideo presents an efficient tool in processing and analyzing videos and increasing interactions in video-based online learning environment. Data from a cybersecurity program with more than 500 students show that applying inVideo to current video material, interactions between student-student and student-faculty increased significantly across 24 sections program-wide.**

***Index Terms*—video processing; video index; big data; learning analytics.**

I. Introduction

Big data analytics are used to collect, curate, search, analyze, and visualize large data sets that are generated from sources such as texts (including blogs and chats), images, videos, logs, and sensors [1]. Video data is a major format of unstructured data, and should be an indispensable area of big data analytics. However, most analytics tools are only effective in analyzing structured data. Due to the nature of the special file format, traditional search engines hardly penetrate into videos, and therefore video indexing becomes a problem [2]–[13].

Videos contain both audio and visual components, and neither of these components is text based. To understand a video, viewers must actually play it and use their eyes and ears to analyze the sounds and visuals being presented to them. Without watching a video, it is hard to glean information from its content or even know whether there is information to be found within. Existing search engines and data analytics tools such as Google, SAS, SPSS, and Hadoop are effective only in analyzing text and image data. Video data, however, are difficult to index and therefore difficult to analyze.

In education, video presents a large opportunity for both classroom and online education [14]. In addition, video is a great teaching format because it can both be more enjoyable and more memorable than other instruction formats [15]. Furthermore, video instruction allows for students to work at their own pace, for teachers to be able to teach more students, and for more reusable teaching materials to be available when compared to an in-person lecture. MOOC creators realize the many benefits of video, as evidenced by the prevalence of video in MOOCs. Many MOOCs focus on video files for the bulk of their instructional material so it is clear that the MOOCs of the future must also focus on videos.

InVideo [16], developed under a US Department of Education grant, is able to analyze video content (language and video frames) prior to initial close researcher review of the video. A highly efficient video indexing engine can analyze both language and video frames based on natural language and referent objects. Once a video is indexed, its content becomes searchable and statistical analysis as well as qualitative analysis are possible. Commenting and tagging add a layer of hyper-information and therefore increase the accuracy of the transcript, which was automatically extracted from the video by the inVideo tool. The indexing technology is especially useful in mining video data in large video collections. inVideo also has an automatic caption system that can transcribe the words spoken in the video. Instructors can use the tool to construct in-place video quizzes for assessments.

Learning is an integration of interaction. The interaction might exist between learners and instructors or between learners and computers. While the traditional approach would be to analyze grades at the end of the semester, this lacks the benefits that come from interactions that occur during the course [17]. As an increasingly large number of educational resources move online, analyzing interactions between students and online course material is becoming more important. Many learning management systems (LMS) have built-in learning analytics tools to look into the data [18]–[20]. Due to the limitation of the data gathering and indexing, the built-in tools are generally not sufficient in assessing study outcomes, especially for video content.

II. Related Work

Automatic video index and search have widely applications in education, public security, and many other video-intensive areas.

An airport traffic and security monitoring system constantly index videos gathers from surveillance cameras and search the suspect based on the graphical and textual information provided by the authority [9].

A video content indexing and retrieval tool index digital videos automatically on a 34 hours of TV news broadcast. The sampled frames are then used in providing the basis for various analysis [21].

Big data and learning analytics can become part of the solutions integrated into administrative and instructional functions of higher education [22]. Traditional face-to-face instruction supports traditional data-driven decision-making process. Videos as a form of big data are more extensive and especially time-sensitive learning analytics applications. It is important that instructional transactions are collected as they occur.

Learning analytics can provide powerful tools for teachers in order to support them in the iterative process of improving the effectiveness of their course and to collaterally enhance their students performance [23]. Dyckhoff developed a toolkit to enable teachers to explore and correlate learning object usage, user behavior, as well as assessment results based on graphical indicators. This learning analytics system is able to analyze data such as time spent, areas of interest, usage of resources, participation rates and correlation with grades data and visualize them using a dashboard. However, the system is unable analyze the interactions between students and the online learning systems on videos.

In order to analyze videos for various applications, we have developed a video index engine to look at every word spoken in the video and categorize it using our custom index algorithm. In addition, a content-based pattern recognition engine can search individual frame of the video to recognize objects and individuals being displayed. The collaborative commenting, tagging, and in-place quizzes make videos more accessible and also increase the accuracy of the search engine [7], [8], [10].

III. Video Indexing and Search Algorithm

Videos are a different data type than text and images, in that they are unstructured data. Traditional search engines are mostly text based, with a few tools that allow for searching of images. In order to index a video, a search engine needs

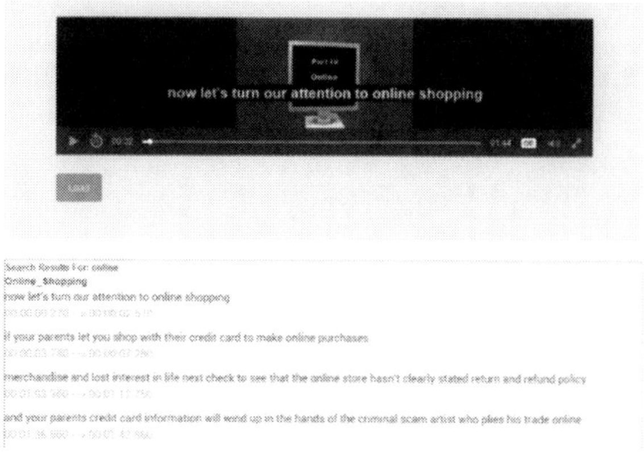

Fig. 1. Analyzing Videos by Keywords

to extract meaningful language from the audio and convert it to text, while simultaneously converting the visual frames into a series of images that can be used to recognize persons and objects in the video. This is an extremely difficult task, given that videos are a compound format. Not only are the audio and visual components integrated, but also within each of these components there is a blend of information being presented in a manner that cannot be distinguished as easily by a computer as by a human brain. For example, the audio of the file may contain speech, music, and background noises that a computer will have a hard time recognizing and analyzing.

A. *Automatic Indexing Algorithm*

The video indexing engine uses the vector space model to represent the document by a set of possible weighted content terms. The weight of the term reflects its importance in relation to the meaning of the document [24].

After calculating the normalized frequency of a term in the document, the weight to measure the relative importance of each concept or single term is obtained. The automatic index algorithm then calculates the final position in n-dimensional space. The result is to be used for generating search results or visualization.

B. *Searching Videos by Keywords*

Video search involves two steps: analyzing by keywords and analyzing by image references. When a keyword is entered, the system looks through the indexed audio transcript to see if there is a match. An image reference may refer to either a picture or keywords that describe an object in the video using an appropriate semantic space. Video clips whose language contains the keywords will be retrieved. Figure 1 shows how indexed videos can be searched using keywords in the spoken language.

C. *Searching Videos by References*

Searching videos by references examines the frames of the video to see if the given picture or keyword is found. If the

Fig. 2. Analyzing Videos by Image References using the CBIR Algorithm

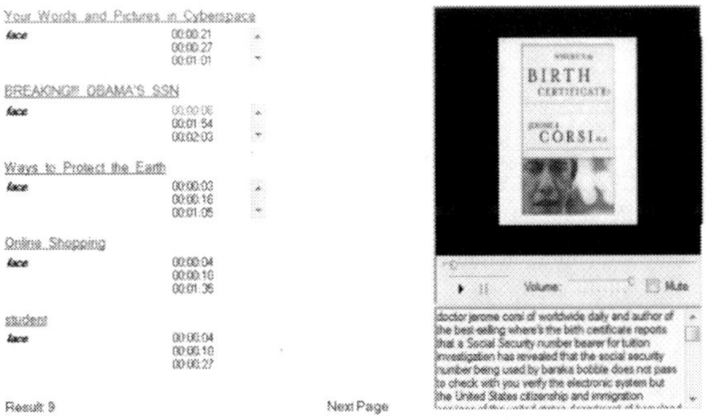

Fig. 3. Analyzing videos by Keyword References using a Knowledge Tree

reference is a picture, then the system uses a Content Based Image Retrieval (CBIR) algorithm to find the match frames and return the video clips that contain the reference picture. Figure 2 shows the image-based CBIR algorithm that retrieves the video frames corresponding to the reference picture (at the bottom).

If the reference is a keyword (e.g. credit card) then the system uses a knowledge tree to find matches in the video. If one video frame contains an object matching the features associated with the keyword, the section of the video is returned. Figure 3 shows how a search for the keyword credit card will retrieve the video frames that contain objects as credit cards.

D. Searching Videos with Multiple Languages

Sometimes multiple languages may be found in videos. Transcribe engines normally only work in one language or in closely-related languages. For other languages, a different transcribe engine may be required. InVideo addresses this problem by allowing videos with different languages to be searched from a single user interface. The inVideo system does not translate between languages. It only transcribe based on the language of original videos. For example, a Chinese video will result in a transcript in Chinese. Figure 4 shows the indexing engine properly analyzing the Chinese language.

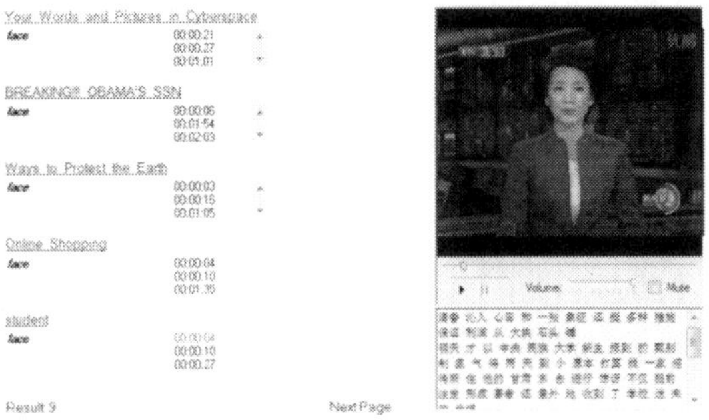

Fig. 4. Analyzing Videos with Different Languages

When entering the word student in Chinese, the video search engine will locate that term in the transcript and return the corresponding frames. Currently, there are multiple languages that can be analyzed by the inVideo system, with more to be added.

E. Elastic Search and Content-aware Elastic Search

Elastic search makes the inVideo application capable of searching video data across distributed environment with HTTP protocol and schema-free JSON documents. Elastic search makes it possible to expand the community by deploying a pluggable cloud architecture, configurable automatic discovery of cluster nodes, persistent connections, and load balancing across all available nodes. Video collections under ACE are no longer restricted to a particular video collection. More importantly, there is no need to move other video collections in a centralized site, which is merely feasible anyway.

Indexed videos can be searched by keywords. When a keyword is entered, the cloud system searches its generated transcript of the audio files to find matches. Video clips whose audio track contains the keywords are retrieved.

The enhanced elastic search partitions videos into individual frames. Thus, users also have the ability to search a video by examining the video frames to see if a given object is found. The enhanced elastic search algorithm matches contents in the frames and return the video clips that contain the reference objects. This process allows us to combine images and words to create hybrid metadata.

For instance, in mathematics education, there is interest in studying the representations students make. The CBIR algorithm allows us to search the videos for particular representations a student would make, for example, images of rods, blocks, tree diagrams. Students may construct these models without talking about them, and thus an audio transcript would miss it. By being able to search the frames of the video, a user interested in tracing a students construction or explanation of a representation can query the database. If a frame of the video contains an object matching the particular representation, this section of the video is returned.

F. Machine Learning and Cloud-based Data Analytics

It should be noted that the goal of the software is not to reproduce the word-for-word accuracy of a human-generated transcript of video files. Rather, the goal is to determine the extent to which voice-to-text analysis and image analysis are able to retrieve desired sections of the video for enriched human analysis. The critical task is for the system to identify a sufficient amount of relevant hits that pertain to the search reference terms or images. Search queries have advanced from keywords to natural language. The inVideo uses artificial intelligence and machine learning technologies to analyze videos and use big data analytics tool to explore, index and visualize videos. InVideo also has security features that secure data and communication in the cloud and protect privacy [2]–[6], [11], [12].

IV. Collaborative and Interactive Learning

Automatically generated video transcripts may have accuracy problems. Besides, the vast numbers of videos in MOOCs make them impossible to be retrieved correctly with just one or a few simple keywords. To solve these problems, we have implemented a collaborative filtering mechanism including commenting, tagging, and in-place quizzes. These features improve accuracy and increase interactions between students and the online learning systems. With collaborative filtering, learning resources retrieval on MOOC systems is greatly improved, and better student achievement is therefore expected.

A. Collaborative Filtering

Collaborative filtering is a process of improving accuracy of the automatic indexing algorithm by leveraging user feedback. This is popular on websites that have millions of users and user-generated content. Users are able to create time-stamped comments on videos. These comments can be hidden or made public so that someone else who views the video can see the comment at a specific time. These comments help increase accuracy of the search tool and transcript and enhance interactions in online learning.

Tagging on videos is another implementation in the inVideo system. It is to attach keyword descriptions to identify video frames as categories or topic. Videos with identical tags can then be linked together allowing students to search for similar or related content. Tags can be created using words, acronyms or numbers. It is also called social bookmarking.

A search term usually yields many related results, which in many cases are hard to differentiate. Commenting and tagging add additional information, refine the knowledge and increase the video search accuracy. At the time when information is exponentially growing, these features are extremely helpful for students to obtain the knowledge with the least amount of time.

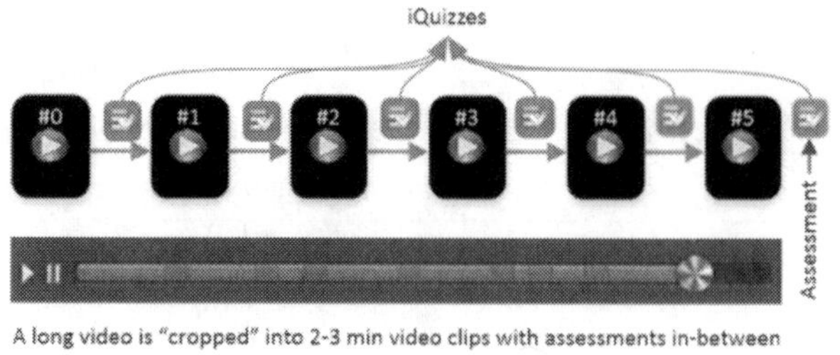

Fig. 5. Transform Linear Videos into Interactive Learning Objects

B. In-place Assessment with iQuiz

Internet computing has the advantage of employing powerful CPUs on remote servers to provide applications across the network. inVideo comes with an Internet Computing-based video quiz system (iQuiz) to utilize the computational power of remote servers to provide video quiz services to users across the Internet. Currently, videos are mostly non-interactive, therefore, there are no interactions between students and the learning content. Students view videos either online or download them to their personal devices. There is no way for educators to know whether a student has understood the content or even to know whether the student has viewed the video or not.

iQuiz can be used to assess learning outcomes associated with video study. Quizzes can be embedded into videos at any place where an instructor wants to assess the outcome of the students study. iQuiz runs as a service on servers. This enables users to execute this resource-intensive application with personal computers or iPads, which would not be possible otherwise.

Instructors can enter into the authoring mode where they can write quizzes by indicating the start and stop positions on the video and adding questions. Video quizzes are stored in XML format, and are automatically loaded while students are watching the video in the learning mode. Answers to the quizzes, either correct or incorrect, are also stored in the XML database for immediate assessments. Assessment of adaptive learning on videos provides better outcomes for students than the traditional video content study with little or no feedback [25].

C. Transform Linear Videos into Interactive Learning Objects

Video are linear in nature. It is hardly interactive nor does it contain branches. Using the inVideo tool, classical videos can be transformed into a series of video clips with assessments in between and at the end. So the video-based learning material becomes interactive. Figure 5 shows a test we conducted that turned a 46-minute video into six selected 2-3 minute video clips. The red segments on the stage bar are the samples. So it is clear that not all videos content was used in the samples.

V. Experimental Results

To test the inVideo system, we selected the 20 most recent videos from National Science Digital Library (NSDL) in cybersecurity and used the inVideo tool to extract keywords that appeared in the transcripts. From this set, we selected the top two ranked keywords: Target (data breach) and encryption (using encryption to secure data). We were confident that those two keywords made good discussion topics that could increase classroom interactions.

As a result, we added two discussion topics to the spring 2014 Masters of Science in Cybersecurity program (24 class sections with each section has 25 student on average).

Videos lack interactions between learners and the online learning environment. Even worse, videos above a certain length will likely never be watched at all because students cannot easily determine what content is within it or how to locate that content. To address this issue, we used the inVideo tool to index the content and break the large videos into a series of small video clips. By doing so, we made it possible for students to watch short video clips covering individual key concepts directly, while retaining the ability to view the whole video if necessary. This served to not only increase student interest and engagement in the lesson, but also more importantly, to improve their ability to comprehend and retain information.

Student responses and interactions can be used as a proxy for their degree of engagement with any particular part of the course. As one example of how the inVideo indexing served to increase this measure, consider Week 2 of the class. In our assessment of past offerings (pre-inVideo) we discovered that this part of the course is a quiet week, because the individual assignment starting in the week will not be due until Week 8. This meant that the interactions in the classrooms dropped significantly from Week 1. Based on this assessment, we decided to use the inVideo intervention in an attempt to generate more interactions during Week 2 of the course.

Our initial observation of one class was very promising; the total number of responses, defined as each posting after viewing a video clip, for Week 2 reached sixty-eight, as compared to only two for the same week in the previous semester. This initial finding encouraged us to investigate the results for all twenty-four sections program-wide. Figure 6 shows the number of responses for the 24 sections comparing Fall 2013 to Spring 2014 during Week 2.

For the research we conducted, Week 2 student responses across the 24 sections were almost seven times higher during Spring 2014 (1,129 responses) than during Spring 2014 (164 responses).

For the cybersecurity online/hybrid class, we have five graded discussions, one individual assignment, one team assignment, and two lab assignments. Two more hands-on exercises (labs) have been added since Spring 2014. Data from the team projects, using the same intervention method, show that student-student and student-faculty interactions were 6.5

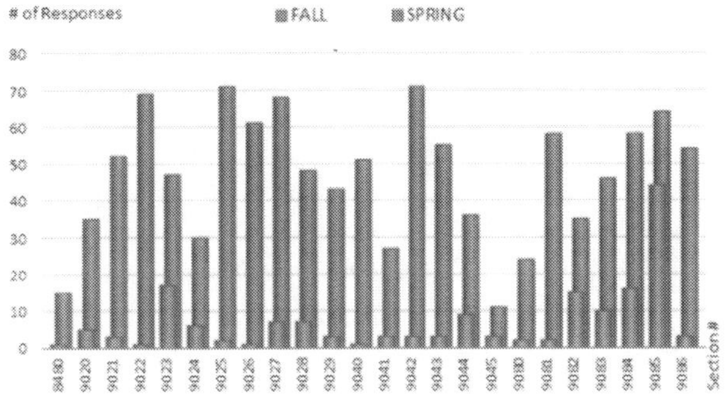

Fig. 6. Number of Responses for 24 Sections - Week 2 Discussions

times greater for the courses with the inVideo intervention (104 responses compared to 16 responses). We also measured student performance against desired learning outcomes. The average grades on both team projects and final grades was higher in Spring 2014 than in Fall 2013. Here we see that the index and data analytics tool inVideo, in combination with just-in-time assessment and intervention, improved learning outcomes.

Based on our finding, we are in the process of breaking up every large learning module into several learning objects using inVideo. The new competency-based learning objects will be used to construct the knowledge cloud. These new learning modules will consist of many competency-based learning objects, and will be more interactive, rational, and accessible.

We will use inVideo to expand the scope of this research to other activities in courses within the cybersecurity program. This tool could also be useful to courses in other disciplines. Using the inVideo tool, linear videos are transformed into a series of interactive learning objects. This is vital in an online learning environment where interactions and learning outcomes are valued the most.

VI. Conclusion and Future Work

This paper discussed a novel video index and analytics tool to analyze video data. Video indexing engines analyze both audio and visual components of a video, and the results of this analysis provide novel opportunities for search. To improve accuracy, we can either improve the transcribe engine, analyze video frames better where there is no audio, or crowd-source accuracy through collaborative filtering. For transcription accuracy, one potential accuracy improvement can come from using a self-learning artificial intelligence (AI) system that could be taught to recognize certain accents or languages. The process or requirements for instituting such a system and the magnitude of the improvement in accuracy are to be studied in the future.

At present, inVideo tool is only limited to analyze native (non-streaming) videos. We will continue our research on analyzing live videos and streaming videos and make inVideo available to broader video collections and applications.

ACKNOWLEDGEMENT

This research is funded in part by grants from US National Science Foundation (NSF) [EAGER-1419055 and DGE-1439570].

REFERENCES

[1] K. Bakshi, "Considerations for big data: Architecture and approach," 2012, pp. 1–7.

[2] S. Wang, "Dual-data defense in depth improves scada security," *Signal*, pp. 42–44, 2016.

[3] S. Wang and W. Kelly, "Smart cities architecture and security in cybersecurity education," *The Colloquium of Information Systems Security Education (CISSE)*, 2017.

[4] P. Wang and W. Kelly, "A novel threat analysis and risk mitigation approach to prevent cyber intrusions," *Colloquium for Information System Security Education (CISSE)*, vol. 3, pp. 157–174, 2015.

[5] S. Wang, A. Ali, and W. Kelly, "Data security and threat modeling for smart city infrastructure," 2015, pp. 1–6.

[6] S. P. Wang and R. S. Ledley, *Computer Architecture and Security*. Wiley, 2013.

[7] S. Wang, W. Kelly, and J. Zhang, "Using novel video indexing and data analytics tool to enhance interactions in e-learning," 2015, pp. 1919–1927.

[8] S. Wang, A. Ali, J. Zhang, and W. Kelly, "invideo - a novel big data analytics tool for video data analytics and its use in enhancing interactions in cybersecurity online education," vol. 60, 2014, pp. 321–328.

[9] S. Wang and J. Zhang, "A video data search engine for cyber-physical traffic and security monitoring systems," 2014, pp. 225–226.

[10] S. Wang and W. Kelly, "invideo - a novel big data analytics tool for video data analytics," 2014, pp. 1–19.

[11] S. Wang and R. Ledley, "Modified neumann architecture with micro-os for security," 2007, pp. 303–310.

[12] S. Wang, F. Shao, and R. S. Ledley, "Connputer - A framework of intrusion-free secure computer architecture," in *Proceedings of the 2006 International Conference on Security & Management, SAM 2006, Las Vegas, Nevada, USA, June 26-29, 2006*, 2006, pp. 220–225.

[13] Á. Serrano-Laguna, J. Torrente, P. Moreno-Ger, and B. Fernández-Manjón, "Tracing a little for big improvements: Application of learning analytics and videogames for student assessment," in *Fourth International Conference on Games and Virtual Worlds for Serious Applications, VS-GAMES 2012, Genoa, Italy, October 29-31, 2012*, 2012, pp. 203–209. [Online]. Available: http://dx.doi.org/10.1016/j.procs.2012.10.072

[14] V. SRideout, U. Foehr, and D. Roberts. (2010) Generation m2: Media in the lives of 8- to 18-year-olds. [Online]. Available: http://kaiserfamilyfoundation.files.wordpress.com/2013/01/8010.pdf

[15] H. Choi and S. Johnson, "The effect of context-based video instruction on learning and motivation in online courses," *The American Journal of Distance Education*, vol. 19, no. 4, pp. 215–217, 2005.

[16] S. Wang and M. Behrmann. (2010) Video indexing and automatic transcript creation.

[17] T. Elias. (2011) Learning analytics: Definitions, processes and potential. [Online]. Available: http://learninganalytics.net/LearningAnalyticsDefinitionsProcessesPotential.pdf

[18] C. E. Hmelo-Silver, C. A. Maher, A. Alston, M. Palius, G. Agnew, R. Sigley, and C. M. Mills, "Building multimedia artifacts using a cyber-enabled video repository: The vmcanalytic," in *46th Hawaii International Conference on System Sciences, HICSS 2013, Wailea, HI, USA, January 7-10, 2013*, 2013, pp. 3078–3087. [Online]. Available: http://dx.doi.org/10.1109/HICSS.2013.122

[19] C. E. Hmelo-Silver, C. A. Maher, G. Agnew, M. Palius, and S. J. Derry, "The video mosaic: design and preliminary research," in *Learning in the Disciplines: Proceedings of the 9th International Conference of the Learning Sciences, ICLS '10, Chicago, IL, USA, June 29 - July 2, 2010, Volume 2*, 2010, pp. 425–426. [Online]. Available: http://dl.acm.org/citation.cfm?id=1854729

[20] G. Agnew, C. M. Mills, and C. A. Maher, "Vmcanalytic: Developing a collaborative video analysis tool for education faculty and practicing educators," in *43rd Hawaii International International Conference on Systems Science (HICSS-43 2010), Proceedings, 5-8 January 2010, Koloa, Kauai, HI, USA*, 2010, pp. 1–10. [Online]. Available: http://dx.doi.org/10.1109/HICSS.2010.438

[21] C. A. F. P. Filho, T. A. Buck, and C. A. S. Santos, "An environment for video content indexing and retrieval base don visual features," in *Proceedings of the XV Brazilian Symposium on Multimedia and the Web*, ser. WebMedia '09. New York, NY, USA: ACM, 2009, pp. 25:1–25:8. [Online]. Available: http://doi.acm.org/10.1145/1858477.1858502

[22] D. M. Norris and L. Baer, "Building organizational capacity for analytics: Panel proposal," in *Proceedings of the 2Nd International Conference on Learning Analytics and Knowledge*, ser. LAK '12. New York, NY, USA: ACM, 2012, pp. 18–19. [Online]. Available: http://doi.acm.org/10.1145/2330601.2330612

[23] A. L. Dyckhoff, D. Zielke, M. Bültmann, M. A. Chatti, and U. Schroeder, "Design and implementation of a learning analytics toolkit for teachers," *Educational Technology & Society*, vol. 15, no. 3, pp. 58–76, 2012. [Online]. Available: http://www.ifets.info/download_pdf.php?j_id=56&a_id=1257

[24] S. Wang, J. Chen, and M. Behrmann. (2004) Visualizing search engine results of data-driven web content. [Online]. Available: http://www.w3.org/WAI/RD/2003/12/Visualization/VisSearch/VisualSearchEngine.htm

[25] S. Wang and M. Behrmann, "Automatic adaptive assessment in mlearning," 2009, pp. 435–438.

Vehicle Detection on Low Altitude Images Based on Edge Density

Antonio J. R. Neves, Manuel Camarneiro and Lucas Cozinheiro

DETI/IEETA, University of Aveiro,
3810-193 Aveiro, Portugal
Email: {an, mcamarneiro, lucas.cozinheiro}@ua.pt

Abstract—**The popularity of unmanned aerial vehicles, usually denoted as drones, is increasing these days due to various factors. Their capability of capturing images from above, allowing new perspectives of a scene, is for sure one of the most significant. It gets even more interesting when captured images are processed using Computer Vision algorithms, creating a powerful technology combination with appliances in several areas. In this paper, we present algorithms under development to process images captured by drones over parking lots in order to detect parked vehicles and further estimate occupancy rates or cars parked in a wrong place. Another application that we are developing is the monitoring of boats in the Aveiro lagoon. As far as we know, the processing of low altitude images is still an open problem in the computer vision community. The preliminary results presented in this paper show the effectiveness of the approaches under development.**

Keywords–Drones; Image processing; object detection.

I. Introduction

Aerial videos captured by unmanned aerial vehicles are becoming popular these days. So called drones are fascinating as they are capable of getting images from places where it used to be impossible to put a recording camera.

Introducing interaction between the drone and its camera creates something much more complex and useful: a device that can be the key for solving a wide range of problems. Autonomous flight with a recording device onboard makes it, for instance, a mobile surveillance camera. But as soon as image processing is added, this device will be able to detect suspicious movements around a property or even follow potential intruders.

Solutions using drones and computer vision are not restricted to security. There is a huge number of possible areas where these devices might be useful [2] [4]. Although, only a few commercial drones are able to perform some basic image processing over obtained images. There is still a long way to go through on scientific research about this technology combination. Lately, a few commercial solutions are available for applications in agriculture mainly used to monitor plants growth, watering levels and fruit maturation. Some prototypes are also being tested for save and rescue tasks or fast mail delivery.

Before the proliferation of drones, monitoring vehicles from aerial imagery was already possible, making use of pictures either taken from satellite or from manned aircraft. For this kind of images there are several approaches regarding algorithms to detect and extract cars position. This is often associated with high altitude or satellite imagery [3] [6]. Even though, as this project assumes the usage of drones in lower altitude flights (about 10 meters from the ground), most of the published work does not apply. Thus, the solution was creating algorithms from scratch for parking lots with three different types of pavement, assuming to have drone's altitude and parking zone location regarding the road as program inputs.

Images were previously captured using a Parrot Bebop 2 [1] flying a selected path over some of the University of Aveiro parking lots, sampling parking zones built on tar, block pavement and both. Algorithms were further developed to detect parked vehicles over each type of pavement identified before.

The algorithms were tested on an external computer used for development but were also adapted for further tests in single boards in order to determine the possibility of having image processing onboard as the drone moves over the parking lots.

We present in this paper experimental results showing the effectiveness of the proposed approach, both in terms of detection ration as well as in terms of processing time.

The paper is organised as follows. In Section II, we present the problem studied in this paper. In Section III, we present an algorithm for car detection in three different type of pavement parks, namely blocks, tar and mixed pavements. In Section IV, we present experimental results. Finally, in Section V, we draw some conclusions.

II. Car Detection in Low Altitude Images

To evaluate parking lots capacity the first mandatory task is image acquisition. Assuming the drone is correctly positioned regarding the road, a frame should be captured and sent to the image processing unit. Once there, the image might need to be corrected in case of heavy distortion effects. After this, the algorithm should try to detect vehicles, compare them with others detected in previous images to check if they were already counted, and finally update the counter. This repetitive pipeline is presented in a circular graphic in Figure 1.

Vehicle detection is obviously a decisive part of software but a broad range of cars might appear in a parking lot. Features as color, size or shape may vary from one to another making it harder to create a global solution capable of detecting them all based only on these features. At the same time, it is necessary to ensure that detected objects are effectively vehicles, distinguishing them from similar objects that might appear.

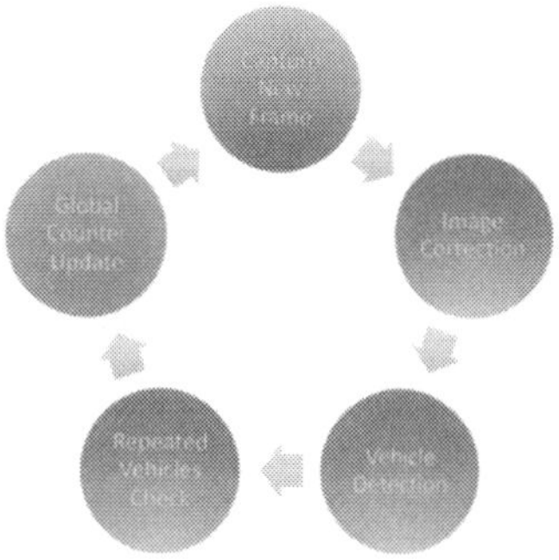

Figure 1. Algorithm Global Pipeline.

Distinguishing pavement from other objects placed above the ground could be a possible solution. Even though, this sets up another challenge. Homogeneous grey concrete or tar might be easily discarded using a color filter threshold. Nevertheless, the same technique will not work in a park built in block pavement.

III. PAVEMENT DETECTION

Distinguishing pavement from other objects placed above the ground could be a possible solution. Even though, this sets up another challenge. Homogeneous grey concrete or tar might be easily discarded using a color filter threshold. Nevertheless, the same technique will not work in a park built in block pavement. In this paper, we developed algorithms for three types of pavement.

A. *Block Pavement Detection*

Canny Edge Detector algorithm [5] was used as a fast and optimized method to perform gradient computations and retrieve the most important edges for each acquired image. Figure 2 shows a fine mesh, which corresponds to the edges of each small block that composes the pavement. Cars, on the other hand, are found in zones of low edge concentration.

Figure 2. At the top, an image of a Block Pavement Parking. On the bottom the corresponding gradient Image.

It would be possible to simply cluster regions with low edge density and compare their size to the expected car size (which estimation would depend on the drone's altitude). Even though this would give space to detection errors, either by including more than one car in a single cluster or by analyzing uninteresting zones in the surrounding areas. Some gardens or sidewalks, for instance, feature smooth surfaces making it harder to distinguish them from parked vehicles.

The solution was finding the road borders to further estimate parking places position. After applying a color filter and Hough lines detector to locate the grids along the road, it is possible to establish the interest regions, on the left, right, or both sides of the road (Figs. 3 and 4).

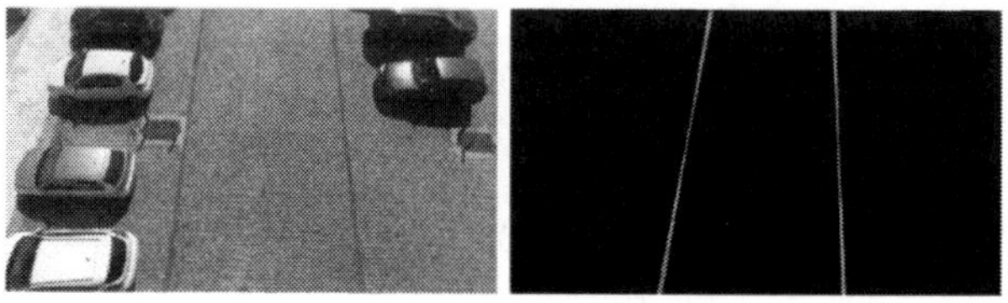

Figure 3. On the left, the image acquired by the drone, on the right the road borders detected.

Figure 4. Road is removed as well as unwanted lateral zones. Parking places' length is very close to access road's width, thus interest region is trunked as presented.

Edge density analysis may now be performed for each one of the interest regions identified before. Vehicle's expected size is compared with the size of detected stains according to their position on the image. Objects on the top appear smaller due to the perspective introduced by the Drone used for image acquiring. To minimize errors edge density analysis is performed only on the bottom half of the image.

Despite the drone is moving with an almost constant speed, it is not possible to capture images without any overlay, meaning that the same vehicle might be present in more than one frame. To avoid double counting, it is required storing color, size and position features of vehicles detected in the last frame to compare them with the vehicles detected at the moment (Figure 5).

B. *Tar Pavement Detection*

Images obtained over tar pavement are smoother and lack of edges when compared to blocks pavement presented before. Despite that fact, it is still possible to reuse the logic from the last algorithm, detecting the road using the limit lines and trunking the interest regions.

As tar is homogeneous either in texture as in colour, checking if a low edge density zone is free or occupied can

Figure 5. New and Repeated Vehicles Detected

Figure 6. On the left, the image acquired by the drone, on the right the road borders detected.

be done using color matching, making sure it is different from the tar found in the road (Figure 7).

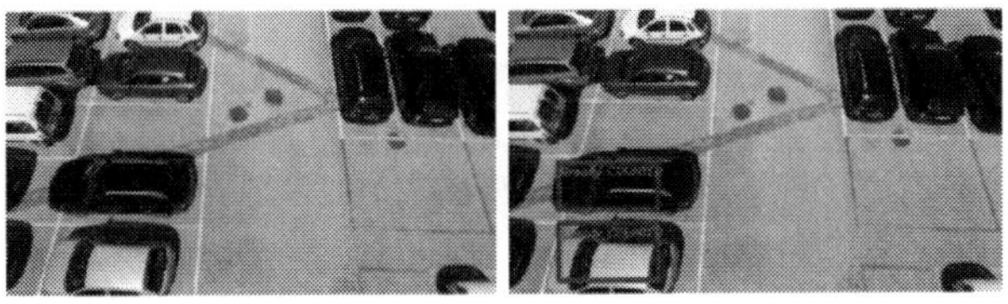

Figure 7. On the left, the image acquired by the drone, on the right the vehicle detection on tar parkings.

C. Mixed Pavement

Most of the studied parking lots are built on both tar (used in the access road) and blocks with different configurations (used in parking places). The algorithm developed for this type of pavement slightly differs from the others, given the impossibility of detecting road based on color filters.

In this case, road limits are determined using the same notion of edge density. Tar zones are not expected to have high gradient values thus road might be easily detected. Further vehicle detection is performed as explained for the block pavement, as well as vehicle repetition check (see Figure 8 and 9).

IV. EXPERIMENTAL RESULTS

This section presents important values measured and analysed for the studied solutions. These are related to detection accuracy and processing times.

All tests were performed using an Unix distribution (Ubuntu 14.04.3) installed on a computer with an Intel Core i5-3340M CPU @ 2.70GHz 4 processor with 4Gb RAM. Images captured were recorded as video and split into frames considering only one frame each half a second. A splitting

Figure 8. Road detection in mixed pavement parking lots. Raster scan window used to evaluate edge density is variable and affects processing times and road detection accuracy.

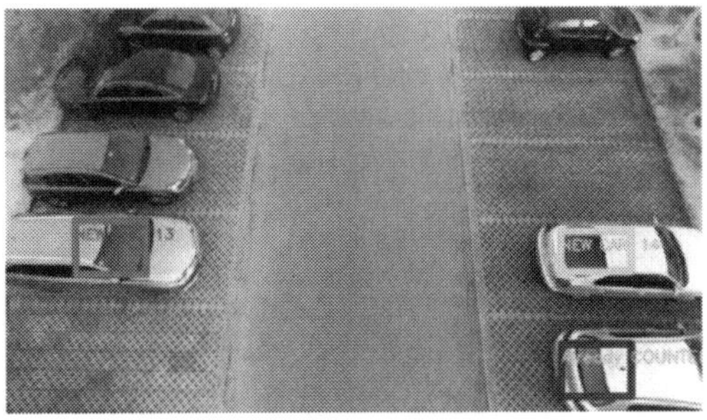

Figure 9. Vehicle detection in mixed pavement parking lots.

tool was also developed to read each video's frame rate and save images every 500 milliseconds in a specific directory previously defined.

Car detection accuracy is evaluated frame by frame comparing manual annotation of the number of cars depicted with detection boxes drawn by the algorithm.

It is crucial to choose a suitable edge detection method since these operations are performed every time a new image is processed. It is important to ensure some points regarding the chosen method:

- Detects low edge concentration over the road pavement (in case the road is made of tar)
- Creates high edge density zones over block pavement, contrasting with uniform surfaces on vehicles.
- Takes a short period of time to compute all the edges in an image.

Choosing the most suitable values enables accurate detection of homogeneous regions as shown in some examples presented in Figure 13.

It is now evident that Canny is an optimised edge detection method, possible to adapt to different situations by conveniently adjusting its parameters. It also features less processing requisites when compared to Sobel making it the best method and the one used for the rest of the algorithm tests.

Finding road limits composes a crucial step in the algorithm's pipeline since this is performed in every park and is essencial to the location of interest zones. It is not relevant to have high accuracy in this procedure as the main goal is to eliminate the major region of the image representing road. It is not decisive to remove every single pixel from the road and

Figure 10. Sliding window influence on road detection.

Figure 11. Cars detected on tar parking lot P1.

Figure 12. Cars detected on block pavement parking lot P5.

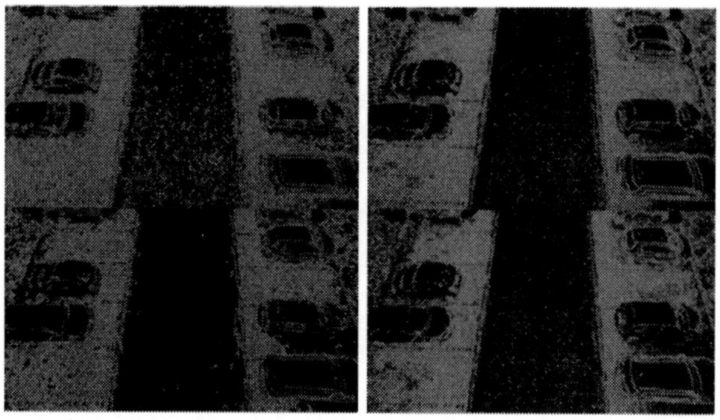

Figure 13. Two different edge detection algorithms tested with different parameters. From left to right, top to bottom: Canny Min=10, Max=50, Sobel X=1, Y=1, Canny Min=2, Max=200, Sobel X=2, Y=2.

preserve all other pixels, what is mandatory is the task to be quickly executed in every frame captured. Even though, road detection methods are distinct for different parking lots and different solutions should be developed for different pavement types.

On the other hand, vehicle detection based on low concentration of edges over the interest regions should be as accurate as possible and is applicable with only a few parameters adjustments to all studied parking lots. The following sections will detail results obtained for each type of parking lot studied.

Parking Lots in homogeneous kind of pavement are perhaps the most simple to deal with. Higher detection rates are then most likely to happen in P1 (Table I and Figure 11).

The block pavement revealed to be a difficult background

TABLE I. RESULTS FOR TAR PARKING LOT.

Parking Lot	Parked Cars	Counted Cars	Repeated Counting	False Positives	Undetected Cars	Detection Rate
P1	17	17	0	0	0	100%

to extract vehicles from. Despite edge density zones concept being easier to imagine in this situation, region segmentation is not easy as there are some homogeneous surfaces in the parking lot borders.

The technique used to detect road borders in the parking lot P5 is based on the grids detection, as referred before. This is very tricky since there is no color differentiation between pavement and grids, all that changes is edges density. Hough Lines detector keeps being used to determine border lines and, as expected, it increases processing time as shown in Table II. Some detection examples are presented in Figure 12.

TABLE II. RESULTS FOR BLOCK PARKING LOT.

Parking Lot	Parked Cars	Counted Cars	Repeated Counting	False Positives	Undetected Cars	Detection Rate
P5	61	61	2	0	2	97%
P5	78	78	1	1	2	97%

In the parking lots 2 and 3, the pavement is mixed. An homogeneous tar surface is found on the road, while the rest is made on block pavement.

Road detection is made based on a sliding window, which runs from the image center to its borders. This window might not move pixel by pixel, it may, for instance, jump 10 pixels every step saving some processing time. On its turn, window

TABLE III. DETAILED PROCESSING TIME FOR BLOCK PARKING LOT USING A RASPBERRY PI 2 MODEL B.

Frame	1	2	3	4	5	6	7	8
Open Time (RGB)	128	125	131	127	130	127	129	127
Gray	36	22	22	22	22	22	22	22
HSV	135	129	131	133	129	127	134	128
Find road	494	478	498	481	491	483	490	481
Car analysis	226	223	234	227	216	224	218	215
Cars found	1	1	2	2	1	1	1	1
Cars on image	1	1	2	2	1	1	1	1
%	100%	100%	100%	100%	100%	100%	100%	100%
TOTAL (ms)	1073	1030	1069	1042	1041	1035	1044	1025
				% AVG	100%			

TABLE IV. DETAILED PROCESSING TIME FOR MIXED PAVEMENT PARKING LOT USING A RASPBERRY PI 2 MODEL B.

Frame	1	2	3	4	5	6	7	8
Open Time (RGB)	141	144	142	146	140	144	137	145
Gray	36	22	23	23	22	22	22	22
HSV	138	128	130	127	128	130	128	129
Find road	431	430	422	428	421	427	422	420
Canny	284	278	272	281	284	280	277	271
Car analysis	226	225	223	218	222	225	245	237
Cars found	1	1	1	1	1	1	2	2
Cars on image	1	1	1	2	1	1	2	2
%	100%	100%	100%	50%	100%	100%	100%	100%
TOTAL (ms)	1309	1280	1265	1276	1269	1280	1284	1276
				% AVG	94%			

size might also be increased, loosing some definition on the road border found but improving algorithm's performance.

To evaluate this, several experiments were made in P2 in order to find a good relation between road borders detection accuracy and processing requisites as shown in Figure 10 and Table V.

TABLE V. RESULTS FOR MIXED PARKING LOTS.

Parking Lot	Parked Cars	Counted Cars	Repeated Counting	False Positives	Undetected Cars	Detection Rate
P2	46	45	0	1	2	96%
P2	20	20	0	0	0	100%
P3	39	39	0	1	1	97%
P3	24	23	0	0	1	96%

Since the goal is the development of fully autonomous drones, we tested the developed algorithms on several single-boards (Raspberry Pi 2 Model B, IGEPv2 DM3730 and EPIA-P910) in order to decide what could be the best hardware solution. Besides the processing time, presented in Tables III and IV we also tested other properties like weight and power consumption. The processing times obviously increase when running the developed algorithms on these single boards. However, we observe that it is possible to reduce the speed of the drone because the images acquired continuously have a considerable repetition of information. With this in mind, and evaluating the experimental results obtained, we consider that Raspberry Pi 2 reaches reasonable values for onboard processing.

V. CONCLUSION

The algorithms presented in this paper showed promising results for the detection of vehicles on low altitude images acquired by Drones, being a solution for parking lots management.

The developed algorithms fulfilled the low processing requirements, which enables the algorithms to process images every second and allows the drone to move at a reasonable speed; the accuracy associated to vehicle detection and counting is also high. Furthermore, results obtained for tests made in three different types of pavement indicated a versatile solution, adaptable to several contexts achieving good performances with slight parameter adjustments from park to park.

As future work, we are developing algorithms for boats detection on water and the preliminaries results were also satisfactory. We think this work can provide an interesting contribution to our future smart cities, as a starting point for monitoring of objects of interest using drones. Moreover, we are optimising the presented algorithms to be used on board of the droned in order to have a fully autonomous solution.

REFERENCES

[1] www.parrot.com/us/Drones/Parrot-Bebop-2, Bebop 2 drone, retrieved April, 2017.

[2] www.amazon.com/b?node=8037720011, Amazon prime air, retrieved April, 2017.

[3] J.-Y Choi and Y.-K. Yang, "Vehicle detection in aerial images", Technical report, College of IT, Kyungwon University, 2009.

[4] dailytech.com, Flying rescue drone prototype to provide lifesaving aid to swimmers, retrieved April, 2017.

[5] R. Maini and H. Aggrwal, "Study and comparison of various image edge detection techniques", Technical report, Punjabi University, India, 2009.

[6] S. Tuermer, J. Leitloff, P. Reinartz and U. Stilla, "Automatic vehicle detection in aerial image sequences of urban areas using 3D HOG features", Technical report, Technische Universitaet Muenchen, German Aerospace Center, 2010.

Face Detection on Infrared Thermal Image

Ricardo F. Ribeiro, José Maria Fernandes, António J. R. Neves

DETI/IEETA, University of Aveiro,
3810-193 Aveiro, Portugal
Email: {rfribeiro, jfernan, an}@ua.pt

***Abstract*—Infrared cameras or thermal imaging cameras are devices that use infrared radiation to capture an image. This kind of sensors are being developed for almost a century now. They started to be used in the military environment, but at that time it took too long to create a single image. Nowadays, the infrared sensors have reached a whole new technological level and are used for purposes other than military ones, as happens in this work, where they are being used for face detection. When comparing the use of thermal images regarding color images, it is possible to see some advantages and some limitations, which will be explored in this paper. This work proposes the development or adaptation of several methods for face detection on infrared thermal images. The well known algorithm developed by Paul Viola and Michael Jones, using Haar feature-based cascade classifiers, is used to compare the traditional algorithms developed for visible light images when applied to thermal imaging. In this paper, we present three different methods for face detection. As far as we know, there is limited research on this topic so we think this work is an important contribution to the field. In the first one, an edge detection algorithm is applied to the binary image and the face detection is based on these contours. In the second method, a template matching method is used for searching and finding the location of a template image with the shape of human head in the binary image. In the last one, a matching algorithm is used. This algorithm correlates a template with the distance transform of the edge image. This algorithm incorporates edge orientation information resulting in the reduction of false detection and the cost variation is limited. The results show that the proposed methods have promising outcome, but the second method is the most suitable for the performed experiments.**

Keywords–Face detection; infrared images;Image processing; robotics; object detection.

I. INTRODUCTION

In the electromagnetic spectrum, the visible light spectrum is the only part that the human eye can see. Due to the fact that infrared radiation is invisible to the human eye, thermal cameras use infrared sensors to capture that radiation, transforming it into visible images. Many objects and even humans emit infrared radiation in function of the temperature: the higher the temperature, the higher the intensity of the emitted radiation.

The use of thermal infrared cameras has been increasing in various scientific areas. A survey providing an overview of the current applications is presented in [1]. Applications include animals, agriculture, buildings, gas detection, industrial, and military fields, as well as detection, tracking, and recognition of humans. In robotics, for computer vision, thermal image analysis and processing is in constant development, being used more often in systems for detection and tracking of objects, humans, among others.

The camera used in this work, which is shown in Figure 1, is a complete long-wave infrared (LWIR) camera module that captures infrared radiation input in the wavelength range from 8 to 14 microns and converts it to infrared thermal image. Figure 2 shows a thermal image complemented with an image in the visual spectrum from the same scene (typically a Red, Green and Blue - RGB - image).

Figure 1. FLIR Lepton thermal camera module with breakout board.

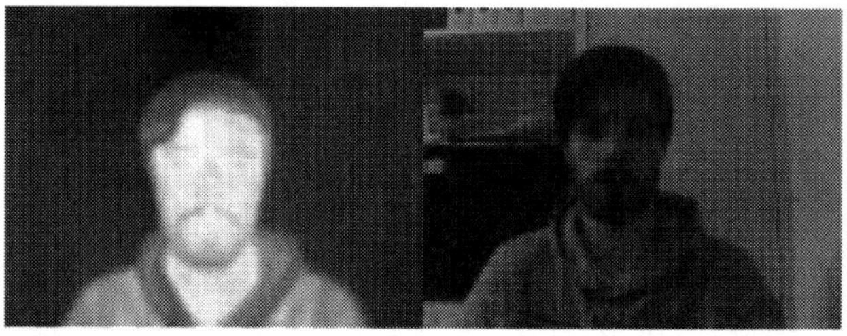

Figure 2. An example of a thermal image and the same scene aquired by a RGB camera.

In this work, we propose algorithms for face detection using thermal infrared cameras. The main goals of this work are the use of these type of sensors in service robots and in monitoring people attention taking into consideration of the temperature of the face over time. We are also working on emotional analysis through thermal images.

This paper is organized as follows. In Section II, we describe some advantages and limitations of thermal images. In Section III, we present the techniques that have been proposed for face detection. In Section IV, we provide experimental results. Finally, in Section V, we draw some conclusions.

II. THERMAL IMAGES

Thermal cameras are advantageous in many applications due to their ability to see in total darkness, their robustness to illumination changes and shadow effects, and less intrusion on privacy [2]. These cameras, when calibrated, are advantageous in temperature measurement compared to point-based methods since temperatures over a large area can be compared, although contact methods are more efficient [3]. In this work, the thermal camera used is not calibrated, so it is not possible to know the exact temperature in the region of interest.

Some algorithms for face detection using color or grayscale images currently have a very high efficiency rate but is not possible to use them directly in the thermal images. In thermal imaging there are some problems that can reduce this efficiency significantly using these algorithms such as occlusion of the face with objects that emit infrared radiation, the uniform temperature in the face, objects with the shape and same temperature of the face, among others. For this reason, only one feature-based algorithm is used, the Haar Cascade [4].

Consequently, with problems regarding face detection, the temperature becomes unstable over time. The face is one of the zones of the human body that is more suitable for the body temperature extraction and posteriorly the emotion analysis. The face detection in this work is represented on a shape of a bounding box obtaining the face and also some surrounding background noise that can affect the detected face for the next modules. The temperature measurement and emotional analysis of the face is being developed, not being included in this current work.

III. Proposed Approach

In this section, different developed algorithms and methods for face detection on thermal images are described. The development of this work was made in C++ programming language, through the use of the OpenCV library, which is an open source computer vision and machine learning software library. The use of these algorithms and methods will be on real-time systems, therefore it is also described in this section the equipment used for the acquisition of the thermal image and the method to obtain these images.

A. *Image Acquisition*

For thermal image acquisition in real-time, it is used a FLIR LEPTON Long Wave Infrared (50 shutterless) camera module, with a focal plane array of 80x60 active pixels. This camera is a non-radiometric version. This camera is also not calibrated, therefore it is not possible to obtain temperature values of each pixel. The output value also changes with the temperature value of the infrared sensor of the camera and the temperature of the scene.

It is also used a Raspberry Pi 3 model B for communication and image processing. For the acquisition of the output values on the Raspberry Pi 3, Serial Peripheral Interface (SPI) communication is used. It also supports a command and control interface (CCI) hosted on a Two-Wire Interface (TWI) similar to Inter-Integrated Circuit (I2C) for software interface [5]. This image acquisition process is based on a project developed by the company Pure Engineering [6]. The obtained output values are received in an 14-bits data, then they are arranged in an 8-bits with one channel image matrix format provided by OpenCV. The image on the left presented in Figure 2 shows an example of a thermal image. Darker areas correspond to colder regions in the scene.

B. *Haar Cascades*

Haar Cascades is a machine learning algorithm where a cascade function is trained from positive and negative images. This approach uses the Viola and Jones algorithm [4].

Haar Cascades is one of the algorithms implemented by OpenCV library. This algorithm was studied by Mekyska et al. [7] showing a machine learning approach for face detection and it requires a high number of images of the object to be detected for the cascade training. A similar study was made in this work, but the results of the face detection are considered of low accuracy. The thermal images with faces that were used for the cascade training can be obtained on the online dataset [8]. The result of the cascade training for Haar Cascade is shown in the results section.

C. *Implementation Details*

As far as we know, face detection on thermal images did not received too much attention on computer vision as the counterpart on visible light images. There are some possible ways using some functionalities of OpenCV library. Thermal image is, on a first stage, segmented and filtered with morphological operators in order to obtain a binary image for the later use of some methods or algorithms.

Segmentation uses the Otsus method that is a thresholding binarization method [9] and filtering is performed using morphological operators, such as dilation, erosion, opening and closing [10]. We developed and implemented the following algorithms:

- **Face Contours** - Acquisition and filtering of the contours in order to obtain the longest contour in the binary image and detect the face through it [11].
- **Template Matching** - Technique for finding areas of an image that match to a template image [12].
- **Chamfer Matching** - Technique to find the best alignment between two edge maps [13].

1) Face Contours: Through the binary image is created an edges map, using the Canny edge detector algorithm [14], where the contours are found [11]. These contours are filtered in order that only the contour of larger area are obtained. Due to the contour of having some parts of the human body that are not relevant for face detection, for example neck and shoulders, it is found the highest point of the contour. This point matches to the highest point on the face. Starting at this point, the two points that correspond to the largest width of the face are found. The detection of the face is made with this two points and the highest point in the face contour.

2) Template Matching: Template Matching is a technique that uses a template to search and find in an image the best match of this template. There are different matching methods to perform the template matching technique. This work uses the Normalized Cross-Correlation method that remains a viable choice for some if not all applications [12].

Researchers in [15] use a Image Pyramid to perform the template matching for objects with different sizes. In this work it is used image pyramid to detect faces of different sizes increasing the performance of the template matching. Due to the image captured by the camera having a reduced resolution, few levels of the pyramid image are used. Each level of the image is downsized. A good template is needed to obtain better results in the template matching.

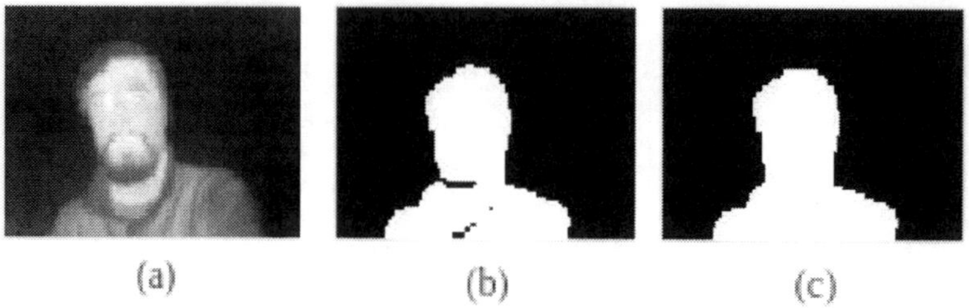

Figure 3. In (b) the segmentation of the thermal image (a). The result of applying the morphological operation is presented in (c).

3) Chamfer Matching: The Chamfer Matching algorithm lies on shape matching using distance transform. This technique uses an edges image of the image being tested and the template to create an Distance Transform map [16]. The value of each pixel in this map is the distance to the nearest background pixel. After this, chamfer distance map is created that contains the computed matching cost through the distance transform maps and the position of the edge orientation contours [13]. The face is detected finding the pixel location of the minimal chamfer distance.

IV. Results

In this section, we present experimental results to verify the effectiveness of the developed algorithms. Since our goal is the real time use of this contribution, the examples were obtained in real time with the camera connected to the single board computer. The obtained output values used to form the thermal images were processed in order to obtain an 8-bit grayscale image. An example of this type of images is represented in Figure 3(a).

A. Haar Cascades

The study made by Mekyska et al. [7] used the Viola and Jones algorithm [4] applied to thermal image. The results of this study show that in order to obtain a good accuracy, a large amount of training data is needed. The disadvantage of this algorithm is also the detection time, which is dependent on the amount of training data.

In this work, there was an attempt of performing cascade training for face detection. An example of the application of this algorithm is presented in Figure 4. However, in comparison with the study mentioned it has an inferior performance. Face detection is unstable since it does not detect the face if the image does not contain the neck and shoulders of the person.

Figure 4. Face detected using Haar Cascades.

B. Proposed Methods for Face Detection

Figures 3(b) and 3(c) show and example of the segmentation obtained in this type of images and the use of morphological operators, respectively.

The methods and algorithms mentioned in Section 3.3 use and input the image presented on Figure 3(c).

1) Face Contours: Using Canny algorithm the edge map presented in Figure 5 is obtained. Figure 6 shows an example of face detection using contours. These results can be influenced if the contours of the face are discontinued for some reason. This method is not the most suitable for face detection since there are some variations in the bounding box of the detected face.

Figure 5. Edge map obtained from a thermal image.

2) Template Matching: When using template matching a good template is needed. Figure 9 shows the template used. This method slides the template over the image of Figure 3(c) and calculates an error for the match between the template and the image being tested [15]. A method based on image pyramids is also used in order to improve the result of template matching since it takes the scale in consideration. The best match is found as a global maximum value. Figure 7(b) shows some examples of application.

3) Chamfer Matching: This algorithm uses the same template of Figure 9, but it is converted to an edge using the Canny edge detector algorithm to be used later in the construction of the cost image. A distance transform map is created from the edge image and from the template, which specifies the distance from each pixel to the nearest edge pixel in the query image.

Figure 10 represents the two images of distance transform maps. Then a map with the matching cost of each pixel is created. The pixel location of the minimal cost is the location of the region of interest. Some results applying the Chamfer Matching [13] are shown in Figure 8.

C. Processing Time

All experimental results have been obtained in real time using a Raspberry Pi 3 model B.

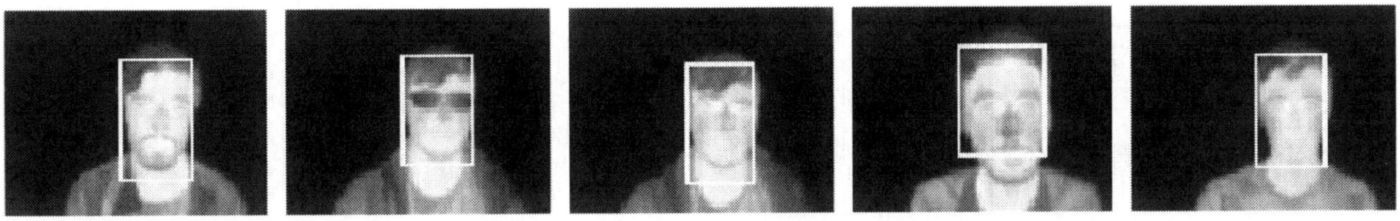

Figure 6. Some examples of face detection in different conditions using contour detection.

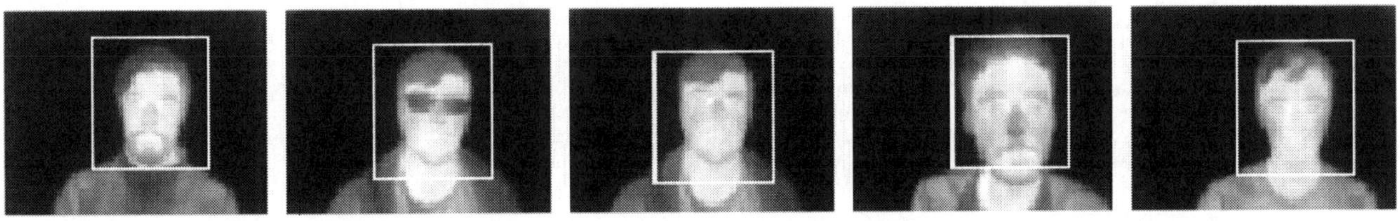

Figure 7. Some examples of face detection in different conditions using Template Matching.

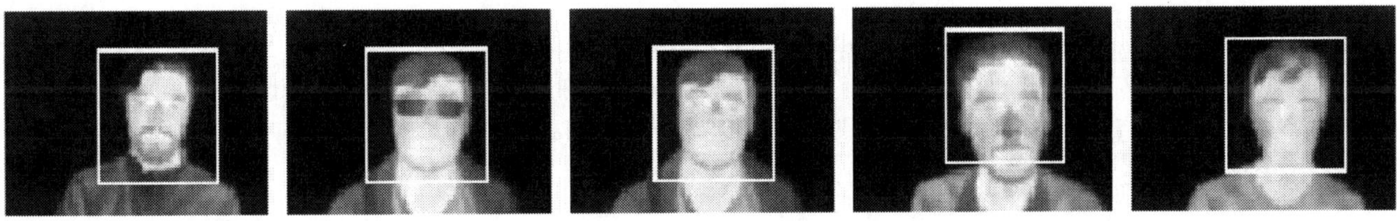

Figure 8. Some examples of face detection in different conditions using Chamfer Matching.

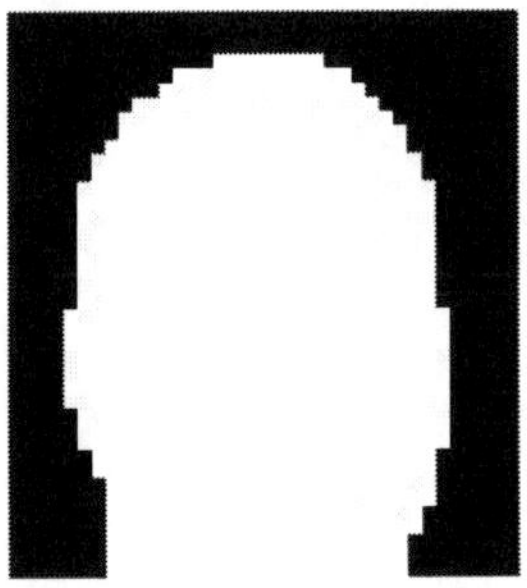

Figure 9. Template used for template matching.

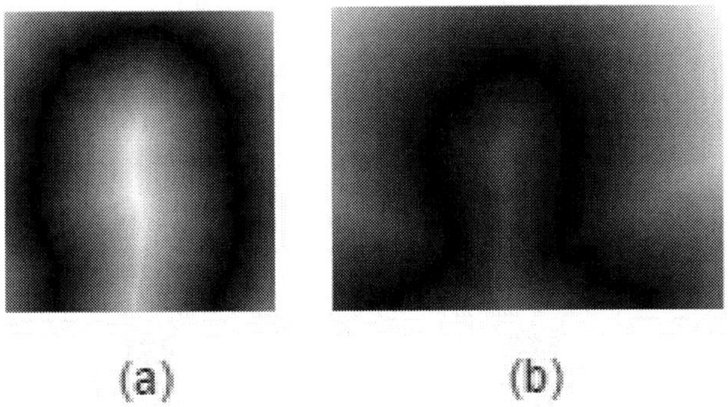

Figure 10. Distance Transform image of template (a) and query image (b).

The processing time of Haar Cascade is approximately 72ms.

The average processing time obtained by the proposed methods applied during an experiment of 70 seconds with a frame rate limited to 4 frames per seconds are the following:

- **Face Contours** - 68ms.
- **Template Matching** - 69ms.
- **Chamfer Matching** - 257ms.

Chamfer Matching has the highest processing time, because this method involves several steps which require more processing time, for example distance transform, edge orientation, among others.

V. Conclusion and Future Work

In this paper, we presented a study regarding the development of three different methods for face detection in thermal images using image segmentation.

Haar Cascade using Viola and Jones algorithm has better performance and accuracy based on [7]. However, this algorithm needs a large amount of data and time for training to obtain good results. Face detection in thermal image using Haar Cascade can be improved using one of the proposed methods for image segmentation and create a lot of thermal images that contain only the face for training database.

Face detection through thermal imaging using segmentation has a good accuracy in single face detection. Comparing the proposed methods, Template Matching is the most suitable. Although Face contours has a processing time similar to Template Matching, the bounding box with the face detected is more unstable. Chamfer Matching has a similar detection to Template Matching but processing time of this method is almost 4 times slower.

In this work, the thermal camera used is not calibrated, so it is not possible to know the exact temperature in the region of interest. As future work, we intend to improve the developed algorithms for face detection and develop algorithms for calibration of this sensor in order to measure absolute temperatures. We are also working on a calibration procedure for the simultaneous use of this camera and an RGB camera.

References

[1] R. Gade, and T. B. Moeslund, "Thermal cameras and applications: a survey", *Machine vision and applications* 25.1: 245-262, 2014.

[2] A. Berg, J. Ahlberg and M. Felsberg, "A thermal object tracking benchmark", *Advanced Video and Signal Based Surveillance (AVSS), 12th IEEE International Conference on.* IEEE, 2015.

[3] A. Berg, *Detection and Tracking in Thermal Infrared Imagery* Diss. Linkping University Electronic Press, 2016.

[4] P. Viola and M. Jones, "Rapid object detection using a boosted cascade of simple features," *Computer Vision and Pattern Recognition, CVPR 2001, Proc. of the 2001 IEEE Computer Society Conference on.* vol. 1. IEEE, 2001.

[5] FLIR LEPTON Long Wave Infrared (LWIR) Datasheet. http://www.flir.com/uploadedFiles/OEM/Products/LWIR-Cameras/Lepton/Lepton%20Engineering%20Datasheet%20-%20without%20Radiometry.pdf, retrieved April, 2017.

[6] Pure Engineering LEPTON project. http://www.pureengineering.com/projects/lepton, retrieved April 2017.

[7] J. Mekyska, V. Espinosa-Dur and Marcos Faundez-Zanuy, "Face segmentation: A comparison between visible and thermal images", *Security Technology (ICCST 2010), IEEE International Carnahan Conference on*, IEEE, 2010.

[8] Terravic Facial Infrared Database. http://vcipl-okstate.org/pbvs/bench/Data/04/download.html, retrieved April, 2017.

[9] R. F. Moghaddam and M. Cheriet, "AdOtsu: An adaptive and parameterless generalization of Otsu's method for document image binarization", *Pattern Recognition* 45.6: 2419-2431, 2012.

[10] H. Heijmans, "Connected morphological operators for binary images," *Computer Vision and Image Understanding* 73.1: 99-120, 1999.

[11] S. Suzuki, "Topological structural analysis of digitized binary images by border following", *Computer vision, graphics, and image processing* 30.1: 32-46, 1985.

[12] J. P. Lewis, "Fast normalized cross-correlation", *Vision interface*, vol. 10. no. 1, 1995.

[13] M. Liu, et al., "Fast directional chamfer matching,", *Computer Vision and Pattern Recognition (CVPR 2010), IEEE Conference on*, IEEE, 2010.

[14] J. Canny, "A computational approach to edge detection", *IEEE Transactions on pattern analysis and machine intelligence* 6: 679-698, 1986.

[15] L. Ferreira, A. J. R. Neves, A. Pereira, E. Pedrosa, J. Cunha, "Human detection and tracking using a Kinect camera for an autonomous service robot", Advances in Aritificial Intelligence - Local Proceedings, EPIA 2013 - XVI Portuguese Conference on Artificial Intelligence, Angra do Herosmo, Azores, Portugal, p. 276-288, 2013.

[16] G. Borgefors, "Distance transformations in digital images", *Computer vision, graphics, and image processing* 34.3: 344-371, 1986.

Transmit Beamforming Strategies with Iterative Equalization for Hybrid mmW Systems

Roberto Magueta, Daniel Castanheira, Adão Silva, and Atílio Gameiro.
DETI, Instituto de Telecomunicações
University of Aveiro
Aveiro, Portugal
e-mail: rlm@av.it.pt, dcastanheira@av.it.pt, asilva@av.it.pt, and amg@ua.pt

Rui Dinis
Instituto de Telecomunicações
Faculdade de Ciências e Tecnologia, Univ. Nova de Lisboa
Lisboa, Portugal
e-mail: rdinis@fct.unl.pt

Abstract– **The aim of this manuscript is to compare the performance of two transmit beamforming approaches with an iterative equalizer for millimeter wave (mmW) systems. At the transmitter, we assume two hybrid beamforming: a sparse beamforming approach recently proposed and fixed random beamforming which the coefficients are computed independently of the instantaneous channel realization. At the receiver, we consider a hybrid iterative block space-time structure to efficiently separate the spatial streams. We consider that both the transmitter and the received are equipped with a large antenna array and the number of radio frequency (RF) chains is lower that the number of antennas. The hardware limitations impose several constraints in the analog domain that are considered when the transmit beamforming/precoder is generated. Our performance results have shown that the performance of the sparse precoder is better for low signal-to-noise ratio (SNR) regime while random precoder outperforms sparse based one for medium to high SNR regime.**

Keywords—massive MIMO, mmWave communications, iterative block equalization, hybrid analog/digital architectures.

I. Introduction

The use of a large number of antennas makes achievable higher data rates for future wireless networks [1]. Additionally, the global bandwidth shortage facing wireless carriers has motivated the exploration of the underutilized millimeter wave (mmW) frequency spectrum for future broadband cellular communication networks [2] and that allows the access to more bandwidth. Due to the small wavelength, the use of mmW with massive MIMO (mMIMO) is very attractive, since the terminals can be equipped with large number of antennas very compacted [3].

In mmW, the channel is very correlated that is critical for a mMIMO implementation, where propagation tends to be line of sight (LOS) or near-LOS. Thus, the use of beamforming to minimize de interference is very important for these systems [3]. MmW massive MIMO systems may exploit new and efficient spatial processing techniques [4], but the design at these techniques should follow different approaches than the ones adopted for lower frequencies counterparts, mainly due to the hardware limitations [5]. The high cost and power consumption of some mmW mixed-signal components, make it difficult to have a fully dedicated radio frequency (RF) chain for each antenna [6] as in conventional MIMO systems [7] and to overcome these limitations, hybrid analog/digital architectures were proposed. At these architectures, some signal processing is done at the digital level and some left to the analog domain, as discussed in [8].

Some beamforming and/or combining/equalization schemes have been proposed for hybrid architectures [9]-[13]. A precoding scheme based on the knowledge of partial channel information at both terminals, in the form of angles of arrival (AoA) and departure (AoD), was proposed in [9]. The authors in [10] designed a joint digital and analog beamforming at the transmitter side, where first a set of fixed analog beamforming coefficients is selected and then a digital eigenmode based precoder is computed, but they consider a fully digital receiver. In [11], a hybrid spatially sparse precoding and combining approach was proposed for mmW massive MIMO systems. The spatial structure of mmW channels was exploited to formulate the single-user multi-stream precoding/combining scheme as a sparse reconstruction problem. A digitally assisted analog beamforming technique for mmW systems was considered in [12], where a digital beamsteering system using coarsely quantized signals assists the analog beamformer. In [13], a turbo-like beamforming was proposed to jointly compute the transmit and receive analog beamforming coefficients, but the digital processing part was not taken into account.

Nonlinear equalizers are considered to efficiently separate the spatial streams in the current MIMO based networks [14]. Iterative block decision feedback equalization (IB-DFE) approach was originally proposed in [15] and it is one of the most promising nonlinear equalization schemes [14]. IB-DFE can be regarded as a low complexity turbo equalizer implemented in the frequency-domain that does not require the channel decoder output in the feedback loop. The IB-DFE principles can be used in mmW massive MIMO context to efficiently separate the spatial streams. However, as discussed, mmW massive MIMO brings new major challenges that prevent a direct plug and play of the iterative equalization based solutions developed for conventional fully digital MIMO systems.

In this paper, we evaluate the performance of two transmit beamforming strategies combined with an efficient iterative block space-time equalizer for hybrid mmW massive MIMO systems. In the first strategy, we consider fixed random precoders computed without the knowledge of the channel state information (CSI) keeping the transmitter with very low complexity. In the second one, we assume a sparse transmit beamforming recently proposed in [11]. At the transmitter side, a space-time encoder structure is employed, before the digital and analog precoders, to 1) ensure that the transmit signal and consequently the noise plus interference, at the receiver side, are Gaussian distributed (which simplifies the receiver optimization), 2) warrant that the signal to interference plus noise ratio (SINR) is independent of each spatial stream and time slot and 3) increase the inherent diversity of the mmW massive MIMO system. At the receiver, we design a hybrid iterative block space-time structure to efficiently separate the spatial streams. We assume a fully connected hybrid architecture where each RF chains are connected to all antennas. The analog and digital parts of the hybrid equalizer are jointly optimized using as a metric the mean square error (MSE) between the transmitted data vector and its estimate after the digital equalizer. The specificities of the analog domain impose several constraints in the joint optimization. To efficiently deal with the constraints the analog part is selected from a dictionary based on the array response vectors.

The remainder of the paper is organized as follows: Section II describes the hybrid mmW massive MIMO systems model. Section III, presents the random precoder. Section IV, starts by briefly describing the iterative space-time receiver structure. Then, the fully digital equalizer is presented and finally the proposed hybrid space-time equalizer is derived in detail. Section V presents the main performance results and the conclusions will be drawn in section VI.

Notations: Boldface capital letters denote matrices and boldface lowercase letters denote column vectors. The operation $(.)^H$ represents the Hermitian transpose of a matrix. Consider a vector $\mathbf{a}$ and a matrix $\mathbf{A}$, then diag($\mathbf{a}$) and diag($\mathbf{A}$) correspond to a diagonal matrix with diagonal entries equal to vector $\mathbf{a}$ and a diagonal matrix with entries equal to the diagonal entries of the matrix $\mathbf{A}$, respectively. $\mathbf{A}(j,l)$ denotes the element at row j and column l of the matrix $\mathbf{A}$. $\mathbf{I}_N$ is the identity matrix with size $N \times N$.

II. SYSTEM CHARACTERIZATION

In this section, we present the mmW massive MIMO signal definition, the transmitter and receiver characterization. We consider a hybrid based architecture, as shown in Fig 1. Furthermore, we assume a single-user mmW system with N_t transmit antennas and N_r receive antennas, where the transmitter sends N_s data streams to the receiver, per time-slot.

We considered a clustered channel, $\mathbf{H} \in \mathbb{C}^{N_r \times N_t}$, that is the sum of the contribution of N_{cl} clusters, each of which contribute N_{ray} propagation paths which follows the clustered sparse mmW channel model discussed in [11]. It may be expressed as

$$\mathbf{H} = \mathbf{A}_r \mathbf{\Lambda} \mathbf{A}_t^H \tag{1}$$

where $\mathbf{\Lambda}$ is a diagonal matrix, with entries (j,l) corresponding to the paths gains of the lth ray in the ith scattering cluster. $\mathbf{A}_t = [\mathbf{a}_t(\theta^t_{1,1}),\ldots,\mathbf{a}_t(\theta^t_{N_{cl},N_{ray}})]$, $\mathbf{A}_r = [\mathbf{a}_r(\theta^r_{1,1}),\ldots,\mathbf{a}_r(\theta^r_{N_{cl},N_{ray}})]$ are the matrix of array response vectors at the transmitter and receiver, whereas $\theta^r_{j,l}$ and $\theta^t_{j,l}$ are the azimuth angles of arrival and departure, respectively. The channel path gains and the angles are generated according to the random distributions discussed in [11]. We consider a block fading channel, i.e., the channel remains constant during a block, with size T, but it varies independently between blocks.

III. RANDOM PRECODER

In this section, we present a low complexity transmitter. We assume that the transmitter have no access to CSI simplifying the overall system design. The transmitter processing is decomposed into two parts, the digital baseband and the analog circuitry that are modeled mathematically by precoder matrices $\mathbf{F}_a \in \mathbb{C}^{N_t \times N_t^{RF}}$ and $\mathbf{F}_d \in \mathbb{C}^{N_t^{RF} \times N_s}$, respectively. The digital part has N_t^{RF} transmit chains, with $N_s \le N_t^{RF} \le N_t$. Due to hardware constraints, the analog part is implemented using a matrix of analog phase shifters, which force all elements of matrix $\mathbf{F}_a$ to have equal norm ($|\mathbf{F}_a(i,l)|^2 = N_t^{-1}$). As such the analog precoder matrix is generated randomly accordingly to

$$\mathbf{F}_a = [e^{j2\pi\phi_{n,p}}]_{1\le n\le N_t, 1\le p\le N_t^{RF}}, \tag{2}$$

where $\phi_{n,p}$, $n \in \{1,\ldots,N_t\}$, $p \in \{1,\ldots,N_t^{RF}\}$ are i.i.d uniform random variables with support $\phi_{n,p} \in [0,1]$.

We assume that all RF resources are used by transmitter, i.e., $N_s = N_t^{RF}$, and then we can assume that digital precoder is equal to identity matrix, $\mathbf{F}_d = \mathbf{I}_{N_s}$. The transmitter total power constraint is $\|\mathbf{X}\|_F^2 = N_s T$. The transmit signal is given by

$$\mathbf{X} = \mathbf{F}_a \mathbf{F}_d \mathbf{C}, \tag{3}$$

where $\mathbf{C} = [\mathbf{c}_1,\ldots,\mathbf{c}_T] \in \mathbb{C}^{N_s \times T}$ denotes a codeword constructed by using a space-time block code (STBC) that can be mathematically described by

$$\mathbf{z}_t = \mathbf{S}\mathbf{f}_t, \tag{4}$$

$$\mathbf{c}_t = \mathbf{\Pi}_t \mathbf{z}_t, \tag{5}$$

where $t = 1,\ldots,T$ denotes the time index, $\mathbf{f}_t \in \mathbb{C}^T$ denotes column t of a T-point DFT matrix ($\mathbf{F}_T = [\mathbf{f}_1,\ldots,\mathbf{f}_T]$), $\mathbf{\Pi}_t \in \mathbb{C}^{N_s \times N_s}, t = 1,\ldots,T$ is a random permutation matrix, known both at the transmitter and receiver sides and $\mathbf{S} = [s_{s,t}]_{1\le s\le N_s, 1\le t\le T} \in \mathbb{C}^{N_s \times T}$, with $s_{t,s}$, $t \in \{1,\ldots,T\}$, $s \in \{1,\ldots,N_s\}$ denoting a complex data symbol chosen from a QAM constellation with $\mathbb{E}[|s_{s,t}|^2] = \sigma_s^2$, where $\sum_{s=1}^{N_s} \sigma_s^2 = N_s$. For the sake of simplicity and, without loss of generality, in this work we consider only QPSK constellations. To compute codeword $\mathbf{C}$ we need to apply an FFT transform to the rows of the symbol matrix $\mathbf{S}$ (see (4)) and then permute each of the resulting T columns with a random permutation $\mathbf{\Pi}_t$, $t = 1,\dots,T$ (see (5)).

IV. Hybrid Iterative Space-Time Receiver Design

In this section, we derive the hybrid iterative block space-time feedback equalizer shown in Fig. 2. We start by designing the fully digital receiver, that can serve as lower bound for the hybrid one and then a detailed formulation of the iterative approach is presented. The received signal is given by

$$\mathbf{Y} = \mathbf{H}\mathbf{X} + \mathbf{N}, \quad (6)$$

where $\mathbf{Y} = [\mathbf{y}_1,\dots,\mathbf{y}_T] \in \mathbb{C}^{N_r \times T}$ denotes the received signal matrix, $\mathbf{X} = [\mathbf{x}_1,\dots,\mathbf{x}_T] \in \mathbb{C}^{N_t \times T}$ is the transmitted signal and $\mathbf{N} = [\mathbf{n}_1,\dots,\mathbf{n}_T] \in \mathbb{C}^{N_r \times T}$ a zero mean Gaussian noise with variance σ_n^2. The received signal is firstly processed through the analog phase shifters, modeled by the matrix $\mathbf{W}_a \in \mathbb{C}^{N_r^{RF} \times N_r}$, then follows the baseband processing, composed of N_r^{RF} processing chains. All elements of the matrix $\mathbf{W}_a$ must have equal norm ($|\mathbf{W}_a(j,l)|^2 = N_r^{-1}$). Specifically, the baseband processing includes a digital feedback closed-loop comprising a forward and a feedback path. For the forward path the signal first passes through a linear filter $\mathbf{W}_d \in \mathbb{C}^{N_s \times N_r^{RF}}$, then follows the decoding of the STBC (demodulation included). In the feedback path, the data recovered in the forward path is first modulated and encoded using the STBC, then it passes through the feedback matrix $\mathbf{B}_d \in \mathbb{C}^{N_s \times N_s}$. The encoding of the STBC follows (4) and (5), and its decoding obeys

$$\tilde{\mathbf{Z}} = [\mathbf{\Pi}_1^H \tilde{\mathbf{c}}_1,\dots,\mathbf{\Pi}_T^H \tilde{\mathbf{c}}_T], \quad (7)$$

$$\tilde{\mathbf{S}} = \tilde{\mathbf{Z}}\mathbf{F}_T^H. \quad (8)$$

The feedback and feedforward paths are combined by subtracting the signal output of the feedback path from the filtered received signal $\mathbf{W}_d \mathbf{W}_a \mathbf{Y}$. At the ith iteration the received signal at the tth time slot, after the de-interleaver, is given by

$$\tilde{\mathbf{z}}_t^{(i)} = \mathbf{\Pi}_t^H (\mathbf{W}_{d,t}^{(i)} \mathbf{W}_{a,t}^{(i)} \mathbf{y}_t - \mathbf{B}_{d,t}^{(i)} \mathbf{\Pi}_t \hat{\mathbf{z}}_t^{(i-1)}), \quad (9)$$

$$\hat{\mathbf{Z}}^{(i-1)} = \hat{\mathbf{S}}^{(i-1)} \mathbf{F}_T, \quad (10)$$

where $\mathbf{\Pi}_t^H \in \mathbb{C}^{N_s \times N_s}$ is the de-interleaver matrix and $\hat{\mathbf{Z}}^{(i-1)} = [\hat{\mathbf{z}}_1^{(i-1)},\dots,\hat{\mathbf{z}}_T^{(i-1)}] \in \mathbb{C}^{N_s \times T}$ is the DFT of the detector output $\hat{\mathbf{S}}^{(i-1)}$. The matrix $\hat{\mathbf{C}}^{(i)} = [\mathbf{\Pi}_1 \hat{\mathbf{z}}_1^{(i)},\dots,\mathbf{\Pi}_T \hat{\mathbf{z}}_T^{(i)}]$ is the hard estimate of the transmitted codeword $\mathbf{C}$ and $\hat{\mathbf{S}}^{(i)} = \mathrm{sign}(\tilde{\mathbf{S}}^{(i)})$ the hard decision associated to QPSK data symbols $\mathbf{S}$, at iteration i.

From the central limit theorem the entries of vector $\mathbf{z}_t$, $t \in \{1,\dots,T\}$ are Gaussian distributed, then as the input-output relationship between variables $\mathbf{z}_t$ and $\hat{\mathbf{z}}_t^{(i)}$, $t \in \{1,\dots,T\}$ is memoryless, follows

$$\hat{\mathbf{z}}_t^{(i)} = \mathbf{\Psi}^{(i)} \mathbf{z}_t + \hat{\boldsymbol{\epsilon}}_t^{(i)}, \quad t \in \{1,\dots,T\}, \quad (11)$$

where $\mathbf{\Psi}^{(i)}$ is a diagonal matrix given by

$$\mathbf{\Psi}^{(i)} = \mathrm{diag}\left(\psi_1^{(i)},\dots,\psi_s^{(i)},\dots,\psi_{N_s}^{(i)}\right), \quad (12)$$

$$\psi_s^{(i)} = \frac{\mathbb{E}\left[\hat{\mathbf{z}}_t^{(i)}(s)\mathbf{z}_t^*(s)\right]}{\mathbb{E}\left[|\mathbf{z}_t(s)|^2\right]}, s \in \{1,\dots,N_s\}, \quad (13)$$

and $\hat{\boldsymbol{\epsilon}}_t^{(i)}$ is a zero mean error vector uncorrelated with $\mathbf{z}_t$, $t \in \{1,\dots,T\}$, with $\mathbb{E}\left[\hat{\boldsymbol{\epsilon}}_t^{(i)} \hat{\boldsymbol{\epsilon}}_t^{(i)^H}\right] = \left(\mathbf{I}_{N_s} - \left|\mathbf{\Psi}^{(i)}\right|^2\right)\sigma_s^2$, and then it can be proven that the average error power is given by

$$\begin{aligned} \mathrm{MSE}_t^{(i)} &= \mathbb{E}[\|\tilde{\mathbf{z}}_t^{(i)} - \mathbf{z}_t\|^2] \\ &= \left\|(\mathbf{W}_{ad,t}^{(i)})^{\Pi} \mathbf{H}_t^{\Pi} - \mathbf{I}_{N_s} - (\mathbf{B}_{d,t}^{(i)})^{\Pi} \mathbf{\Psi}^{(i-1)}\right\|_F^2 \sigma_s^2 \quad (14) \\ &+ \left\|(\mathbf{B}_{d,t}^{(i)})^{\Pi} (\mathbf{I}_{N_s} - |\mathbf{\Psi}^{(i-1)}|^2)^{1/2}\right\|_F^2 \sigma_s^2 + \left\|(\mathbf{W}_{ad,t}^{(i)})^{\Pi}\right\|_F^2 \sigma_n^2, \end{aligned}$$

where $\mathbf{H}_t^{\Pi} = \mathbf{H}\mathbf{F}_a\mathbf{F}_d\mathbf{\Pi}_t$, $(\mathbf{W}_{d,t}^{(i)})^{\Pi} = \mathbf{\Pi}_t^H \mathbf{W}_{d,t}^{(i)} \mathbf{\Pi}_t$, $(\mathbf{W}_{a,t}^{(i)})^{\Pi} = \mathbf{\Pi}_t^H \mathbf{W}_{a,t}^{(i)}$, $(\mathbf{W}_{ad,t}^{(i)})^{\Pi} = (\mathbf{W}_{d,t}^{(i)})^{\Pi} (\mathbf{W}_{a,t}^{(i)})^{\Pi}$ and $(\mathbf{B}_{d,t}^{(i)})^{\Pi} = \mathbf{\Pi}_t^H \mathbf{B}_{d,t}^{(i)} \mathbf{\Pi}_t$.

A. *Design of Digital Iterative Space-time Receiver*

Firstly, we design the fully digital iterative space-time receiver based on the IB-DFE principles. The performance of this approach can be regarded as a lower bound for the hybrid iterative block equalizer designed in the next section. The equalizer is designed by minimizing the MSE

$$\begin{aligned} \left((\mathbf{W}_{ad,t}^{(i)})_{opt}^{\Pi}, (\mathbf{B}_{d,t}^{(i)})_{opt}^{\Pi}\right) &= \arg\min \mathrm{MSE}_t^{(i)} \\ \text{s.t.} \sum_{t=1}^{T} \mathrm{diag}((\mathbf{W}_{ad,t}^{(i)})^{\Pi} \mathbf{H}_t^{\Pi}) &= T\mathbf{I}_{N_s}. \end{aligned} \quad (15)$$

In this case, the number of receiver RF chains is equal to the number of receiver antennas, and thus we only have a digital

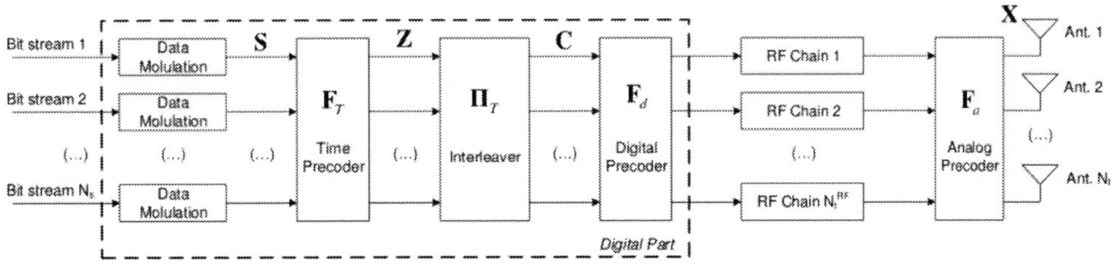

Fig 1. Transmitter block diagram.

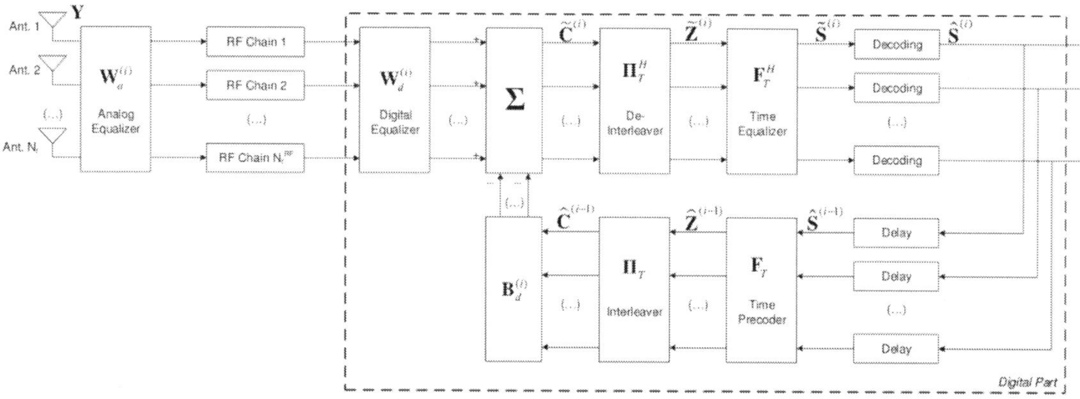

Fig 2. Receiver block diagram.

linear feedforward filter referred as $\mathbf{W}_{ad,t}$ and a feedback filter $\mathbf{B}_{d,t}$. The solution to the optimization problem (15) is

$$(\mathbf{W}_{ad,t}^{(i)})_{opt}^{\Pi} = \mathbf{\Omega}\left(\mathbf{R}_t^{(i-1)}\right)^{-1}(\mathbf{H}_t^{\Pi})^H, \tag{16}$$

$$(\mathbf{B}_{d,t}^{(i)})_{opt}^{\Pi} = \left((\mathbf{W}_{ad,t}^{(i)})_{opt}^{\Pi}\mathbf{H}_t^{\Pi} - \mathbf{I}_{N_s}\right)\left(\mathbf{\Psi}^{(i-1)}\right)^H, \tag{17}$$

$$\mathbf{\Omega} = T\left(\sum_{t=1}^{T}\mathrm{diag}\left(\left(\mathbf{R}_t^{(i-1)}\right)^{-1}(\mathbf{H}_t^{\Pi})^H\mathbf{H}_t^{\Pi}\right)\right)^{-1}, \tag{18}$$

$$\mathbf{R}_t^{(i-1)} = (\mathbf{H}_t^{\Pi})^H\mathbf{H}_t^{\Pi}(\mathbf{I}_{N_s} - |\mathbf{\Psi}^{(i-1)}|^2) + \sigma_n^2\sigma_s^{-2}\mathbf{I}_{N_s}. \tag{19}$$

B. Design of Hybrid Iterative Space-time Receiver

In this section, we design the hybrid iterative block space-time receiver. Clearly, the previous optimization problem of (15) does not take into account the analog domain constraints. Let us denote by $\mathcal{W}_a$ the set of feasible RF equalizers, i.e., the set of $N_t \times N_t^{RF}$ matrices with constant-magnitude entries, then the reformulated optimization problem for the hybrid iterative equalizer is as follows

$$\left((\mathbf{W}_{a,t}^{(i)})_{opt}^{\Pi}, (\mathbf{W}_{d,t}^{(i)})_{opt}^{\Pi}, (\mathbf{B}_{d,t}^{(i)})_{opt}^{\Pi}\right) = \arg\min \mathrm{MSE}_t^{(i)}$$
$$\text{s.t.} \sum_{t=1}^{T}\mathrm{diag}((\mathbf{W}_{d,t}^{(i)})^{\Pi}(\mathbf{W}_{a,t}^{(i)})^{\Pi}\mathbf{H}_t^{\Pi}) = T\mathbf{I}_{N_s} \tag{20}$$
$$(\mathbf{W}_{a,t}^{(i)})^{\Pi} \in \mathcal{W}_a.$$

Due to the digital nature of the feedback equalizer $(\mathbf{B}_{d,t}^{(i)})^{\Pi}$ and since the new constraint does not impose any restriction on this matrix, the feedback equalizer for the hybrid iterative equalizer is similar to the fully digital iterative equalizer discussed in the previous section, and thus given by

$$(\mathbf{B}_{d,t}^{(i)})_{opt}^{\Pi} = \left((\mathbf{W}_{d,t}^{(i)})_{opt}^{\Pi}(\mathbf{W}_{a,t}^{(i)})_{opt}^{\Pi}\mathbf{H}_t^{\Pi} - \mathbf{I}_{N_s}\right)\left(\mathbf{\Psi}^{(i-1)}\right)^H. \tag{21}$$

From (14) and (21), the MSE expression simplifies to is equal (up to a constant) to

$$\overline{\mathrm{MSE}}_t^{(i)} = \left\|\left((\mathbf{W}_{d,t}^{(i)})^{\Pi}(\mathbf{W}_{a,t}^{(i)})^{\Pi} - (\overline{\mathbf{W}}_{ad,t}^{(i)})_{opt}^{\Pi}\right)\left(\tilde{\mathbf{R}}_t^{(i-1)}\right)^{1/2}\right\|_F^2, \tag{22}$$

$$\tilde{\mathbf{R}}_t^{(i-1)} = \mathbf{H}_t^{\Pi}(\mathbf{I}_{N_s} - |\mathbf{\Psi}^{(i-1)}|^2)(\mathbf{H}_t^{\Pi})^H + \sigma_n^2\sigma_s^{-2}\mathbf{I}_{N_r}, \tag{23}$$

$$(\overline{\mathbf{W}}_{ad,t}^{(i)})_{opt}^{\Pi} = (\mathbf{I}_{N_s} - |\mathbf{\Psi}^{(i-1)}|^2)\mathbf{\Omega}^{-1}(\mathbf{W}_{ad,t}^{(i)})_{opt}^{\Pi}, \tag{24}$$

where $(\overline{\mathbf{W}}_{ad,t}^{(i)})_{opt}^{\Pi}$ and $\tilde{\mathbf{R}}_t^{(i-1)}$ denote a non-normalized version of the optimum fully digital feedforward matrix and the correlation of the ISI plus channel noise.

Due to the non-convex nature of the feasible set $\mathcal{W}_a$, an analytical solution to the problem (20) is difficult to obtain, if not impossible. Nevertheless, we find an approximate solution to problem (20) by assuming that the matrix $(\mathbf{W}_{a,t}^{(i)})^{\Pi}$ is a N_r^{RF} sparse linear combination of vectors $\mathbf{a}_{r,u}(\theta_{j,l}^{r,u})$ or equivalently a N_r^{RF} sparse linear combination of the columns of matrix $\mathbf{A}_r = [\mathbf{A}_{r,1}, \ldots, \mathbf{A}_{t,U}]$. We may say that $(\mathbf{W}_{a,t}^{(i)})^{\Pi}$ has a N_r^{RF} term representation over the dictionary $\mathbf{A}_r$. Therefore, optimization problem can be approximated as follows

$$\begin{aligned}(\ddot{\mathbf{W}}_{d,t}^{(i)})_{opt}^{\Pi} &= \arg\min \left\|\left((\ddot{\mathbf{W}}_{d,t}^{(i)})^{\Pi}\mathbf{A}_r^H - (\overline{\mathbf{W}}_{ad,t}^{(i)})_{opt}^{\Pi}\right)\left(\tilde{\mathbf{R}}_t^{(i-1)}\right)^{1/2}\right\|_F^2 \\ &\text{s.t.} \sum_{t=1}^{T}\mathrm{diag}((\ddot{\mathbf{W}}_{d,t}^{(i)})^{\Pi}\mathbf{A}_r^H\mathbf{H}_t^{\Pi}) = T\mathbf{I}_{N_s} \\ &\left\|\mathrm{diag}(((\ddot{\mathbf{W}}_{d,t}^{(i)})^{\Pi})^H(\ddot{\mathbf{W}}_{d,t}^{(i)})^{\Pi})\right\|_0 = N_t^{RF},\end{aligned} \tag{25}$$

where $\left\|\mathrm{diag}(((\ddot{\mathbf{W}}_{d,t}^{(i)})^{\Pi})^H(\ddot{\mathbf{W}}_{d,t}^{(i)})^{\Pi})\right\|_0 = N_t^{RF}$ represents the sparsity constraint and enforces that only N_r^{RF} columns of matrix $(\ddot{\mathbf{W}}_{d,t}^{(i)})^{\Pi}$ are non-zero. The optimum digital feedforward matrix $(\mathbf{W}_{d,t}^{(i)})_{opt}^{\Pi}$ is obtained from $(\ddot{\mathbf{W}}_{d,t}^{(i)})_{opt}^{(i)} = [(\mathbf{W}_{d,t}^{(i)})_{opt}^{\Pi}, \mathbf{0}]$ by removing the zero columns and the optimum analogue feedforward matrix $(\mathbf{W}_{a,t}^{(i)})_{opt}^{\Pi}$ is obtained from $\mathbf{A}_r^H$ by selecting the rows corresponding to the non-zero columns of $(\ddot{\mathbf{W}}_{d,t}^{(i)})^{\Pi}$.

From optimality condition (associated Lagrangian equal to zero), we obtain $\mathbf{W}_{res,t}^{(i)}$ that is the residue matrix that is given by

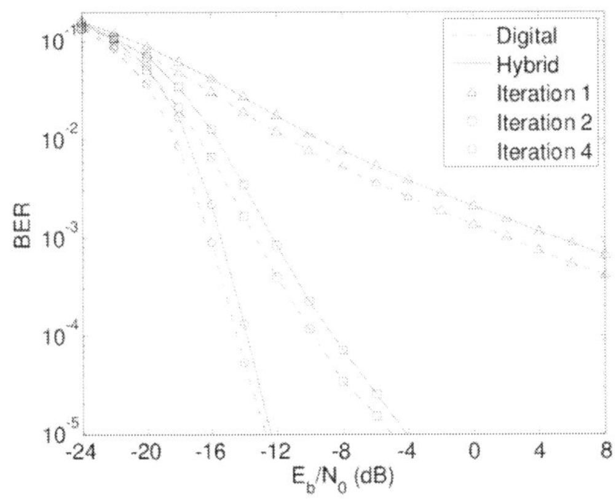

Fig 3. Performance for sparse precoder.

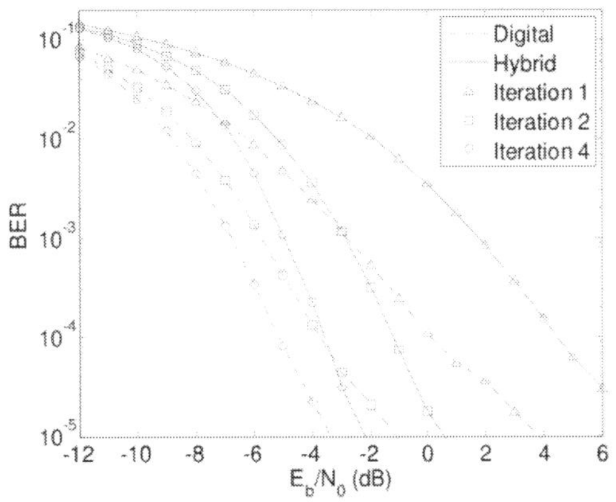

Fig 4. Performance for hybrid random precoder.

$$\mathbf{W}_{res,t}^{(i)} = \left((\ddot{\mathbf{W}}_{d,t}^{(i)})^{\Pi}\mathbf{A}_r^H - (\overline{\mathbf{W}}_{ad,t}^{(i)})_{opt}^{\Pi}\right)\left(\tilde{\mathbf{R}}_t^{(i-1)}\right) + \mathbf{U}_d(\mathbf{H}_t^{\Pi})^H . \quad (26)$$

From the definition of matrices $\tilde{\mathbf{R}}_t^{(i-1)}$, $\mathbf{R}_t^{(i-1)}$, $(\overline{\mathbf{W}}_{ad,t}^{(i)})_{opt}^{\Pi}$ and $(\mathbf{W}_{ad,t}^{(i)})_{opt}^{\Pi}$ equation (26) simplifies to

$$\mathbf{W}_{res,t}^{(i)} = (\dddot{\mathbf{W}}_{d,t}^{(i)})^{\Pi}\mathbf{A}_r^H\tilde{\mathbf{R}}_t^{(i-1)} - \mathbf{\Omega}_d(\mathbf{H}_t^{\Pi})^H , \quad (27)$$

where $\mathbf{\Omega}_d = \mathbf{I}_{N_s} - |\mathbf{\Psi}^{(i-1)}|^2 + \mathbf{U}_d$ denotes a redefined Lagrangian multipliers matrix, that must be selected so that the constraint of the optimization problem (25) is respected. The matrix $\mathbf{U}_d = \text{diag}(\mu_1,\ldots,\mu_{N_s})$ is a diagonal matrix where $\mu_s, s\in\{1,\ldots,N_s\}$ are the Lagrange multipliers.

To enforce the sparsity constraint, the best columns of the dictionary $\mathbf{A}_r$ are selected using an iterative greedy method. At each iteration the column of $\mathbf{A}_r$ that is most correlated with the actual value of the residue $\mathbf{W}_{res,t}^{(i)}$ is selected. In the first iteration, the residue is set to the trivial value $\mathbf{W}_{res,t}^{(i)} = -(\overline{\mathbf{W}}_{ad,t}^{(i)})_{opt}^{\Pi}\left(\tilde{\mathbf{R}}_t^{(i-1)}\right)$. Then, after identifying a set of columns of the matrix $\mathbf{A}_r$ (one column per iteration) to form the analog feedforward equalizer matrix $(\mathbf{W}_{a,t}^{(i)})_{opt}^{\Pi}$, we obtain the optimum digital feedforward equalizer matrix $(\mathbf{W}_{d,t}^{(i)})_{opt}^{\Pi}$ using the orthogonality condition. It can be proven that the optimum digital feedforward matrix is

$$(\mathbf{W}_{d,t}^{(i)})_{opt}^{\Pi} = \mathbf{\Omega}_d\left((\mathbf{W}_{a,t}^{(i)})_{opt}^{\Pi}\mathbf{H}_t^{\Pi}\right)^H\left(\mathbf{R}_{d,t}^{(i-1)}\right)^{-1}, \quad (28)$$

where $\mathbf{R}_{d,t}^{(i-1)} = (\mathbf{W}_{a,t}^{(i)})_{opt}^{\Pi}\tilde{\mathbf{R}}_t^{(i-1)}((\mathbf{W}_{a,t}^{(i)})_{opt}^{\Pi})^H$ and to respect the constraint of problem (25) $\mathbf{\Omega}_d$ is given by

$$\mathbf{\Omega}_d = T\left(\sum_{t=1}^{T}\text{diag}\left(\left((\mathbf{W}_{a,t}^{(i)})_{opt}^{\Pi}\mathbf{H}_t^{\Pi}\right)^H\left(\mathbf{R}_{d,t}^{(i-1)}\right)^{-1} \times(\mathbf{W}_{a,t}^{(i)})_{opt}^{\Pi}\mathbf{H}_t^{\Pi}\right)\right)^{-1}, \quad (29)$$

After obtaining the optimum value of the digital feedforward matrix $(\mathbf{W}_{d,t}^{(i)})^{\Pi}$ the residue matrix (26) is updated. The previous steps iterate on the updated residue value to obtain the N_r^{RF} index set to index the dictionary $\mathbf{A}_r$.

The proposed iterative hybrid space-time equalizer is identical to the equalizer proposed in [11] when the block length is equal to one ($T=1$) and for iteration one ($i=1$).

V. PERFORMANCE RESULTS

In this section, we access the performance of the two transmit beamforming approaches combined with the iterative space-time equalizer. We consider a clustered channel model with $N_{cl}=8$ clusters, each with $N_{ray}=10$ rays, with Laplacian distributed azimuth angles of arrival and departure. The average power of all N_{cl} clusters is the same and the angle spread at both the transmitter and receiver is set to 8 degrees. We assume that the transmitter's sector angle is 60º wide in the azimuth domain and the receiver antenna array has omnidirectional antenna elements. The antenna element spacing is assumed to be half-wavelength. The channel remains constant during a block, with size $T=32$, and takes independent values between blocks.

We present results for a scenario whose the parameters are $N_r=32$, $N_t=128$, $N_s=8$, $N_r^{RF}=N_t^{RF}=8$. These results are presented for iteration 1, 2 and 4 of the digital and hybrid iterative space-time receivers, which are referred as *digital* and *hybrid*, in the following.

The performance metric considered is the BER, which is presented as a function of the E_b/N_0, with E_b denoting the average bit energy and N_0 denoting the one-sided noise power spectral density. We consider $\sigma_1^2=\ldots=\sigma_{N_s}^2=1$ and then the average E_b/N_0 is identical for all streams $s\in\{1,\ldots,N_s\}$.

From Figs. 3 and 4 we can see the performance improves as the number of iterations increases as expected. Furthermore, the proposed hybrid equalizer is quite close to the digital counterpart for the 2-4th iterations. From these results, we verify that the gaps from the 1st to the 2nd iteration are much higher than from the 2nd iteration to the 4th.This larger gap is mainly due to the removal of the residual ISI which enables the added benefit of a larger diversity. From the 2nd to the 4th iteration there is also a benefit from ISI removal, but the gains are smaller since most of the ISI is removed in the 4nd iteration. At iteration 1, the BER target of 10^{-3} is achieved for an E_b / N_0 of 6 and 2dB, for sparse precoder and random precoder, respectively. However, at iteration 4, the BER target of 10^{-3} is achieved for an E_b / N_0 of -15.4 and -4.5dB, respectively. Therefore, the random precoder get a better performance for iteration 1, but the gain for sparse precoder was higher and the sparse precoder has a better performance than random precoder at iteration 4. This happens because the mmW massive MIMO are very correlated. The random precoder deals better with interference, but we get a higher beamforming gain with sparse precoder that despite dealing worse with interference, this one can be mitigated with an efficient non-linear equalizer.

VI. Conclusion

In this paper, we compared the performance of two hybrid transmit beamforming approaches, with different levels of CSI knowledge, combined with a hybrid iterative space-time equalizer for mmW massive MIMO systems. The analog part considers the specific hardware limitation inherent to the analog domain processing. A space-time encoder was used, before the analog precoders, to ensure transmit Gaussian based signals, which allowed to simplify the receiver optimization and to increase the system diversity.

The results have shown that the sparse precoder with a hybrid iterative space-time receiver achieved the best performance, mainly for low SNR regime, with a very few number of iterations. This happens because a larger beamforming gain can be achieved with sparse precoder and the interference can be efficiently removed with the iterative receiver structure. On the other hand, the random precoder explores the diversity and overcomes the problem of very correlated mmW massive MIMO channels. Therefore, the random precoder achieved the best performance for a linear equalizer (single iteration), because the signal at receiver suffers of less interference. Thus, we can conclude that the random precoder based transmitter structure is interesting for practical mmW massive MIMO based systems, where the channels are very correlated and it does not require CSI.

Acknowledgment

This work was supported by the Portuguese Fundação para a Ciência e Tecnologia (FCT) PURE-5GNET (UID/EEA/50008/2013) project.

References

[1] F. Rusek et al. "Scaling up MIMO: opportunities and challenges with very large arrays," *IEEE Signal Process. Mag.*, vol. 30, no. 1, pp. 40-60, Jan. 2013.

[2] S. Rangan, T. S. Rappaport, and E. Erkip, "Millimeter-wave cellular wireless networks: potentials and challenges", *Proceedings of the IEEE*, vol. 102, no. 3, pp. 366-385, March 2014.

[3] A. Swindlehurts, E. Ayanoglu, P. Heydari, and F. Capolino, "Millimeter-wave massive MIMO: The next wireless revolution?," *IEEE Commun. Mag.*, vol. 52, no. 9, pp. 52–62, Sep. 2014.

[4] W. Roh et. al., "Millimeter-wave beamforming as an enabling technology for 5G Cellular communications: theoretical feasibility and prototype results," *IEEE Commun. Mag.*, vol. 52, no. 2, pp. 106-113, 2014.

[5] T. Rappaport et. al., Millimeter wave wireless communications, *Prentice Hall*, 2014.

[6] T. S. Rappaport, J. N. Murdock, and F. Gutierrez, "State of art in 60 GHz integrated circuits and systems for wireless communications," *Proceedings of the IEEE*, vol. 99, no. 8, pp. 1390-1436, 2011.

[7] M. Vu, and A. Paulraj," MIMO wireless linear precoding," *IEEE Signal Processing Mag.*, vol. 24, no. 5, pp. 86-105, 2007.

[8] S. Han, Chih-Li I, Z. Xu, and C. Rowell, "Large-scale antenna systems with hybrid analog and digital beamforming for millimeter wave 5G,", *IEEE Commun. Mag.*, vol. 53, no. 1, pp. 186–194, 2015.

[9] A. Alkhateeb, O. El Ayach, G. Leus, and R. Heath, "Hybrid precoding for millimeter wave cellular systems with partial channel knowledge,", *in Proc. Information Theory and Applications Workshop (ITA)*, 2013.

[10] T. Obara, S. Suyama, J. Shen, and Y. Okumura, "Joint fixed beamforming and eigenmode precoding for super high bit rate massive MIMO systems using higher frequency bands", *in Proc. IEEE PIMRC*, 2014.

[11] O. Ayach, S. Rajagopal, S. Surra, Z. Piand, and R. Heath., "Spatially Sparse Precoding in millimeter wave MIMO systems", *IEEE Trans. Wireless Commun.*, vol. 13, no. 3, pp. 1499–1513, Mar. 2014.

[12] A. Kokkeler, and G. Smit, "Digitally assisted analog beamforming for millimeter-wave communications," *in Proc. ICC'15-Workshop on 5G & Beyond* – Enabling Technologies and Applications, 2015.

[13] X. Gao, L. Dai, C. Yuen, and Z. Wang, "Turbo-like beamforming based on Tabu search algorithm for millimeter-wave massive MIMO systems", *IEEE Trans. Veh. Technol.*, Jul. 2015 (online).

[14] N. Benvenuto, R. Dinis, D. Falconer, and S. Tomasin, "Single carrier modulation with non linear frequency domain equalization: An idea whose time has come - Again," *Proceedings of the IEEE*, vol. 98, no. 1, pp. 69-96, Jan. 2010.

[15] N. Benvenuto, and S. Tomasin, "Block iterative DFE for single carrier modulation," *Electron. Lett.*, vol. 39, issue 19, pp.1144-1145, Sep. 2002

Secure Video Multicast over Wireless Ad-hoc Networks using Network Coding

Du Yang, Valdemar Monteiro and Jonathan Rodriguez
Instituto de Telecomunicações
Universidade Aveiro, Campus Universitário,
Aveiro, 3810-193, Portugal
vmonteiro@av.it.pt

Tasos Dagiuklas and Charalambos Mysirlidis
Hellenic Open University, Computer Science
Patras, 263 65, Greece
ntan@ece.upatras.gr

Abstract—**Video streaming over wireless networks has been continuously increasing, which results in significant energy consumption and growing security concerns, especially for safety-related services such as video surveillance. Advanced transmission and security mechanisms are required to improve video quality, protect video transmissions, and in the same time achieve energy efficiency. One of the promising solutions is to exploit network coding. In this research paper, we provide network coding aided transmission as well as security mechanisms, and compare them to non-network coding schemes. It is proved that using network coding is capable of significantly improving the achievable video quality, and reducing the computation complexity as well as signaling overhead for data encryption.**

Keywords- *secure video streaming; network coding; SVC.*

I. Introduction

Media Applications such as broadcasting IPTV video and video on demand (VoD) services have become extremely popular to both service providers that perceive them as a mean to expand their revenues and market share, and subscribers that can have access to all-IP based services and traditional TV on any device, through the Internet. The H264/SVC (Scalable Video Coding) as specified in Annex G of H.264/AVC allows the construction of bit-streams that contain sub-bit streams that conform to H.264/AVC [1].

Network Coding is a promising technique that could be used for network content distribution. The concept behind network coding relies on XOR/linear combination among the packets in order to optimize throughput [2]. However, one of the constraints is because it necessitates considering coding distortion conveyed in a video packet in order to construct the network information flows in an efficient way [3].

The wireless media but other hand, is vulnerable for a wide range of attacks because of its broadcasting nature, which motivates a continuous research interest in this area [4][5] with the objective of providing sufficient security protection in an resource efficient manner.

This paper examines the use of secure network coding for video applications over wireless environments. It is proved that using network coding is capable of achieving the max-min-cut network capacity [6], and providing weak information-theoretical security [7].

The rest of the paper is organized as follows. The target scenario is introduced in section II, followed by a brief introduction of scalable video coding and network coding in section III. Video transmission schemes on multi-hop wireless network with and without network coding are detailed in section IV. In section V, two network coding assisted security mechanisms are described. The simulation results are demonstrated in section VI, followed by conclusion and future work in section VII.

II. Target Scenario

We are interested in considering an ad-hoc network, where nearby nodes are organized into clusters. One of the trustworthy nodes such as a desktop/router is selected as the cluster head. This cluster head is responsible of connecting to other cluster heads or severs. The example two-hop network as shown in Figure 1 consists of one source node (Node-S), three relay nodes (Node-R1, Node-R2 and Node-R3), and two destination nodes (Node-A and Node-B). The wireless links are denoted in dashed lines, which results in three disjoint paths from source node to each destination node via three different relay nodes. All the nodes are connected to other clusters or servers via the cluster-head R2.

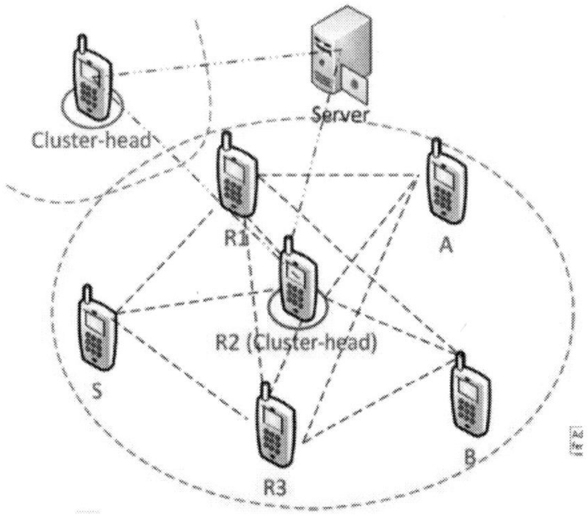

Figure 1. Target scenario example: a two-hop wireless ad-hoc network consisting of five nodes.

Besides serving as a portal, the cluster-head is also evolved in key management. At the beginning of clustering, the cluster head broadcasts its presence. Each member node responses with a joining request, and negotiate a shared key using Diffie-Hellman key exchange algorithm [8].

Our target is to multicast a video sequence within this network in an efficient and secure manner. Without loss of generality, we focus on the communication within a single cluster. As shown in Figure 1, a H.264/SVC encoded video sequence is generated at Node-S, and transmitted to Node-A and Node-B. We will demonstrate in the rest of the paper that network coding could be applied in both transmission and security mechanisms so as to improve the efficiency.

III. NETWORK CODING AIDED TRANSMISSION MECHANISMS

In this section, we start introducing some preliminary concepts, followed with introducing the common procedure of video transmission. Then we detail in single hop scenario, how the video packets are transmitted without and with network coding. After that, we discuss the additional benefits of using network coding in a multi-hop scenario.

A. *Scalable Video Coding and Network Coding concepts*

There are different ways of introducing scalability in H.264 SVC. The bit stream supports the following scalability modes: Coarse-Grain Scalability (CGS: the transform coefficients are encoded in a non-scalable way), Medium Grain Scalability (MGS the transform coefficients can be split in several fragments) and Fine-Grain Scalability (FGS: the transform coefficients are arranged as an embedded bit stream). Without loss of generality, MGS has been used in this research work.

Network coding is a revolutionary idea proposed in [6], which considered information bits as flow instead of commodity. It allows intermediate nodes in the network to store-recode-forward received information, instead of simply store-forward. Network coding algorithms can be classified according to various criteria [9]. Based on the present/absent of network topology knowledge, there are state-aware/stateless network coding algorithms.

The delay-sensitive nature of video streaming requires fast en-/decoding operation. Considering these two factors, stateless random linear network coding (RLNC) and the simply XOR operation have been widely recognized as good candidates [3,5,9] for video multicast over wireless network, which are also deployed in this paper.

B. *Common video transmission procedure*

A general video transmission involves three entities: source node, network, and sink node. Video is sampled at the source node frame by frame with a constant sampling interval Tf(s). Each frame is compressed and encoded into a sequence of packets. As demonstrated in Figure 2, each frame is encoded into two layers of packets, a base-layer (l = 1) and an enhancement layer (l = 2) (Without loss of generality, we assume 2 layers generated using MGS). It is crucial for all destinations to receive base-layer packets. The enhancement layer packets are optional and not decodable without receiving the base-layer.

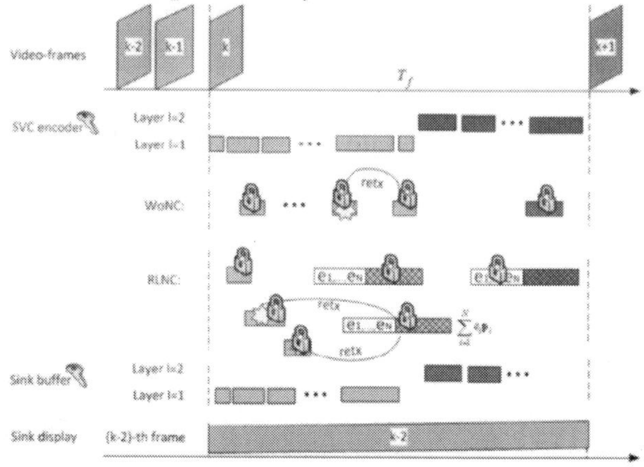

Figure 2. Illustration of video transmission and data encryption 1) without network coding; and 2)with network coding in a single-hop scenario.

It is essential for a sink node to buffer a few packets or frames before replaying the video. At a certain time slot, source node is in the process of compressing and encoding the k -th frame. Concurrently, packets belonging to the (k −1) -th video frame are transmitted and retransmitted over the network, and buffered at sink nodes. In the meantime, the (k − 2) -th video frame is displayed. As a result, the total transmission and retransmission time for each frame is equal to Tf.

The H.264 SVC bit stream is organized in autonomous entities called NAL Units. Each NAL Unit contains a header and payload. NAL units are encapsulated in RTP packets. IETF has specified different modes of encapsulating NAL Units in RTP packets namely: Single NAL Unit (SNU), Aggregating NAL Unit from one frame to RTP (STAP), Aggregating NAL Units from different frames to RTP (MTAP), Fragmenting NAL Units to Multiple RTP Packets. There are 3 transmission modes for SVC namely: Single Session Transmission (SST), Multi-Session Transmission (MST) and Media-Aware Network Element (MANE). Without loss of generality, we use SNU for each layer and MST SVC Transmission Mode (Each layer sends independently its packets). We are interested in using network coding to reduce the packet loss ratio of RTP video packets, in order to improve the video quality.

C. *Single-hop scenario*

The transmission in a single-hop scenario is illustrated in Figure 2 without and with network coding.

Without network coding scheme (WoNC): In the absent of network coding, the RTP video packets capsulated into IP packets by appending the IP header, and then pass to media access control (MAC) layer. Whenever a mobile node seizes an opportunity to transmit, adaptive modulation and coding is applied on the MAC layer packets based on the channel condition. An acknowledgement is fed back to the transmitter when a packet is received. Otherwise, this MAC-layer packet is marked as lost, and will be retransmitted later. Note that although end-to-end retransmission is forbidden in RTP/UDP/IP protocols, single-hop retransmission at MAC layer is allowed.

<u>*With RLNC:*</u> When we have equal length data packets, RLNC scheme logically re-organized the original packets { p1, p2,... } at source nodes into generations, each of which is a set of packets with adjacent packet-ids. We use a pair of parameters (g_{id} , g_{size}) to denote a generation to which packets with packet-ids equal to or larger than (g_{id} -1)*g_{size} , and smaller than g_{id} g_{size} . A coded packet is generated by linear combination, where e_k is an element in a certain finite field F. In the header of a coded packet, the encoding vector e = (e_1, K, e_{size}) as well as g_{id} is stored for later decoding at the receivers. A destination must receive equal or more than g_{size} number of linear independent coded packets in order to decode the original packets via Gaussian elimination.

However, SVC video packets have several features very distinct from non-real-time data packets. First of all, the video packets do not have equal length, but varies from several bytes to 1000 bytes according to frame type and scene complexity. Simple padding will introduce a significant amount of overhead. Second, video service is sensitive to delay, which could not tolerant a big generation size. Third, some video packets are more important than others. For example, base-layer video packets are more important than enhancement-layer ones. Mixing those packets with different importance may introduce video quality degradation.

Considering the aforementioned video features, we improve the network coding algorithm proposed in [3][10][11], and propose the following alterations:

- Base-layer video packets are first transmitted without using network coding.
- During base-layer packet retransmission, RLCN is applied over several packets. Supposed that four packets {p_1,p_2,p_3,p_4} are transmitted from Node-S. Only p_2 is lost at Node-R1, and p_3 is lost at Node-R2. Both nodes can recover their lost packet if Node-S retransmits one coded packet $\sum_{i=1}^{4} e_i p_i$
- Enhancement layer video packets are transmitted and retransmitted using RLCN, since they usually have a longer packet length and smaller variation.
- Enhancement layer video packets can be encoded with base layer video packets so as to provide higher protection to base-layer packets. Packet length variation is coped with the generation size allowed to change.

As we demonstrate in the simulation section, the proposed RLNC scheme reduces the Packet Loss Ratio (PLR) compared to WoNC scheme, and improves the video quality.

D. Multi-hop scenario

Using network coding provides an additional benefit in a multi-hop scenario. More explicitly, RLNC provides a nature way to exploit multiple paths from the source to the destinations. This is because that coded packets are mixture of original packets. All relay nodes are free to send several coded packets, which will all be useful for decoding at the sink node. The CodeCast protocol proposed based on RLNC in [11] demonstrates benefits in terms of throughput and robustness improvement. By contrast, without network coding, relay nodes must be careful to avoid sending redundant packets, which results in a more complicated and less efficient routing protocol.

IV. NETWORK CODING ASSISTED SECURITY MECHANISMS

As shown in last section, network coding can be applied on video transmission for higher throughput. It can also be used in synergy with security mechanism [5] [12] [13]. In this section, we explain network coding assisted security mechanism in two aspects: video data encryption and multicast group key agreement.

A. Lightweight encryption algorithm

<u>WoNC</u>: In the absent of network coding, the data payload must be encrypted in order to protect data confidentiality against eavesdropping attack. Assuming that only the legitimate sink nodes have the decryption key, any intermediate node is not able to interpolate the video content based on the received encrypted packets. A comprehensive encryption methods for H.264 video can be found in [4].

<u>RLNC</u>: Network coded packets using RLNC are linear combinations of several original packets. If an intermediate node is not able to decode network code packets, it is not capable of interpolating the video content, which provides some degree of security. It also provides a lightweight solution as suggested in [12]. In this scheme, the network coding coefficients are encrypted using a secrete key at source node, then the encrypted coefficients becomes a part of the payload. Normal RLNC is further applied at relay nodes. The sink nodes who have the secrete key will first decode the coded packets using Gaussian elimination, then decrypt the source-node coding coefficients using the secrete key, and finally obtain the original video data by using Gaussian elimination again. The video content is protected at relay nodes who do not have the knowledge if the encryption key. Since the coding coefficient is significantly less than the payload, this mechanism significantly reduce the amount of encryption data.

We illustrate the above-mentioned encryption methods in Figure 2. Due to the adjustment explained in Section 6-B, RLNC is not applied on layer-1 video packets. Hence, the reduction using the lightweight encryption algorithm of [12] can only be achieved for enhancement layer video packets. In some use-cases, enhancement layer video packets also need to be encrypted. For example, in video-on-demand services, higher video quality is offer only to those users subscribe to this service.

B. *Efficient multicast group key agreement*

Aided with a trustworthy cluster-head as well as the connected authentication server (if available), it is possible to set up pair-wise keys between each cluster member node and the cluster head. We have explained this in Section II. However, for video multicast, a common group key is required between source node and all sink nodes. The management of group key is a difficult problem. Each time a new member is added or an old member is evicted from the group, the group key must be changed to ensure backward and forward security, which means a new member cannot figure out any past group key, and an evicted member is not able to guess any new group key neither.

Many algorithms have been proposed for group key management [8]. One of them is called One-way function tree (OFT) assuming the presence of a centralized trust framework. Taking the example scenario shown in Figure 1, we illustrates the conventional OFT algorithm in Figure 3. More explicitly, the cluster-head Node-R2 is serves as a central trust point. At the beginning, Node-S, Node-A and Node-B have an individual symmetric key with the cluster-head Node-R2 denoted as Ks, KA and KB, respectively. Then, these group members are divided into subgroups of size 2, and a new shared key between these two members is derived. For example, a new shared key between Node-S and Node-A is calculated as

$$K_{SA} = f\left(h(k_A), h(K_S)\right) \qquad (1)$$

where h(.) is a one-way hash function, and f (.) is a mixing function such as concatenation. These new shared keys are further divided into subgroups of size 2, and a higher-level shared key is agreed using the same method. This process continues until a single shared key is agreed among all member nodes. Since the cluster head have all the individual keys, this shared key could be calculated at cluster head. However, for better security, it is not a good idea to directly transmit this group key to each member nodes. Instead, the cluster head encrypts the one-way hash value using individual secret keys, and distribute them to group member nodes, so that the group key could be derived locally at each member node. For example, the cluster head transmits two encrypted message to Node-A E_(K_A) (h(K_S)) and E_(K_A) (h(K_B)) where E_(K_A) (.) represents encrypting a message using Node-A's symmetric key KA .Similarly, the cluster-head must transmit 2 encrypted messages to Node-B and Node-S, which results in 6 messages in total. The reason of having a tree structure is to facilitate updating or regeneration of new keys when the group membership changes [8].

The above-mentioned communication overhead for group key initialization could be reduced by using a simple XOR network coding operation. Instead of transmitted two messages E_(K_A) (h(K_S)) and E_(K_A) (h(K_B)) to Node-A and Node-B respectively, the cluster-head could simply broadcast one message XOR (h(K_A),h(K_S)) to both Node-A and Node-B. Since they already have the hash value of its own key, it is easy to obtain the hashed value of the other key using XOR. Although the message is not encrypted, it is secure since only Node-A has the knowledge of its own key. As a result, this XOR-aided OFT algorithm could reduce 50% of the communication overhead in group key initialization process.

V. SIMULATION RESULTS

A. *Simulation Setup*

An end-to-end test-bed platform has been used for the experiments comprising video encoder, streamer, network emulator and decoder. The test-bed has been used to evaluate video quality of two video sequences. The video encoder uses an H.264/SVC encoder configured to create two Medium Grain Scalability (MGS) layers of one base and one enhancement layer. More specifically, two video sequences namely Crew and Soccer with 4-CIF (704x576) resolution has been used during the experimentation phase. The frame rate is 60 fps, and there are 600 frames lasting for 10 seconds. The intra period is set to 8 frames. The quantization parameters are set to 36-30 for both layers.

An H.264/SVC Streamer/Receiver has been implemented in order to transmit and receive each video sequence through the network using RTP/UDP/IP protocol stack. Each generated packet of the streamer has a single Network Abstraction Layer Unit (NALU) with a total size of 1400 bytes. Also an additional path is responsible for the transmission of the Parameter Sets (PS) to the client through a TCP/IP connection for more reliability because of their importance.

Between the streamer and the client, we consider the two-hop network shown in Figure 1. Video packets are generated at Node-S, relayed by Node-R1, Node-R2 and Node-R3. Node-A and Node-B are destination nodes. The whole experiment has been repeated quite a few times in order to be statistically correct.

B. *Simulation Results*

Figure 4 illustrates the PSNR versus time for both RLNC and WoNC schemes. For low packet loss rates, RLNC provides better robustness as opposed to WoNC in terms of PSNR variations. As packet loss rate increases above 5% the two schemes starting to converge.

Table 1 compares the amount of data needs to be encrypted using WoNC and RLNC scheme propose in Section VI. B and Section V.A. In both schemes, the payload in base-layer video packets needs to be encrypted. For enhancement-layer video packets, WoNC scheme encrypts all the payload, while RLNC scheme only encrypts the coding coefficients. We have set Galois Filed size equal to 2^8 , and variable generation size with three options 2, 3 and 4.

For both video sequence Crew and Soccer, about 50% reduction is achieved using RLNC scheme.

TABLE I: AMOUNT OF ENCRYPTION DATA FOR TWO VIDEO SEQUENCES USING 1) WONC SCHEME AND 2) RLNC SCHEME, AS WELL AS THEIR RATIO.

		WoNC (Bytes)	RLNC (Bytes)	(RLNC/WoNC) %
Crew	Layer-1	3823027	3823027	100%
	Layer -2	3477276	3419	0.09%
	Total	7300303	3826446	52.41%
Soccer	Layer-1	3757378	3757378	100%
	Layer-2	3226585	3418	0.1%
	Total	6983963	3760796	53.8%

VI. CONCLUSIONS AND FUTURE WORK

In this paper, we have explored the idea of using network coding for video multicast over wireless ad-hoc networks. We have examined three schemes: network coding aided video transmission, network coding aided encryption, and XOR-aided one-way-function tree group key initialization. The simulation results using two video sequences have proved that network coding significantly improves the video quality because of its capability of utilizing multi-paths and retransmission efficiency. Using network coding also reduces about 50% of the amount of data for encryption, as well as 50% of the communication overhead in group key initialization. We could conclude that network coding is a promising energy efficient solution for video multicast in future network. In summary, using network coding for secure video multicast over wireless ad-hoc network is a promising technical, and worth further in-depth investigation.

ACKNOWLEDGMENT

The research leading to the present results has been undertaken within the European Union's Horizon 2020 research and innovation programme under grant agreement H2020-MSCA-ITN-2016 SECRET-722424

REFERENCES

[1] H. Schwarz, D. Marpe and T. Wiegand, "Overview of the Scalable Video Coding Extension of the H.264/AVC Standard", IEEE Trans. On Circuits and Systems for Video Technology, Vol. 17, No. 9, September 2007

[2] E. Magli, M. Wang, P. Frossard, and A. Markopoulou, "Network Coding Meets Multimedia: a Review," IEEE Trans. Multimed., vol. 15, no. 5, pp. 1195 – 1212, 2012.

[3] H. Seferoglu and A. Markopoulou, 'Video-Aware Opportunistic Network Coding over Wireless Networks", IEEE JSAC, Vol. 27, No.5, pp. 1-16, 2009

[4] T. St and A. Uhl, "A Survey of H . 264 AVC / SVC Encryption," Technical report, 2010.

[5] L. Lima, S. Gheorghiu, J. Barros, M. Medard, and A. L. Toledo, "Secure network coding for multi-resolution wireless video streaming," IEEE J. Sel. Areas Commun., vol. 28, no. 3, pp. 377–388, Apr.2010

[6] R. Ahlswede, N. Cai, S.-Y. R. Li, and R. W. Yeung, "Network Information Flow," IEEE Trans. Inf. Theory,, vol. 46, pp. 204–1216, 2000

[7] Ning Cai and T. Chan, "Theory of Secure Network Coding," Proc. IEEE, vol. 99, no. 3, pp. 421–437, Mar. 2011.

[8] B. Wu, J. Wu, and M. Cardei, "Chapter 30: A Survey of Key Management in Mobile Ad Hoc Networks," in in Handbook of research on wireless security, 2008, pp. 176–188

[9] T. Matsuda, T. Noguchi, and T. Takine, "Survey of Network Coding and Its Applications," IEICE Trans. Commun., vol. E94-B, no. 3, pp. 698–717, 2011.

[10] H. Wang, J. Liang, and C. Kuo, "Overview of robust video streaming with network coding," J. Inf. Hiding Multimed. Signal Process., vol. 1, no. 1, pp. 36–50, 2010

[11] J. Park, M. Gerla, and D. Lun, "Codecast: a network-coding-based ad hoc multicast protocol," IEEE Wirel. Commun., vol. 13, no. 5, pp. 76–81, 2006

[12] J. Vilela, L. Lima, and J. Barros, "Lightweight Security for Network Coding," in IEEE International Conference on Communications (ICC '08), 2008, pp. 1750 - 1754

[13] R. Zeng, Y. Jiang, C. Lin, Y. Fan, and X. (Sherman) Shen, "A scalable and robust key pre-distribution scheme with network coding for sensor data storage," Comput. Networks, vol. 55, no. 10, pp. 2534–2544, Jul. 2011

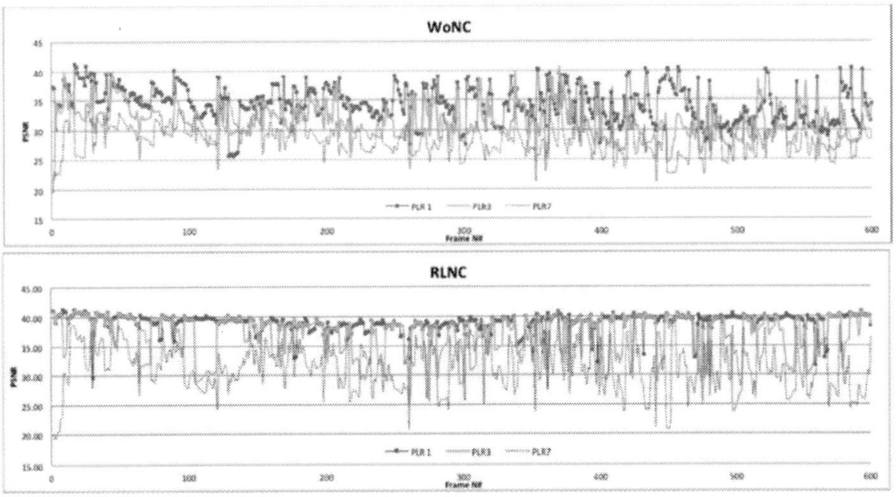

Figure 3. PSNR versus time for both RLNC and WoNC for various packet loss rates (1%, 3%,7%).

Joint Beamforming, Terminal Scheduling, and Adaptive Modulation with Imperfect CSIT in Rayleigh Fading Correlated Channels with Co-channel Interference

Ramiro Sámano-Robles

Research Centre in Real-time and Embedded Computing Systems
Intituto Politécnico do Porto, Porto, Portugal
Email: rasro@isep.ipp.pt

***Abstract*—This paper presents a resource allocation algorithm for multi-user wireless networks affected by co-channel interference. The analysis considers a network with one base station (BS) that uses a multiple antenna transmitter (beamformer) to schedule (in a time-division manner) transmissions towards a set of J one-antenna terminals in the presence of K persistent interferers. The transmitter is assumed to employ Maximum-Ratio Combining (MRC) beamforming with spatially-correlated branches and channel envelopes modelled as Rayleigh-distributed processes. The BS has access to an imperfect (outdated) copy of the instantaneous Channel State Information (CSI) of each terminal. Based on this CSI at the transmitter side (CSIT), the BS proceeds to select (at each time interval or time-slot) the terminal with the highest channel strength for purposes of transmission. This imperfect CSIT is also used to calculate the coefficients of the beamformer that will be used to transmit information towards the scheduled terminal, as well as for selecting the most appropriate modulation format (threshold-based decision). In addition, the transmission towards each scheduled terminal is assumed to experience persistent co-channel interference that will degrade the quality of the information reception process. The main merits of this work are the following: 1) joint analysis of MRC-based beamforming, terminal scheduling based on maximum channel strength, and modulation assignment, and 2) joint modelling of the effects of spatial correlation, co-channel interference and imperfect CSIT. Results suggest that scheduling helps in rejecting co-channel interference and the degrading effects of imperfect CSIT. Spatial correlation could some times lead to better performance than the uncorrelated case, particularly in the low SNR (Signal-to-Noise Ratio) regime. Conversely, uncorrelated branches always outperform the correlated case in the high SNR regime. The use of higher numbers of antennas also improve performance of the system. However, spatial correlation tends to accumulate over the antenna array thus leading to a more noticeable performance degradation and more allocation errors due to the outdated CSIT assumption.**

Keywords–Beamforming; Scheduling; Resource allocation, Imperfect CSIT, Maximum Ratio Combining (MRC)

I. Introduction

Multiple antenna systems (also known as MIMO or Multiple-Input Multiple-Output systems) are expected to proliferate in the coming years, particularly in the context of 5G or fifth generation of mobile systems [1]. The growing demand for wireless connectivity, the limited transmission resources, and the outdated spectrum allocation paradigm have created the need for more efficient and higher capacity transmission systems. MIMO technology offers considerable capacity growth that escalates with the number of transmit-receive antenna pairs. In addition to this, MIMO also offers improved energetic efficiency and reduced interference with minimum spectrum expenditure [2].

From the many different types of multiple antenna systems, perhaps *beamforming* technology represents the option with higher potential for commercial solutions, mainly due to its maturity, flexible implementation, and low computational costs. Beamforming refers to the ability to dynamically steer the phases of an antenna array and change the directionality properties of the resulting radiation beams. This enables a wide set of applications in multi-user settings, such as: interference rejection/management [3], spatial multiplexing [4], and more recently (with a few modifications) 3D beamforming with massive MIMO in 5G [5], beam-division multiple access [6], and interference alignment [7]. In future networks, beamforming will be key for efficiently organizing spectrum resources in dense small cells, as well as minimizing energy expenditure, reducing leakage and/or interference to adjacent cells or terminals, and also for improving security against potential attacks of signal jamming or eavesdropping in the network.

All these recent advances in the physical layer of multiple antenna systems need to be integrated with upper layer algorithms. This has opened several issues regarding the cross-layer design and optimization of beamforming and in general multiple-antenna systems. One particularly important topic in this field is the modelling of the underlying multiple antenna signal processing tools to be used in resource allocation and system-level evaluation frameworks. In large network set ups with tens or hundreds of BSs and hundreds or thousands of terminals, all the details of the PHYsical (PHY) layer cannot be usually included in full detail in the analysis or simulation loop. Therefore, a trade-off must be found between the accuracy of the model that represents the underlying PHY-layer and its flexibility for purposes of resource allocation and optimisation at the system-level.

This paper attempts to partially fill these gaps by addressing the link-layer interface modelling in Rayleigh fading correlated channels of an adaptive wireless multi-user network using Maximum-Ratio Combining (MRC) beamforming and terminal scheduling based on limited (outdated) feedback. The transmitter selects the most adequate Modulation and Coding Schemes (MCSs) and beamforming vectors based on an estimated Channel State Information (CSI). This imperfect CSI at the transmitter side (i.e., CSIT) is assumed to have been initially collected by the receiver (perfect estimation), and subsequently reported back to the transmitter via a feedback channel affected by delay. This paper presents the analysis of the statistics of correct reception process conditional on the decision made by the transmitter (*modulation format selection, beamforming and scheduling*) based on the inaccurate CSIT. Link-layer throughput is evaluated by means of an *interface model* based on an instantaneous Signal-to-Interference-plus-Noise Ratio (SINR) adaptive switching threshold scheme for modulation assignment. This model aims to provide an accurate but flexible representation of the underlying PHY-layer suitable for upper-layer design. In the proposed model, a packet transmission using a given MCS is considered as correctly received with given values of BLock-Error Rate (BLER) and spectral efficiency whenever the instantaneous SINR exceeds the reception threshold of the selected MCS. The reception parameters of each MCS are obtained from Look-Up-Tables (LUTs) previously calculated via *off-line PHY-layer simulation*. The main contribution of this work is the joint analysis of spatial correlation, imperfect CSIT and co-channel interference in link adaptation and terminal scheduling for MRC-based multiple antenna beamforming systems.

This paper is organized as follows. Section II describes previous works and the achievements of this paper with respect to the state of the art. Section III describes the system model and the assumptions of the paper. Section IV presents the link-layer interface model. Section V deals with the statistics of the estimated SNR and the instantaneous SINR. Section VI presents analytic results and sketches of the statistics of packet reception using different network assumptions. Finally, Section VII presents the conclusions of this paper.

II. PREVIOUS WORKS

The simplest multiple antenna system is the MRC transceiver, which provides a relatively flexible framework for statistical analysis and interface modelling. The literature of MRC transceivers has focused on the derivation of outage and bit error probability distributions (see [18]-[26]). The effects of imperfect channel knowledge on the performance of MRC receivers in Rayleigh fading correlated channels can be found in [18]-[19] following the analysis with perfect channel estimation presented in [20]. A series expansion of the statistics of MRC systems with correlated Rician channels is given in [21]. A unified approach for analysis of two-stage MRC systems with hybrid selection in generalized Rice correlated channels was proposed in [22]. Extensions to the case of co-channel interference are given in [23]-[26].

The present work considers the extension of outage probability analysis of MRC transmitters (beamformers) to the study of Adaptive Modulation and Coding (AMC) in Rayleigh fading correlated channels with imperfect/outdated CSIT and co-channel interference. To the best of our knowledge, this is the first attempt in the literature that addresses these issues under the same framework. This work attempts to extend the analysis of MRC systems towards including resource allocation aspects which are typical of upper layer design (radio resource management). In addition, network design and in particular resource allocation for multiple antenna systems is usually conducted under the assumption perfect CSIT. Imperfect CSIT has been addressed in [27] for distributed systems and in [28] for energy efficient MIMO link adaptation. In comparison with these works, which are focused on numerical evaluation of imperfect CSIT, this work provides an analytic framework for obtaining the statistics of errors in MCS assignment for correlated MRC transmitters.

A related topic is the analysis of the effects of limited feedback in adaptive modulation for beam-forming and multiple antenna systems. The work in [29] provides a review of the state of the art of limited feedback in adaptation schemes for MIMO systems. The work in [30] presents the analysis of adaptive modulation for two-antenna beam-formers considering mean CSI at the transmitter side. The work in [31] addressed the impact of outdated feedback on AMC and user selection diversity systems for MIMO systems in Rayleigh uncorrelated channels. Other works with limited feedback for different types of system can be found in [33]-[35]. All these previous works consider uncorrelated MIMO channels. This work goes beyond this assumption searching for a joint analysis of limited feedback and spatial correlation for adaptive MRC transmitters with co-channel interference.

Notation: Bold lower case letters (e.g., $\mathbf{x}$) denote vector variables, bold upper case letters (e.g., $\mathbf{A}$) denote matrices, $(\cdot)^T$ is the vector transpose operator, $E[\cdot]$ is the statistical average operator, $(\cdot)^*$ is the complex conjugate operator, f_z, F_z and $\bar{F}_z$ denotes, respectively, the Probability Density Function (PDF), Cumulative Density Function (CDF) and Complementary Cumulative Density Function (CCDF) of any random variable z, Z^+ denotes the set of positive integers, $Re(\cdot)$ denotes the real part operator, $\mathbf{0}_N$ is the vector of N zeroes, $\mathbf{I}_N$ is the identity matrix of order N, and $\begin{pmatrix} J-1 \\ \mathbf{l} \end{pmatrix} = \begin{pmatrix} J-1 \\ l_0, l_1, \ldots l_N \end{pmatrix} = \frac{(J-1)!}{l_0! l_1! \ldots l_N}$ is the multinomial combinatorial number of $J-1$ and N coefficients $l_0, l_1, \ldots l_N$ arranged in the vector $\mathbf{l} = [l_0, l_1, \ldots, l_N]^T$.

III. SYSTEM MODEL AND ASSUMPTIONS

Consider the network depicted in Figure 1 with one Base Station (BS) scheduling transmissions towards J terminals (in a time-division fashion), each one with one receiving antenna, and a set of K persistent single-antenna interferers. The BS uses an N-antenna Maximum-Ratio Combining (MRC) beamformer that is used to transmit information to a given terminal at specific time slots. The channel vector between the BS and the jth terminal is denoted by $\mathbf{h}_j = [h_j(1), h_j(2), \ldots h_j(N)]^T$. All instantaneous channel variables will be modelled as zero-mean complex circular Gaussian random variables with variance γ: $\mathbf{h}_j(n) \sim \mathcal{CN}(\mathbf{0}_N, \gamma \mathbf{I}_N)$. The estimated channel variable available at the transmitter side is given by $\hat{\mathbf{h}}_j = [\hat{h}_j(1), \hat{h}_j(2), \ldots \hat{h}_j(N)]^T$. This information is used by the BS for purposes of beamforming, terminal scheduling and resource allocation (modulation format assignment). The channel between the interferer k towards terminal j is denoted by $h_{k,j}$ and is modelled as a zero-mean complex circular Gaussian random variable with variance λ: $h_{k,j} \sim \mathcal{CN}(0, \lambda)$.

The transmitter selects one of M modulation formats, which are arranged in increasing order according to their target Signal-to-Interference plus Noise Ratio (SINR). The target SINR of the mth MCS will be denoted by β_m. The variables θ_m and η_m will denote, respectively, the BLER and spectral efficiency (in bps/Hz) considering operation at the target SINR of the mth MCS. It is assumed that the receiver monitors the quality of the channel and reports it back to the transmitter. Based on this collected Channel State Information (CSI), the transmitter selects the most appropriate MCS using a correction for the decision thresholds denoted here by $\hat{\beta}_m$. This paper considers perfect channel estimation at the receiver side and imperfect channel state information at the transmitter side (CSIT). Imperfect CSIT is assumed to be mainly due to a

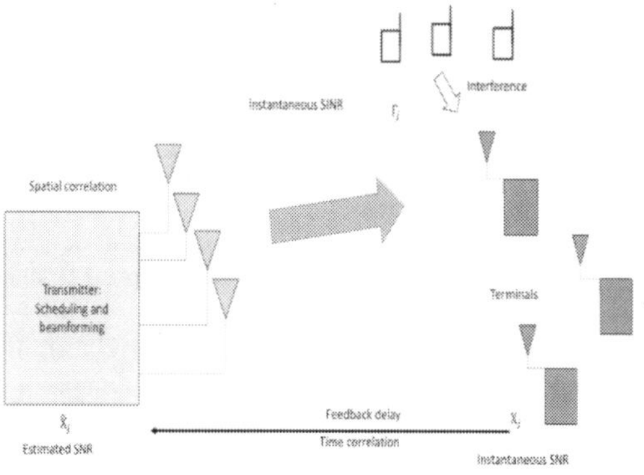

Figure 1. Wireless network with one transmitter using imperfect CSIT for scheduling, modulation assignment and beamforming information to a set of terminals in the presence of co-channel interference.

feedback channel affected by delay. The beamforming vector is denoted by $\mathbf{w}_j = [w_j(1), w_j(2), \ldots, w_j(N)]^T$, which using the MRC criterion is given by $\mathbf{w}_j = \mathbf{h}_j^*$. Therefore, the signal received by the scheduled terminal can be mathematically written as follows

$$r_j = \mathbf{w}_j^T \mathbf{h}_j s_j + \sum_{k=1}^{K} h_{k,j} \check{s}_k + v_j, \tag{1}$$

where s_j is the information symbol transmitted towards terminal j, $\check{s}_k$ is the symbol transmitted by interferer k, and v_j is the additive white Gaussian noise experienced by terminal j with variance σ_v^2: $v_j \sim \mathcal{CN}(0, \sigma_v^2)$. Considering the symbol transmit power constraint $E[s_j^* s_j] = P$, the estimated SNR at the transmitter side from(1) is given by:

$$\hat{X}_j = \frac{\hat{\mathbf{h}}_j^H \hat{\mathbf{h}}_j E[s_j^* s_j]}{\sigma_v^2} = \frac{\sum_{n=1}^{N} P|\hat{h}_j(n)|^2}{\sigma_v^2}. \tag{2}$$

Note that in this paper it is assumed that an estimate of interference $I_j = \sum_{k=1}^{K} h_{k,j} \check{s}_k$ in (1) is not available at the transmitter. Therefore, all decisions will be based on an estimate of the SNR in (2). The estimated channels will be generated using the following linear correlation model:

$$\hat{h}_j(n) = \sqrt{1-\rho} Z_j(n) + \sqrt{\rho} G_j, \tag{3}$$

where ρ is the spatial correlation coefficient and the terms $Z_j(n)$ and G_j are the zero-mean complex circular Gaussian variables with variance γ. Note that this correlation model complies with $E[\hat{h}_j(n)^* \hat{h}_j(\tilde{n})] = \rho\gamma$, $n \neq \tilde{n}$, and $E[\hat{h}_j(n)^* \hat{h}_j(n)] = \gamma$. This correlation model constitutes an approximation of real-life settings by assuming that all elements experience the same correlation with each other. In real-life systems, antennas farther apart from each other experience less correlation than contiguous elements. The correlation model for imperfect CSIT is given by:

$$h_j(n) = \rho_c \hat{h}_j(n) + \sqrt{1-\rho_c^2} Y_j(n), \tag{4}$$

TABLE I. LIST OF VARIABLES.

Variable	Meaning
N	Number of antennas at the transmitter side
ρ	Spatial correlation coefficient
ρ_c	Temporal correlation coefficient
P	Transmit power
σ_v^2	Noise variance
γ	Channel variance
λ	Interferer channel variance
J	Number of terminals
M	Number of modulation formats
$\mathbf{h}_j$	Channel vector of terminal j
$\mathbf{w}_j$	Beamforming vector for terminal j
$\hat{\mathbf{h}}_j$	Estimated channel vector
$\hat{X}_j$	Estimated SNR for terminal j
Γ_j	Instantaneous SINR of terminal j
I_j	Interference experienced by terminal j
$h_{k,j}$	Channel between interferer k and terminal j
K	Number of persistent interferers
s_j	Symbol transmitted towards terminal j
$\check{s}_k$	Symbol transmitted by interferer k
β_m	Reception SINR target threshold for modulation format m
θ_m	BLER for modulation format m @ β_m
η_m	Spectral efficiency of modulation format m @ β_m
T	Link Layer throughput
$\hat{\beta}_m$	Selection SNR threshold of modulation format m

where ρ_c is the temporal correlation coefficient that describes the accuracy of the CSIT. This correlation model complies with $E[h_j(n)^* h_j(n)] = \rho_c \gamma$. The instantaneous SINR is given by:

$$\Gamma_j = \frac{Re(P\hat{\mathbf{h}}_j^H \mathbf{h}_j)}{I_j + \sigma_v^2} \tag{5}$$

where $I_j = \sum_{k=1}^{K} P|h_{k,j}|^2$ is the interference created by K co-channel persistent interferers. Table I presents a list of the main variables used throughout this paper.

IV. LINK LAYER MODEL

The probability of selection of a modulation format m is given by the probability that the estimated SNR $\hat{X}_j$ at the transmitter side lies within the interval $[\hat{\beta}_m, \hat{\beta}_{m+1}]$:

$$\Pr\{\hat{\beta}_m \leq \hat{X}_j < \hat{\beta}_{m+1}\} \tag{6}$$

Link-layer throughput (denoted by T) will be expressed as a linear contribution of all possible MCSs with their respective selection probabilities from (6) and conditional reception probabilities, each one weighted by their conditional throughput performance (T_m):

$$T = \sum_{m=1}^{M} E_{\Gamma_{j^*}}[T_m(\Gamma_{j^*}) | \hat{\beta}_m \leq \hat{X}_{j^*} < \hat{\beta}_{m+1}]$$
$$\Pr\{\hat{\beta}_m \leq \hat{X}_{j^*} < \hat{\beta}_{m+1}\} \Pr\{j^* = \arg\max_j \hat{X}_j\}, \tag{7}$$

where $T_m(\Gamma_j)$ indicates of the link-layer throughput of terminal j when using the mth MCS conditional on a given value of the operational SINR Γ_j in (5) of the selected terminal. In this paper, we consider a simplification of this expression, by assuming that the term $T_m(\Gamma)$ in (7) is a step function defined by a switching SINR threshold β_m above which all packet transmissions are assumed to be correctly received with a given BLER θ_m and spectral efficiency η_m. The simplification can be expressed as follows:

$$T = \sum_{m=1}^{M} \Delta_B W \eta_m (1-\theta_m) \Pr\{\Gamma_{j^*} \geq \beta_m | \hat{\beta}_m \leq \hat{X}_{j^*} < \hat{\beta}_{m+1}\}$$

$$\Pr\{\hat{\beta}_m \leq \hat{X}_{j^*} < \hat{\beta}_{m+1}\} \Pr\{j^* = \arg\max_j \hat{X}_j\} \quad (8)$$

where Δ_{BW} is the operational bandwidth in Hz, $\Pr\{j^* = \arg\max_j(\hat{X}_j)\}$ is the probability of terminal to experience the highest estimated SNR and therefore being scheduled for transmission by the BS, and $\Pr\{\Gamma_{j^*} \geq \beta_m | \hat{\beta}_m \leq \hat{X}_{j^*} < \hat{\beta}_{m+1}\}$ is the probability of the instantaneous SINR Γ_{j^*} to surpass the threshold β_m provided the estimated SNR $\hat{X}_{j^*}$ (used for MCS selection and terminal scheduling) lies in the range $[\hat{\beta}_m, \hat{\beta}_{m+1}]$.

Note that this last conditional probability term captures the effects of imperfect CSIT on the performance of the beamforming, scheduling and adaptation scheme. In the case of perfect CSIT ($\rho_c \to 0$), correct reception occurs with probability one. Also, note that the link-layer throughput expression in (8) represents only an approximation (compression) of the real performance of the system. The simplified model in (8) assumes packets are erroneous when the instantaneous SINR drops below the reception threshold β_m, when in practice there might be some cases where correct reception can still occur. Conversely, some cases with higher instantaneous SNR than the reception threshold could also lead to erroneous packet transmissions. This type of compression/abstraction model as in (8) has been proved accurate for system-level simulation of networks with considerable excursions of path-loss values, which are typical of cellular systems where terminals lie at different distances from the access point.

V. Performance Analysis

The following subsections present the derivation of analytic expressions of the different terms of the link-layer throughput model in (8) . For convenience, it is useful to derive the statistics of the estimated SNR (presented in Section V-A) and then deal with the statistics of the instantaneous SINR (presented in Section V-B) conditional on the MCS selection, terminal scheduling, and beamforming processes.

A. Statistics of estimated SNR

Let us now substitute the correlation model described by (3) in the expression of the estimated SNR in (2), which yields:

$$\hat{X}_j = \frac{\sum_{n=1}^{N} P|\hat{h}_j(n)|^2}{\sigma_v^2} = \sum_{n=1}^{N} \frac{P|\sqrt{1-\rho} Z_j(n) + \sqrt{\rho} G_j|^2}{\sigma_v^2}. \quad (9)$$

The statistics of the estimated SNR have been investigated in our previous work in [36]. The sub-index j is dropped in subsequent derivations due to the symmetrical network assumption. The probability density function (PDF) and complementary cumulative distribution function (CCDF) are given, respectively, by [36]:

$$f_{\hat{X}}(y) = \frac{A}{\tilde{\gamma}} e^{-\frac{y}{\tilde{\gamma}}} + e^{-\frac{y}{\tilde{\gamma}}} \sum_{n=1}^{N-1} \frac{B_n y^{n-1}}{\tilde{\gamma}^n (n-1)!}, \quad (10)$$

and

$$\bar{F}_{\hat{X}}(y) = A e^{-\frac{y}{\tilde{\gamma}}} + e^{-\frac{y}{\tilde{\gamma}}} \sum_{n=1}^{N-1} \sum_{u=0}^{n-1} \frac{B_n y^u}{\tilde{\gamma}^u u!} =$$

$$= A e^{-\frac{y}{\tilde{\gamma}}} + e^{-\frac{y}{\tilde{\gamma}}} \sum_{u=0}^{N-2} \frac{y^u}{\tilde{\gamma}^u u!} \sum_{n=1}^{N-1-u} B_n, \quad (11)$$

where $\tilde{\gamma} = \frac{P(1-\rho)\gamma}{\sigma_v^2}$, $\check{\gamma} = \alpha\gamma + \tilde{\gamma}$, $\alpha = \frac{PN\rho}{\sigma_v^2}$, $A = \left(1 - \frac{\tilde{\gamma}}{\check{\gamma}}\right)^{1-N}$ and $B_n = \left(-\frac{\tilde{\gamma}}{\check{\gamma}}\right)\left(1 - \frac{\tilde{\gamma}}{\check{\gamma}}\right)^{n-N}$. The effects of terminal scheduling on the statistics of the estimated SNR will be obtained via the theory of order statistics. The statistics of the random variable with maximum value are given by the following formula [37]:

$$f_{\hat{X}^*}(y) = J f_{\hat{X}}(y) F_{\hat{X}}(y)^{J-1}. \quad (12)$$

By substituting the expressions for the PDF and CDF of $\hat{X}^*$ in (12) and using the formula for multinomial theorem we obtain the following expression:

$$f_{\hat{X}^*}(y) = \sum_{\mathbf{l}; \sum_{t=0}^{N} l_t = J-1} \tilde{\alpha}_{\mathbf{l}} e^{-\tilde{\mu}_{\mathbf{l}} y} y^{\tilde{\eta}_{\mathbf{l}}}$$

$$+ \sum_{\mathbf{l}; \sum_{t=0}^{N} l_t = J-1} \alpha_{\mathbf{l}} e^{-\mu_{\mathbf{l}} y} \sum_{n=1}^{N-1} B_n y^{\eta_{\mathbf{l},n}} \quad (13)$$

where

$$\alpha_{\mathbf{l}} = J \binom{J-1}{\mathbf{l}} (-A)^{l_{N-1}} \prod_{t=0}^{N-2} \left(\sum_{u=1}^{N-1-t} -\frac{B_u}{t!} \right)^{l_t}, \quad (14)$$

$$\tilde{\alpha}_{\mathbf{l}} = \frac{\alpha_{\mathbf{l}} A}{\check{\gamma} \tilde{\gamma}^{\tilde{\eta}_{\mathbf{l}}}}, \quad (15)$$

$$\tilde{\mu}_{\mathbf{l}} = \frac{\tilde{\eta}_{\mathbf{l}}}{\tilde{\gamma}} + \frac{l_{N-1} + 1}{\check{\gamma}}, \quad (16)$$

$$\tilde{\eta}_{\mathbf{l}} = \sum_{t=0}^{N-2} t l_t, \quad (17)$$

$$\mu_l = \frac{1 + \tilde{\eta}_{\mathbf{l}}}{\tilde{\gamma}} + \frac{l_{N-1}}{\check{\gamma}}, \quad (18)$$

$$\eta_{\mathbf{l},n} = n - 1 + \tilde{\eta}_{\mathbf{l}}, \quad (19)$$

$$\tilde{B}_n = \frac{B_n}{\tilde{\gamma}^{n+\tilde{\eta}_{\mathbf{l}}} (n-1)!}, \quad \{l_t, t\} \in Z^+, 0 \leq t \leq N \quad (20)$$

For details of this derivation please see the Appendix.

B. Statistics of instantaneous SINR

Let us now substitute the correlation model described by (4) into the expression of the instantaneous SINR in (5):

$$\Gamma_j = \frac{P\rho_c \hat{\mathbf{h}}_j^H \hat{\mathbf{h}}_j + Re[P\sqrt{1-\rho_c^2} \sum_{n=1}^{N} \hat{h}_j(n)^* Y_j(n)]}{I_j + \sigma_v^2}. \quad (21)$$

Since we are interested in the reception probability term $\Pr\{\Gamma_j > \beta_m\}$ we can use (21) to express the term $\Pr\{\Gamma_j > \beta_m\}$as follows:

$$\Pr\{\Gamma_j > \beta_m\} =$$

$$\Pr\left\{\frac{P\rho_c\hat{\mathbf{h}}_j^H\hat{\mathbf{h}}_j + Re[P\sqrt{(1-\rho_c^2}\sum_{n=1}^{N}\hat{h}_j(n)^*Y_j(n)]}{I_j+\sigma_v^2} > \beta_m\right\}$$

By rearranging the terms of the inequality we obtain:

$$\Pr\{\Gamma_j > \beta_m\} =$$

$$\Pr\{P\rho_c\hat{\mathbf{h}}_j^H\hat{\mathbf{h}}_j + Re[P\sqrt{(1-\rho_c^2)}\sum_{n=1}^{N}\hat{h}_j(n)^*Y_j(n)] - \beta_m I_j$$

$$> \beta_m\sigma_v^2\} = \Pr\{\psi_j > \sigma_v^2\}.$$

The characteristic function of ψ_j conditionally on a particular value of $\hat{\mathbf{h}}_j$ is the addition of two random variables: a Gaussian process with mean $P\rho_c X_j$ and variance $P\sqrt{(1-\rho_c^2)}X_j/2$ and a chi-square random variable with K degrees of freedom and parameter $-\beta\lambda$. This can be mathematically written as follows:

$$\Psi_{\psi_j|\mathbf{h}_j}(i\omega) = \frac{e^{jP\rho_c X_j+\omega^2 P\sqrt{(1-\rho_c^2)}X_j/2}}{(1+i\omega\beta_m\lambda)^K}.$$

The CF conditional on the decision made by the transmitter can be obtained as follows:

$$\Psi_{\psi_j|\beta_m<X_j<\beta_{m+1}}(i\omega) = \int_{\beta_m}\Psi_{\psi_j|X_j}(i\omega)f(X_j)dX_j.$$

This term will be evaluated numerically and then transformed into the PDF domain to obtain the statistics of instantaneous SINR conditional on the decion made by the transmitter.

VI. Results

This section presents graphical results of the statistics of the MRC beamformer with adaptive modulation, scheduling and co-channel interference with imperfect CSIT. Figure 2 displays the results of the Cumulative Distribution Function (CDF) of the SNR of the scheduler conditional on the decision made by the transmitter based on imperfect CSIT using a hypothetical MCS selection threshold equal to ($\hat{\beta} = 2$). The results in Figure 2 have been obtained using fixed transmit power settings ($P\gamma/\sigma_v^2 = 1$) assuming no interference with different numbers of antennas ($N = 2, N = 4$) and different values of correlation coefficients ($\rho = 0.2$, $\rho = 0.95$, $\rho_c = 0.2$ and $\rho_c = 0.95$).

Figure 3 shows the results for the CDF of the SNR using the same settings as in the previous example, except for the transmit power which is now set to $P\gamma/\sigma_v^2 = 5$. The objective of investigating the conditional CDF is to observe the effects of imperfect CSIT on the instantaneous SNR experienced by the scheduled terminals. The results show the heavy influence of imperfect CSIT on the characteristics of the CDF. Low values of the correlation coefficient $\rho \to 0$, see a considerable degradation on the probability of correct reception. Note that all curves of the CDF depart from the hypothetical decision threshold set to $\hat{\beta} = 2$. This departure to the left-hand side of the figure is a measure of the incorrect reception due to imperfect CSIT. All the curves at the top left of the figure are indeed the curves with worse CSIT conditions. It is observed that spatial correlation degrades performance at high values of SNR, but it could be beneficial in the low SNR regime. In some cases, spatial diversity provided by higher numbers of antennas can even compensate for the effects of imperfect CSIT, particularly at with low values of spatial correlation. In all cases in both figures, it is observed that the performance of the CDF is superior with higher numbers of terminals in the scheduler, but this gain is more noticeable in channels with low spatial correlation. It can be also observed that user scheduling reduces the effects of spatial correlation. Spatial correlation reduces the diversity gains of the combining beamformer, and it can be accumulated over the several antennas resulting in a more noticeable performance reduction. User scheduling provides extra diversity gains that can compensate this reduction.

TABLE II. SINR(dB) vs BLER FOR WiMAX MODULATION AND CODING SCHEMES [39].

QPSK 1/3		QPSK 1/2		QPSK 2/3	
SINR	BLER	SINR	BLER	SINR	BLER
-1.14	4.10e-3	1.32	4.13e-3	3.47	6.50e-3
QPSK 3/4		**QPSK 4/5**		**16 QAM 1/3**	
SINR	BLER	SINR	BLER	SINR	BLER
4.78	3.30e-3	5.46	4.97e-3	3.66	7.15e-3
16 QAM 1/2		**16 QAM 2/3**		**16 QAM 3/4**	
SINR	BLER	SINR	BLER	SINR	BLER
6.52	5.70e-3	9.37	3.80e-3	10.98	1.57e-3

The results presented in Figure 3 and Figure 4 have been obtained using the same settings used in the previous two examples, except for the interference assumption. The channel power settings of the $K = 2$ persistent interferers were all set to $\lambda/\gamma = 0.1$. The results show the CDF of the instantaneous SINR instead of the SNR. The CDF results show how affected the system becomes by the presence of interference. It becomes evident that the presence of interference affects also how the spatial correlation plays a role on the performance of the system. This will become more evident in the results of throughput presented in the following figures.

To test the performance of the algorithm in a full wireless transmission system with different modulation formats, we have used the settings of the WiMAX standard and its different modulation schemes (see Table II). The results in Figure 4 and Figure 5 present the overall throughput for a network with different numbers of users included in the scheduler versus different values of transmit average SNR. Figure 4 shows the results with no interference, while Figure 5 shows the results with $K = 2$ interferers using set to $\lambda/\gamma = 0.1$. The results with interference show several changing patterns due to the complex relation between interference and the received signal by the terminals. Surprisingly at high values of transmit SNR some of the curves with low spatial correlation tend to perform worse that the correlated cases, which can only be explained by the increased importance of the interference term and the parameters of the modulation formats used in the simulation.

VII. Conclusions

This paper has presented an analytical framework for the study of joint MRC beamforming, terminal scheduling and resource allocation (modulation assignment) algorithms for multiuser networks in the presence of persistent co-channel

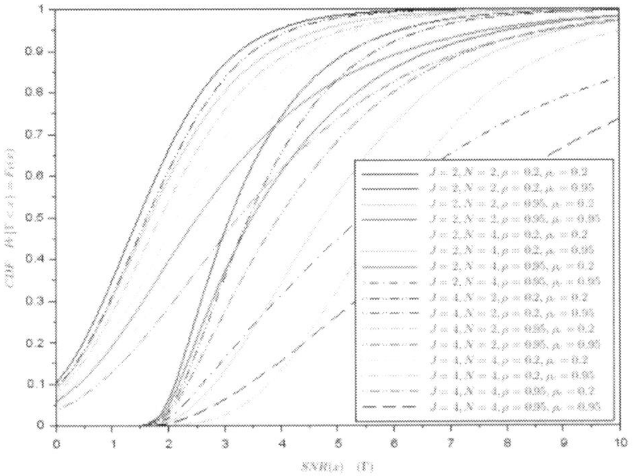

Figure 2. CDF of instantaneous SNR conditional on the estimated SNR being above the threshold $\hat{\beta} = 2$ with fixed Tx power settings $(P\gamma/\sigma_v^2) = 5)$ without interference and different vales of antennas and correlation coefficients.

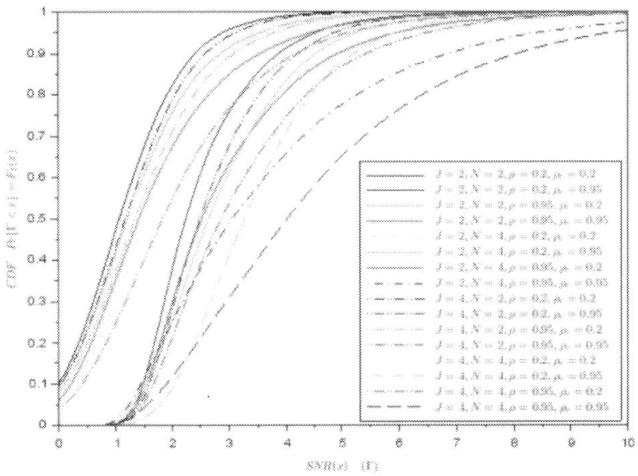

Figure 4. CDF of instantaneous SINR conditional on the estimated SNR being above the threshold $\hat{\beta} = 2$ with fixed Tx power settings $(P\gamma/\sigma_v^2) = 1)$ in the presence of cochannel interference $(K = 2, \lambda/\gamma = 0.1)$ and different vales of antennas and correlation coefficients.

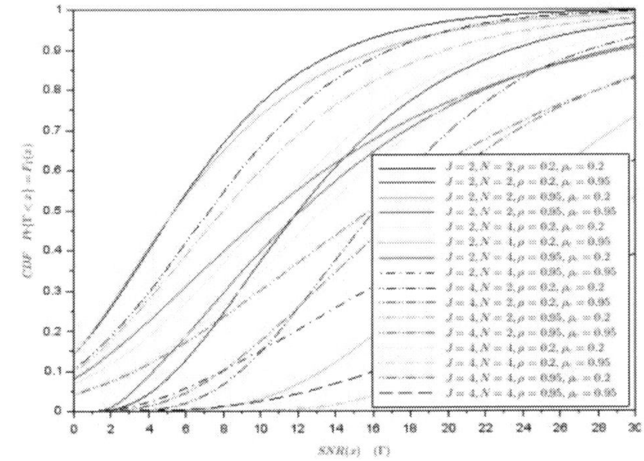

Figure 3. CDF of instantaneous SNR conditional on the estimated SNR being above the threshold $\hat{\beta} = 2$ with fixed Tx power settings $(P\gamma/\sigma_v^2) = 5)$ without interference and different vales of antennas and correlation coefficients.

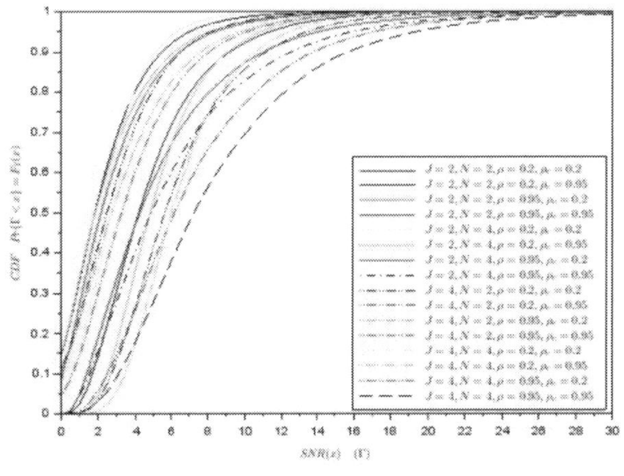

Figure 5. CDF of instantaneous SINR conditional on the estimated SNR being above the threshold $\hat{\beta} = 2$ with fixed Tx power settings $(P\gamma/\sigma_v^2) = 5)$ in the presence of co-channel interference $(K = 2, \lambda/\gamma = 0.1)$ and different vales of antennas and correlation coefficients.

interference. The results show that co-channel interference can considerably affect the performance of beamforming, being counteracted by the effects of scheduling and higher degree of accuracy of channel state information at the transmitter side. The number of antennas tends to reduce the effects of imperfect CSIT and interference. However, channel correlation can affect these gains, particularly in the high SNR regime. Conversely, in the low SNR regime it seems that channel correlation can outperform the case on uncorrelated channels. Spatial correlation effects tend to be accumulated when the number of antennas increases and therefore its effects will be more clearly observed in the high SNR regime.

ACKNOWLEDGMENTS

This work has received funding from project SCOTT (www.scottproject.eu) within the Electronic Component Systems for European Leadership Joint Undertaking under grant agreement No 737422. This Joint Undertaking receives support from the European Unions Horizon 2020 research and innovation programme and Austria, Spain, Finland, Ireland, Sweden, Germany, Poland, Portugal, Netherlands, Belgium, Norway. Funded also by FCT/MEC (Fundacão para a Ciência e a Tecnologia), ERDF (European Regional Development Fund) under PT2020, and by CISTER Research Unit (CEC/04234) .

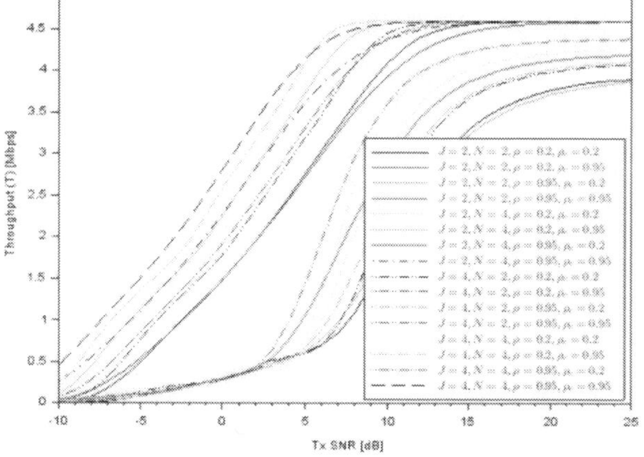

Figure 6. Throughput vs. transmit SNR for the MRC beamforming, scheduling and resource allocation algorithm without interference and different vales of antennas and correlation coefficients.

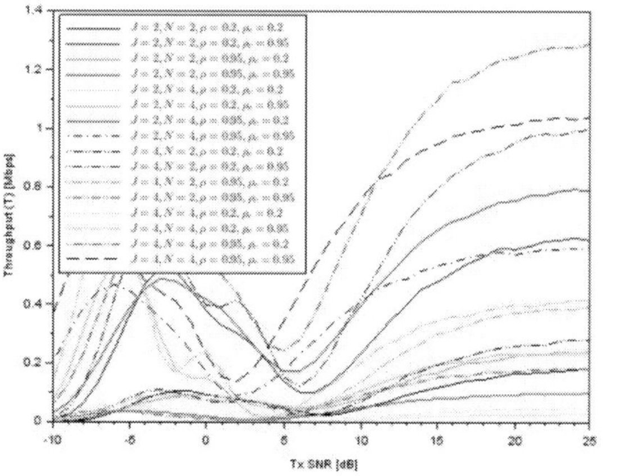

Figure 7. Throughput vs. transmit SNR for the MRC beamforming, scheduling and resource allocation algorithm in the presence of cochannel interference ($K = 2$, $\lambda/\gamma = 0.1$) and different vales of antennas, numbers of terminals and correlation coefficients.

References

[1] H. Kim, "Coding and modulation techniques for high spectral efficiency transmission in 5G and Satcom," 23rd European Signal Processing Conference (EUSIPCO) 2015; Nice, France, pp. 2746-2750. DOI: 10.1109/EUSIPCO.2015.7362884

[2] A. Goldsmith, S. A. Jafar, N. Jindal, and S. Vishwanath. "Capacity limits of MIMO channels," IEEE Journal on Selected Areas in Communications, Vol. 21, No. 5, pp. 684-702, 2003, DOI: 10.1109/JSAC.2003.810294

[3] W. Ge, J. Zhang, and G. Xue, "MIMO-Pipe Modeling and Scheduling for Efficient Interference Management in Multihop MIMO Networks," IEEE Transactions on Vehicular Technology. 2010; Vol. 59, No. 8, pp. 3966-3978. DOI: 10.1109/TVT.2010.2060376

[4] R. Smano-Robles and A. Gameiro, "Joint Scheduling, link adaptation and space division multiplexing for distributed antenna systems" TELFOR (Telecommunications Forum) Belgrade, Serbia, 2012.

[5] D. Soldani and A. Mazalini, "On the 5G Operating System for a True Digital Society," IEEE Vehicular Technology Magazine. 2015 March, pp. 32-42. DOI: 10.1109/MVT.2014.2380581

[6] A. Sasi and P. Santhiva. "Quantum internet using 5G NanoCore with Beam Division Multiple Access." International Conference on Advanced Computing and Communication Systems, Jan. 2015; Coimbatore, India. 2015.

[7] H. J. Yang,W.-Y. Shin, B. C. Jung, C. Suh, and A. Paulraj. "Opportunistic Downlink Interference Alignment for Multi-Cell MIMO Networks." IEEE Transactions on Wireless Communications. 2017;(99):1-1. DOI: 10.1109/TWC.2017.2647942

[8] F. Rashid, K. J. Ray Liu, and L. Tassiulas, "Transmit beamforming and power control for cellular wireless systems." IEEE Journal on Selected Areas in Communications. 1998; Vol. 16, No. 8, pp. 1437-1450. DOI: 10.1109/49.730452

[9] H. Dahrouj and W. Yu. "Coordinated beamforming for the multi-cell multi-antenna wireless system." IEEE Transactions on Wireless Communications. 2010; Vol. 9, No. 5, pp. 1748-1759.

[10] Y. Huang, G. Zheng, M. Bengtsson, K. Wong, L. Yang, and B. Ottersten. "Distributed Multicell Beamforming With Limited Intercell Coordination". IEEE Transactions on Signal Processing. 2010;59(2):728-738. DOI: 10.1109/TSP.2010.2089621

[11] Deliverable D5.1: System level evaluation metrics and interfacing, "FP7 CODIV: Enhanced Wireless Communication Systems Employing COoperative DIVersity,", Available at: http://www.ict-codiv.eu/

[12] Deliverable D5.4: Final report on link level and system level channel models, "FP7 WINNER: Wireless World Initiative New Radio,", Available at: http://www.ist-winner.org

[13] Deliverable D7.1: System level interfacing, metrics and simulation scenarios, "FP7 FUTON: Fibre-Optic Networks for Distributed Extendible Heterogeneous Radio Architectures and Servic,", Available at: http://www.ict-futon.eu/

[14] K. Brueninghaus, et al., "Link performance model models for system level simulations of broadband radio access systems," *Proceedings IEEE International Symposium on Personal, Indoor and Mobile Radio Communications*, vol. 4, pp. 2306-2311, March 2005.

[15] J. Murkovic, G. Orfanos, and H. J. Reumermann, "MIMO link modeling for system-level simulations," *The 17th annual IEEE International Symposium on Personal, Indoor and Mobile Radio Communications, PMRC*, , vol. 4, pp. 1-6, 2006.

[16] M. Wrulich and M. Rupp, "Efficient link measurement model for system-level simulations of Alamouti encoded MIMO HSDPA transmissions," *2008 ITG Workshop on smart antennas* pp. 351-355.

[17] A. Perez-Niera and M Campalans, "Cross-Layer Resource Allocation in Wireless Communications: Techniques and Models from PHY and MAC Layer Interaction." *Academic Press, Oxford, 2010*

[18] F. A. Dietrich and W. Utschick, "Maximum ratio combining of correlated Rayleigh fading channels with imperfect channel knowledge," *IEEE Communications Letters*, vol. 7, no. 9, pp. 419-421, 2003.

[19] Y. Ma, R. Schober, and S. Pasupathy, "Effect of channel estimation errors on MRC diversity in Rician fading channels," *IEEE Trans. on Vehicular Technologies*, vol. 54, no. 6, pp. 2137-2142, November 2005.

[20] Y. Ma, "Impact of correlated diversity branches in Rician fading channels," *IEEE International Conference on Communications (ICC)*, vol. 1, pp. 473-477, 2005.

[21] H. T. Hui, "The performance of the maximum ratio combining method in correlated Rician-Fading channels for antenna-diversity signal combining," *IEEE Trans. on Antennas and Propagation*, Vol. 53, no. 3, pp. 958-964, 2009.

[22] P. Loskot and N.C. Beaulieu, "A unified approach to computing error probabilities of diversity combining schemes over correlated fading channels," *IEEE Transactions on Communications*, vol. 57, no. 7, pp. 2031-2041, 2009.

[23] N.C. Beauliu and X. Zhang, "On selecting the number of receiver diversity antennas in Ricean fading cochannel interference," *IEEE Global Telecommunications Conference (Globecom) 2006*, pp. 1-6.

[24] N.C. Beauliu and X. Zhang, "On the maximum number of receiver diversity antennas that can be usefully deployed in a cochannel interference dominated environment," *IEEE Transactions on Signal Processing*, vol. 55, no. 7, pp. 3349-3359, July 2007.

[25] N.C. Beauliu and X. Zhang, "On the maximum useful number of receiver antennas for MRC diversity in cochannel interference and noise," *IEEE International Conference on Communications (ICC)*,pp. 5103-5108.

[26] Y. Dong, B. L. Hughes, and G. Lazzi "Performance analysis of maximum ratio combining with imperfect channel estimation in the presence of cochannel interferences," *IEEE Transactions on Wireless Communications*, vol. 8, no. 3, pp. 1080-1085, March 2009.

[27] R. Samano-Robles and A. Gameiro, "Joint Spectrum Selection and Radio Resource Management for Distributed Antenna Systems with Cognitive Radio and Space Division Multiplexing" *Workshop on Smart Antennas, Stuttgart, Germany*, 2013.

[28] L.Chen, Y. Yang, X. Chen, and G. Wei, "Energy-Efficient Link Adaptation on Rayleigh Fading Channel for OSTBC MIMO System With Imperfect CSIT" *IEEE Transactions on Vehicular Technology*, vol. 62, no. 4, pp. 1577-1585, 2013.

[29] A. E. Ekpenyong and Y.F. Huang, "Feedback Constraints for Adaptive Transmission" *IEEE Signal Processing Magazine*, May 2007, pp. 69-78.

[30] S.i Zhou and G. B. Giannakis, "Adaptive Modulation for Multi-antenna Transmissions With Channel Mean Feedback " *IEEE Transactions on Wireless Communications*, Vol. 3, No. 5 September 2004, pp. 1626-36.

[31] M. Torabi and J.F. Frigon "Impact of Outdated Feedback on the Performance of M-QAM Adaptive Modulation in User Selection Diversity Systems with OSTBC over MIMO Rayleigh Fading Channel" *IET Communications*, vol. 6, no. 4, pp. 458-463, March 6 2012

[32] P. Yang, Y. Xiao, Y. Yu, L. Li, Q. Tang, and S. Li, "Simplied Adaptive Spatial Modulation for Limited-Feedback MIMO Systems " *IEEE Signal Processing Magazine*, May 2007, pp. 69-78.

[33] P. Xia, S. Zhou, and G. B. Giannakis, "Multiantenna Adaptive Modulation With Beamforming Based on Bandwidth Constrained Feedback" *IEEE Transactions on Communications* vol. 53, no. 3, March 2005

[34] Z. Bouida, A. Ghrayeb, and K. A. Qaraqe "Adaptive Spatial Modulation for Spectrum Sharing Systems With Limited Feedback" *IEEE Transactions on Communications*, vol. 63, No. 6, June 2015

[35] Z. Bouida, A. Ghrayeb, and K. A. Qaraqe "Joint Adaptive Spatial Modulation and Power Adaptation for Spectrum Sharing Systems with Limited feedback" *IEEE Wireless Communications and Networking Conference (WCNC 2015)*

[36] R. Samano Robles, E. Lavendelis, and E. Tovar "Performance Analysis of MRC Receivers with Adaptive Modulation and Coding in Rayleigh Fading Correlated Channels with Imperfect CSIT" *Wireless Communications and Mobile Computing*, Volume 2017 (2017), Article ID 6940368,.

[37] http://mathworld.wolfram.com/OrderStatistic.html

[38] J. Proakis, *Digital Communications*, McGraw-Hill, 4th edition 2001.

[39] WiMAX Forum Standard,"*WiMAX system level evaluation methodology, V.0.0.1*," 2006.

APPENDIX

Derivation of order statistics of estimated SNR in (2)

Using the multinomial theorem, it is possible to obtain a formula for the term $F_{\hat{X}}(y)^{J-1}$ considering the expression in (11):

$$F_{\hat{X}}(y)^{J-1} = \sum_{l_0,l_1,\ldots l_N=J-1} \begin{pmatrix} J-1 \\ \mathbf{l} \end{pmatrix} (-A)^{l_{N-1}} e^{-\frac{l_{N-1}y}{\bar{\gamma}}}$$

$$\prod_{t=0}^{N-2} \left(e^{-y\bar{\gamma}} \frac{y^t}{\bar{\gamma}^t t!} \sum_{u=1}^{N-1-t} -B_u \right)^{l_t}$$

where l_t is the exponent index of the t-th element of the multinomial expression$(x_0 + x_1 + x_2 + x_t + x_N)^{J-1}$, considering that $x_t = e^{-y\bar{\gamma}} \frac{y^t}{\bar{\gamma}^t t!} \sum_{u=1}^{N-1-t} -B_u$, $0 \leq t \leq N-2$, $x_{N-1} = -Ae^{-\frac{y}{\bar{\gamma}}}$, $x_N = 1$. The previous expression can be reorganized as follows:

$$F_{\hat{X}}(y)^{J-1} = \sum_{l_0+l_1+l_N=J-1} \begin{pmatrix} J-1 \\ \mathbf{l} \end{pmatrix} (-A)^{l_N}$$

$$e^{-y\left(\frac{\sum_{t=0}^{N-2} l_t}{\bar{\gamma}} + \frac{l_{N-1}}{\bar{\gamma}}\right)} \left(\frac{y}{\bar{\gamma}}\right)^{\sum_{t=0}^{N-2} t l_t} \prod_{t=0}^{N-2} \left(\sum_{u=1}^{N-1-t} -\frac{B_u}{t!} \right)^{l_t}$$

By substituting the previous expression back in (12) we then obtain:

$$f_{\hat{X}^*}(y) = J \sum_{l_0+l_1+l_N=J-1} \begin{pmatrix} J-1 \\ \mathbf{l} \end{pmatrix} (-A)^{l_{N-1}}$$

$$e^{-y\left(\frac{\sum_{t=0}^{N-2} l_t}{\bar{\gamma}} + \frac{l_{N-1}}{\bar{\gamma}}\right)} \left(\frac{y}{\bar{\gamma}}\right)^{\sum_{t=0}^{N-2} t l_t} \prod_{t=0}^{N-2} \left(\frac{1}{t!} \sum_{u=1}^{N-1-t} -B_u \right)^{l_t}$$

$$\left(\frac{A}{\bar{\gamma}} e^{-\frac{y}{\bar{\gamma}}} + e^{-\frac{y}{\bar{\gamma}}} \sum_{n=1}^{N-1} \frac{B_n y^{n-1})}{\bar{\gamma}^n (n-1)!} \right),$$

which can be rewritten as follows

$$f_{\hat{X}^*}(y) = \sum_{l_0+l_1+l_N=J-1} \alpha_{\mathbf{l}} e^{-y\left(\frac{\sum_{t=0}^{N-2} l_t}{\bar{\gamma}} + \frac{l_{N-1}}{\bar{\gamma}}\right)} \left(\frac{y}{\bar{\gamma}}\right)^{\sum_{t=0}^{N-2} t l_t}$$

$$\left(\frac{A}{\bar{\gamma}} e^{-\frac{y}{\bar{\gamma}}} + e^{-\frac{y}{\bar{\gamma}}} \sum_{n=1}^{N-1} \frac{B_n y^{n-1})}{\bar{\gamma}^n (n-1)!} \right)$$

where $\alpha_{\mathbf{l}} = J \begin{pmatrix} J-1 \\ \mathbf{l} \end{pmatrix} (-A)^{l_N} \prod_{t=0}^{N-2} (\sum_{u=1}^{N-1-t} -\frac{B_u}{t!})^{l_t}$. A further modification of this expression leads to:

$$f_{\hat{X}}^*(y) = \sum_{\mathbf{l};l_0+l_1+l_N=J-1} \tilde{\alpha}_{\mathbf{l}} e^{-y\left(\frac{\sum_{t=0}^{N-2} l_t}{\bar{\gamma}} + \frac{l_{N-1}+1}{\bar{\gamma}}\right)} y^{\sum_{t=0}^{N-2} t l_t}$$

$$+ \sum_{\mathbf{l};l_0+l_1+l_N=J-1} \alpha_{\mathbf{l}} e^{-y\left(\frac{1+\sum_{t=0}^{N-2} l_t}{\bar{\gamma}} + \frac{l_{N-1}}{\bar{\gamma}}\right)}$$

$$\sum_{n=1}^{N-1} \frac{B_n y^{n-1+\sum_{t=0}^{N-2} t l_t}}{\bar{\gamma}^{n+\sum_{t=0}^{N-2} t l_t} (n-1)!}$$

where $\tilde{\alpha}_{\mathbf{l}} = \alpha_l \frac{A}{\bar{\gamma}\bar{\gamma}^{\sum_{t=0}^{N-2} t l_t}}$. This can be rewritten as the intended expression in (13), which finalizes the derivation.

Stability and Delay of Network-Diversity Multiple Access with Backlog Retransmission Control

Ramiro Sámano-Robles

Research Centre in Real-time and Embedded Computing Systems
Intituto Politécnico do Porto, Porto, Portugal
Email: rasro@isep.ipp.pt

***Abstract*—This paper proposes two strategies for retransmission control of backlog traffic in the family of algorithms known as Network Diversity Multiple Access (NDMA). This type of algorithm has been shown to achieve (in ideal conditions) the following aspects: 1) collision-free performance for contention-based traffic, 2) low latency values, and 3) reduced feedback complexity. These features match the machine-type traffic, real-time, and dense object connectivity requirements in 5G. This makes NDMA a candidate for contention traffic support in 5G systems. However, existing analysis ignores the effects of backlog traffic generated by the imperfect detection conditions that arise in settings with finite Signal-to-Noise Ratio (SNR). This paper aims to partially fill this gap, by providing analytic expressions for the performance of symmetrical training-based NDMA protocols with two different types of backlog traffic retransmission schemes. In the first strategy, all terminals involved in an unsuccessful resolution period retransmit immediately in the subsequent resolution periods or epoch slots. This procedure is repeated continuously (*persistent retransmission*) by inducing the same collision event under different channel outcomes until all the contending signals are correctly detected and received. In the second retransmission strategy, the terminals in backlog state retransmit at a randomly selected time-slot with a probability that that is assumed (for simplicity) to match the transmission rate of the system. In both strategies, expressions are here obtained of the maximum stable throughput and the average delay experienced by any packet to be correctly received by the destination. This allows us to determine the capabilities of NDMA for achieving low-latency, reduced feedback complexity, as well as highly stable and real-time throughout performance. The results shown here suggest that NDMA can achieve attractive low latency and high throughput figures mainly at high SNR values and moderate traffic loads.**

Keywords–Multiple Access in 5G; Retransmission Diversity; Signal Processing; Multi-User Detection; Cross-layer Design; Random Access; Multi-Packet Reception.

I. Introduction

Some of the main requirements in future 5G systems are the following: 1) low latency for real-time and machine-type communications, 2) increased spectral efficiency and throughput performance for broadband high speed and industrial applications, and 3) reduced signalling load and feedback complexity to cope with the large number of objects and terminals that will be competing for access to network resources. Network Diversity Multiple Access or NDMA is the family of signal-processing-based random access algorithms originally proposed in [1] that represent a good candidate to achieve the main goals of contention-based access in 5G networks. In NDMA, adaptive retransmissions are used to resolve collisions of variable size. For example, if a collision of K terminals occurs, then the system attempts to induce enough diversity via retransmissions to create K or more degrees of freedom. These degrees of freedom or sources of diversity will allow the system to recover the signals of the colliding terminals via multi-user detection tools. NDMA is the perfect example of cross-layer interactions: PHY (PHYsical) layer diversity is created explicitly by retransmissions induced by MAC (Medium Access Control) layer processes.

Training-based NDMA protocols have been proposed in [1] and [2] for non-dispersive and dispersive channels, respectively. Blind versions based on rotational invariance techniques and Independent Component Analysis (ICA) were proposed in [3] and [4], respectively. More recently, a combination of NDMA, Multi-Packet Reception (MPR) and Successive Interference Cancellation (SIC) was shown in [7] to potentially break the barrier of M packets per time-slot, where M is the number of antennas at the receiver. This is the highest throughput potentially found in random access theory. Performance of NDMA combined with Automatic Repeat reQuest (ARQ) has been investigated in [8]. NDMA is expected to be an attractive solution for future 5G systems, mainly because it achieves (in ideal conditions) an almost collision-free throughput performance with low values of latency or access delay and reduced signalling feedback complexity.

There are several open issues that need to be solved in the design of NDMA systems, particularly related to stability. Stability of asymmetrical NDMA systems under perfect detection and reception conditions using the Foster-Lyapunov criterion and the Loynes' theorem were presented in [5]. Stability of symmetrical NDMA protocols with finite SNR using a Markov model for backlog states of the system was presented in [6]. *Stability* is loosely defined here as the ability of a network to deal with the traffic requests of all the terminals within a finite period of time. Stability is often more important but also more difficult to investigate than throughput or delay. Exact stability boundaries of NDMA in the case of imperfect collision multiplicity estimation have not yet been obtained in the literature.

This paper attempts to partially fill this gap, by obtaining more accurate predictions of the stable throughput of conventional NDMA systems considering backlog traffic with two different types of retransmission strategy. In the first strategy, also called *persistent retransmission strategy*, the backlogged terminals immediately engage in a new resolution period in an attempt to correctly decode the colliding packets. This procedure is repeated until the conflict has been successfully resolved. In the second retransmission strategy, backlogged terminals retransmit *randomly* in future time slots assuming, for convenience, a retransmission probability that exactly matches the transmission rate of the system. For both cases, the stability condition is evaluated by means of a balance traffic equation which is the result of a particular application of Loynes' theorem of stability in queuing systems. Delay is evaluated by means of the M/G/1 queue analytical framework, which is commonly used in the literature of NDMA to estimate average delay. The results show that NDMA is capable to surpass by a significant margin its ALOHA counterparts, and when the SNR is high enough and with moderate traffic loads, low latency values and high throughput performance could be attractive for future 5G networks.

The organisation of this paper is as follows. Section II presents the system assumptions and definitions. Section III presents the details of the first retransmission strategy (also called here persistent retransmission strategy) where backlogged terminals continuously retransmit information until the BS correctly resolves the collision. Section IV details the random retransmission strategy. Results of the retransmission schemes are displayed and discussed in Section V. The conclusions of the paper are then presented in Section VI.

Notation: $E[\cdot]$ is the statistical average operator, $E[x|y]$ is the average of random variable x conditional on a particular instance of random variable y, $E_x[\cdot]$ is the statistical average operation over the probability space of random variable x, $\bar{(\cdot)} = 1 - (\cdot)$ is the complement to one operator, $\begin{pmatrix} N_1 \\ N_2 \end{pmatrix} = \frac{N_1!}{(N1-N_2)!N_2!}$ is the combinatorial number of N_1 elements (objects) in N_2 positions.

II. System Model and Assumptions

This section deals with the system model and the assumptions used throughout the paper. The subsections are organised as follows: Subsection II-A describes the scenario and the steps of the original NDMA protocol. Subsection II-B describes the backlog retransmission strategies. Subsection II-C defines the types of collision resolution periods or epoch-slots, and finally Subsection II-D provides illustrative examples of the two proposed retransmission strategies.

A. Scenario description and NDMA protocol operation

Consider the wireless random access network depicted in Figure 1 with one base station (BS) and J terminals. All network elements have only one antenna. Each terminal is assumed to have a buffer experiencing a packet arrival process with Poisson statistics described by the parameter λ. The transmission probability of any terminal at the beginning of any resolution period is denoted by p. All channels are considered non-dispersive, flat and block fading with Rayleigh statistics.

Whenever the terminals are allowed to transmit a packet, they do so at the beginning of a new collision resolution period or epoch-slot. At the beginning of every epoch slot, the BS proceeds to obtain an estimate of the identity of the contending terminals by means of signal processing tools (details can be found in [1]). Each terminal uses as packet header a unique orthogonal code previously assigned. The BS exploits this header using a matched filter receiver and energy detection processing to estimate the presence of each terminal in the collision event. Since this process is prone to errors due to fading and noise, the probability of detection conditional on the terminal having transmitted a packet in the current time-slot is given by P_D (probability of correct presence detection). On the other hand, the probability of presence detection conditional on the terminal not having engaged in transmission is given by P_F or probability of false alarm. In Rayleigh fading channels, it has been shown in [1] that the Receiver Operational Characteristic (ROC) of the terminal presence detector is given by $P_D = P_F^{\frac{1}{1+\gamma}}$, where γ is the average post-detection Signal-to-Noise Ratio (SNR).

SCHEME 1 — Superepoch; e=1, e=2, e=3, e=4

	e=1		e=2		e=3			e=4	
Contending terminals	1,3,8	1,3,8	1,3,8	1,3,8	1,3,8	1,3,8	1,3,8	1,7	1,7
Detected terminals	3,8	3,8	1,5	1,5	1,3,8	1,3,8	1,3,8	1,7	1,7
Feedback flag 1	1	0	1	0	1	1	0	1	0
Feedback flag 2		0		0			1		1

SCHEME 2 — Superepoch for terminal 1; e=1, e=2, e=3, e=4

	e=1		e=2		e=3			e=4	
Contending terminals	1,3,8	1,3,8	1,7	1,7	5,3	5,3	5,3,8	9,6	9,6
Detected terminals	3,8	3,8	1,7	1,7	5,3,8	5,3,8	5,3,8		
Feedback flag 1	1	0	1	0	1	1	0	1	0
Feedback flag 2		0		1			0		1

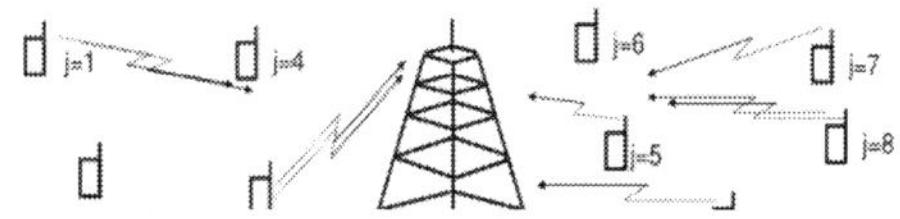

Figure 1. NDMA operation with the two backlog retransmission algorithms. Scheme 1 is also called persistent retransmission scheme. Scheme 2 is also called random retransmission scheme

The detection of the presence of the different active terminals provides the BS with an estimation of the collision size. Based on this information, the BS proceeds to request retransmissions from the contending terminals so as to construct a virtual Multiple-Input Multiple-Output (MIMO) system with the convenient rank conditions that will ensure that the collision can be resolved via multi-user detection.

B. Backlog retransmission schemes

In NDMA, it is conventionally assumed that any detection error at the BS side yields the loss of all packets involved in the collision. Conversely, the collision is successfully resolved only when all the terminals are correctly detected (both active and idle terminals). This paper proposes two backlog retransmission schemes to deal with the packets that were involved in an unsuccessful resolution period or epoch-slot. The first scheme (also called *persistent*) allows the contending terminals to engage immediately in a new resolution period. The BS indicates to the terminals that the previous resolution process did not succeed, and therefore the same contending terminals are induced to collide again at the beginning of the new resolution period. This procedure is repeated until all the packets involved in the collision are correctly decoded by the destination. In the second retransmission strategy, the backlogged terminal retransmits randomly in a future epoch slot with probability p, which is exactly the same probability as the overall system attempt rate. This scheme is also called *random retransmission scheme*.

C. Epoch-slot definition and feedback model

The collision multiplicity at the beginning of any epoch slot will be denoted by the random variable K. The length of a simple collision resolution period will be denoted by the random variable l. The period of time used for a packet to be correctly decoded by the destination will be denoted by L, and it will also be called *super-epoch*. Two types of epoch and super-epoch are further defined: *relevant*, where a particular terminal under analysis is always present, and *irrelevant*, where such incumbent terminal is idle.

The BS has two feedback flags that are considered to be ideal and instantaneous. One flag is used to indicate to the colliding terminals that retransmission is needed in the next time slot for purposes of diversity. The second feedback flag occurs at the end of a collision resolution period and indicates whether the epoch was successful or not. Based on this information, the colliding terminals decide to enter in one of the backlog retransmission schemes presented in this paper.

D. Examples

To further illustrate the proposed algorithms, Figure 1 shows the realization of the two retransmission strategies over 4 epoch-slots. In the first epoch ($e = 1$) of scheme 1, three terminals collide at the beginning of the epoch slot ($\{1,3,8\}$). However, only two of them were detected correctly as active ($\{3,8\}$). The system has requested only one more retransmission when indeed it was necessary to collect two more retransmissions to resolve the collision. This means this epoch $e = 1$ is unsuccessful. The terminals are now in backlog state and retransmit immediately in the next resolution period. Once again, the detection process was incorrect, by miss-detecting two of the contending terminals ($\{3,8\}$) and estimating one of the idle terminals ($\{5\}$) as active (false alarm). The backlogged terminals proceed then to retransmit again in a third consecutive epoch slot ($e = 3$). This time all terminals were correctly detected and the collision is conveniently resolved. The fourth epoch ($e = 4$) allows new terminals to transmit, and it can be observed that this case was a successful epoch. Note that the first collision took three epoch slots to be correctly resolved with total length of $L = 7$. This set of epoch slots that a collision experiences to be resolved is called *super epoch*.

In the second retransmission strategy, the three contending terminals involved in the first resolution period ($\{1,3,8\}$) become backlogged. However, they start retransmission randomly over the next epoch slots. In the second epoch slot, terminal $j = 1$ retransmits the backlogged packet and this time the resolution is successful. By contrast, the third epoch sees terminal $j = 3$ to experience again an incorrect detection with one case of false alarm. The last epoch shows that two non-backlogged terminals experience a successful collision resolution. Note that the super-epoch for terminal $j = 1$ is given by the first and second resolution periods with a total length of $L = 4$.

III. Persistent Retransmission Strategy

In the first retransmission strategy, all the terminals involved in an incorrect resolution period are forced to retransmit immediately in the next resolution period(s). This process is repeated until the collision is correctly resolved. The steps of the persistent retransmission strategy are described in Algorithm 1. Stability will be investigated here by using a modified traffic balance equation. This equation has been used before in [5] for stability analysis of NDMA. The expression states the balance between the incoming and outgoing traffic in the NDMA system. It is a modification of the Loynes' theorem of stability in queuing systems, and it can be written, in our context, as follows:

$$p = \lambda E[L], \tag{1}$$

which states the balance between the transmission attempt rate p and the incoming traffic rate per super-epoch-slot. In conventional NDMA, correct resolution occurs when all terminals are correctly detected. This occurs when all K contending terminals have been correctly detected with probability P_D^K and all $J - K$ idle terminals are not incorrectly detected as active with probability $\bar{P}_F^{J-K}$, where $\bar{P}_F = 1 - P_F$.

Consider now a collision of K out of J terminals. The probability of correct resolution is equal to the joint probability of correct detection of all terminals (active and idle), which can be written as follows:

$$P_{c,K} = P_D^K \bar{P}_F^{J-K}. \tag{2}$$

To obtain the expression for the average length of a super epoch $E[L]$ we consider that the resolution of any collision of size K takes a random number of attempts described by a geometric distribution with parameter $\bar{P}_{c,K}$ from (2) and with average number of attempts given by $1/P_{c,K}$. Therefore the average length of a super epoch conditional on the collision size is given by:

$$E[L|K] = \frac{E[l|K]}{P_{c,K}},$$

where

$$E[l|K] = KP_D + (J-K)P_F + \bar{P}_D^K \bar{P}_F^{J-K}. \tag{3}$$

For details of the derivation of the previous expression please see the Appendix. Averaging over the probability space of all potential collision sizes we obtain:

$$E[L] = \sum_{K=1}^{J} \binom{J}{K} p^K \bar{p}^{J-K} \frac{E[l|K]}{P_{c,K}} \tag{4}$$

The access delay for NDMA is usually approximated by the formula of delay for an M/G/1 queue with vacations [1]:

$$D = E[L_r] + \frac{\lambda E[L_r^2]}{2(1-\lambda E[L_r])} + \frac{E[L_{ir}^2]}{2E[L_{ir}]}, \tag{5}$$

where, $E[L_r]$, $E[L_{ir}]$, $E[L_r^2]$, and $E[L_{ir}^2]$ denote, respectively, the first- and second-order moments of the length of a relevant and irrelevant super-epochs. For the particular case of the persistent retransmission scheme we obtain the following:

$$E[L_r] = \sum_{K=1}^{J} \binom{J}{K} p^{K-1} \bar{p}^{J-K} \frac{E[l|K]}{P_{c,K}} \tag{6}$$

and

$$E[L_{ir}] = \sum_{K=1}^{J-1} \binom{J-1}{K} p^K \bar{p}^{J-1-K} \frac{E[l|K]}{P_{c,K}} \tag{7}$$

The second order moments of the two types of super-epoch are given by

$$E[L_r^2] = \sum_{K=1}^{J} \binom{J}{K} p^{K-1} \bar{p}^{J-K} E[l^2|K] \frac{2-P_{c,K}}{P_{c,K}^2} \tag{8}$$

and

$$E[L_{ir}^2] = \sum_{K=1}^{J-1} \binom{J-1}{K} p^K \bar{p}^{J-1-K} E[l^2|K] \frac{2-P_{c,K}}{P_{c,K}^2} \quad (9)$$

where

$$E[l^2|K] = KP_D(KP_D + \bar{P}_D) + (J-K)P_F[(J-K)P_F + \bar{P}_F] + 2KP_D(J-K)P_F + \bar{P}_D^K \bar{P}_F^{J-K} \quad (10)$$

For details of the derivation of this last expression please see the Appendix.

1) Generate set of colliding terminals using traffic model.
2) Start super-epoch slot.
3) Start of a conventional epoch-slot of NDMA
4) Detect the presence of contenting terminals
5) Request retransmissions to create a virtual MIMO system
6) Attempt the decoding of the colliding terminals
7) Is the collision resolved? If Yes, then end of a super-epoch and go back to step 1. If not, the same contending terminals restart one more epoch slot. Go back to step 3.

Algorithm 1: Algorithm NDMA with persistent backlog retransmission control.

IV. Random Backlog retransmission strategy

In the second retransmission strategy, backlogged terminals use a random retransmission scheme with a probability that is forced to match the transmission probability of the system p. This assumption simplifies the derivation of metrics in the system. In the case of different selection of retransmission probability, it is necessary to use a Markov chain model of the system and a two-state model for each terminal in the network (see [6]). Terminals involved in a collision with an unsuccessful first epoch will retransmit at different time slots randomly selected. The steps of the random retransmission scheme are enumerated in Algorithm 2. To investigate this scheme, we will use a modified traffic balance equation written as follows:

$$p = \lambda E[L] = \lambda(pE[L_r] + \bar{p}E[l_{ir}]), \quad (11)$$

where L_r and l_{ir} indicate, respectively, the length of a relevant super-epoch and irrelevant epochs. It is called relevant because it denotes the super-epoch where a given terminal is involved in transmission. In the random retransmission strategy, the average number of attempts is dictated by the probability of success resolution, denoted here by P_c and given by:

$$P_c = P_D(pP_D + \bar{p}\bar{P}_F)^{J-1}$$

The number of attempts has therefore a geometric distribution with parameter $\bar{P}_c$ and with average given by $\frac{\bar{P}_c}{P_c}$. Now, since the retransmission attempt is randomized, there is a number of resolution periods ignored by the backlogged terminal. Another geometric distribution of this inter attempt process is modelled with parameter $\bar{p}$ and average given by $\frac{\bar{p}}{p}$. The final expression is thus given by:

$$E[L_r] = \frac{\bar{P}_c}{P_c}\left(\frac{\bar{p}}{p}E[l_{ir}] + E[l_r]\right) + E[l_r],$$

where the average length of a relevant and an irrelevant epoch can be written, respectively, as follows:

$$E[l_r] = (J-1)P_A + P_D + \bar{P}_D\bar{P}_A^{J-1} \quad (12)$$

and

$$E[l_{ir}] = (J-1)P_A + P_F + \bar{P}_F\bar{P}_A^{J-1}. \quad (13)$$

For details of the derivation of these previous two expressions we refer the reader to the Appendix. The average delay for NDMA is usually approximated by the formula of delay an M/G/1 queue with vacations [1]:

$$D = E[L_r] + \frac{\lambda E[L_r^2]}{2(1-\lambda E[L_r])} + \frac{E[L_{ir}^2]}{2E[L_{ir}]}, \quad (14)$$

where using the properties of binomial and geometric probability distributions we can obtain:

$$E[L_r^2] = \frac{E[l_r^2]}{P_c^2 p_r^2} \quad (15)$$

$$E[l_r^2] = (J-1)P_A[\bar{P}_A + (J-1)P_A] + 2(J-1)P_AP_D + P_D + \bar{P}_D\bar{P}_A^{J-1} \quad (16)$$

and

$$E[L_{ir}^2] = (J-1)P_A[\bar{P}_A + (J-1)P_A] + 2(J-1)P_AP_F + \bar{P}_F\bar{P}_A^{J-1} \quad (17)$$

For details of the derivations of these expressions we refer the reader to the Appendix.

1) Generate set of colliding terminals using traffic model.
2) Start of a conventional epoch-slot of NDMA
3) Detect the presence of contenting terminals
4) Request retransmissions to create a virtual MIMO system
5) Attempt the decoding of the colliding terminals
6) Is the collision resolved? If Yes, then go back to step 1. If not, terminals backlog randomly the lost packet with probability p. Go back to step 3.

Algorithm 2: Algorithm NDMA with random backlog retransmission control.

V. Results

The results discussed in this section have been obtained with a network configuration with $J = 16$ terminals with an average SNR γ of 7, 10, and 15 dB. The detection threshold has been adjusted to obtain a probability of false alarm of $P_F = 0.01$. Figure 2 shows the stable throughput $T = J\lambda$ versus different traffic load values. Figure 3 shows the delay experienced by the two retransmission schemes. It can be observed that the persistent retransmission scheme only slightly outperforms the random retransmission strategy, particularly at low SNR. Both strategies seem to be able to achieve the maximum throughput previously estimated in [1] for the conventional version of the protocol without backlog traffic. This is a significant result that paves the way for further analysis about the equivalence of stability and throughout metrics of the protocol.

It is worth pointing out that the main virtues of the random retransmission strategy cannot be fully observed in the figures provided here. The random strategy will be optimum in networks affected by deep and long fades, or with terminals with long term degrading channel conditions. Therefore, the reader should keep in mind that random retransmission will play an important role in particular network situations. Future networks are meant to be more adaptive and cognitive to network and channel conditions, and therefore it is expected that different backlog retransmission strategies can be adopted on the fly to maximize performance. Another aspect to point out is that in comparison with ALOHA solutions, NDMA protocols are capable to adopt persistent retransmission strategies, which in ALOHA is practically impossible. Once a collision event occurs in ALOHA, terminals must engage in random backlog retransmission algorithms, mainly because the repetition of the same collision event (used in persistent retransmission schemes) leads inevitably to unstable performance. This is another proof that NDMA is considerably better in terms of stability than its ALOHA counterparts.

Regarding delay in Figure 4, both algorithms seem to achieve the same performance. Delay is degraded as traffic load reaches the maximum channel transmission rate. The values of delay suggest that NDMA has good performance for real time systems only at moderate traffic loads and at relatively high values of SNR. To further illustrate the difference between the conventional NDMA and the proposed retransmission algorithms, Figure 4 shows the average length of the super epochs of the two algorithms. It can be observed that the super-epochs clearly are larger by several orders of magnitude than the conventional NDMA, which is consequence of the retransmission schemes. However, the reader must remember that the original protocol ignores the effects of backlog traffic, whereas in the present approach we estimate the effects of backlog traffic by inducing further retransmissions so that we can evaluate the performance of the algorithm in such conditions. Note that at high SNR the retransmission schemes are closer in performance to the average length of the epoch in the conventional NDMA protocol.

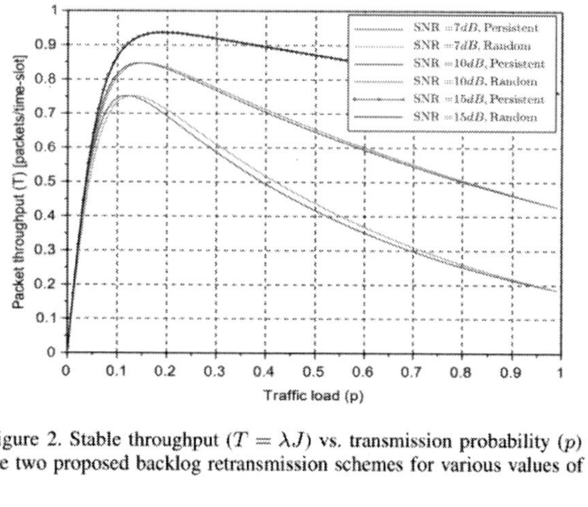

Figure 2. Stable throughput ($T = \lambda J$) vs. transmission probability (p) using the two proposed backlog retransmission schemes for various values of SNR.

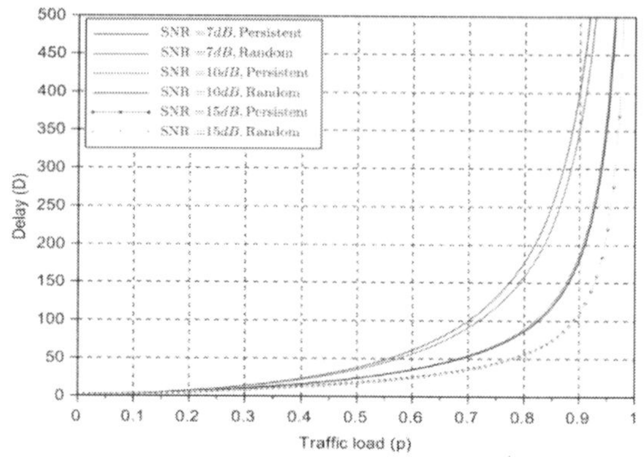

Figure 3. Average Delay (D) vs. transmission probability (p) using the two proposed backlog retransmission schemes for various values of SNR.

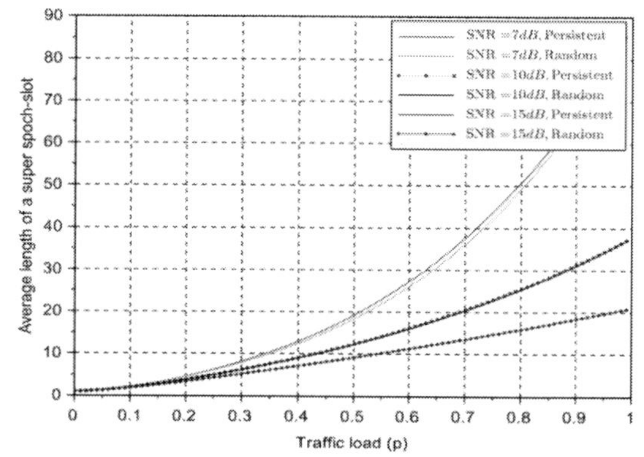

Figure 4. Average length of a super-epoch ($E[L]$) vs. transmission probability (p) using the two proposed backlog retransmission schemes for various values of SNR.

VI. CONCLUSIONS

This paper has presented two retransmission schemes of backlog traffic for the conventional NDMA protocol in Rayleigh block fading and non-dispersive channels. It has been observed that under these assumptions the persistent retransmission strategy, where terminals involved in an unsuccessful resolution keep retransmitting until the collision is resolved, provides the best results achieving an almost identical value as the throughput without backlog traffic consideration. However, the random retransmission strategy with a retransmission probability equal to the system transmission rate performs almost identically, but it has the further advantage of being suitable for scenarios with deep and long-term fades or with terminals with persistent bad channels conditions. The results show that NDMA considerably outperforms stability of ALOHA solutions. It has been also shown that for high SNR values, the persistent retransmission scheme boils down to the conventional NDMA solution. The importance of the results in this paper is that NDMA shows great potential for handling future low-latency traffic, particularly at high values of SNR and moderate traffic loads. Additionally, we have obtained for the first time a figure of the performance of NDMA with backlog traffic, thus helping in the evaluation of the stability properties of this type of protocol.

ACKNOWLEDGMENTS

This work has received funding from project SCOTT (www.scottproject.eu) within the Electronic Component Systems for European Leadership Joint Undertaking under grant agreement No 737422. This Joint Undertaking receives support from the European Unions Horizon 2020 research and innovation programme and Austria, Spain, Finland, Ireland, Sweden, Germany, Poland, Portugal, Netherlands, Belgium, Norway. Funded also by FCT/MEC (Fundacão para a Ciência e a Tecnologia), ERDF (European Regional Development Fund) under PT2020, and by CISTER Research Unit (CEC/04234) .

REFERENCES

[1] M. K. Tsatsanis, R. Zhang, and S. Banerjee, "Network-Assisted Diversity for Random Access Wireless Networks," *IEEE Trans. on Sig. Proc.*, Vol. 48, No. 3, March 2000, pp. 702-711.

[2] M. K. Tsatsanis, R. Zhang, and S. Banerjee, "Network-Assisted Diversity for Random Access systems in dispersive channels," *IEEE Trans. on Commun.*, Vol. 50, No. 4, 2002, pp. 623-632.

[3] R. Zhang, N. D. Sidiropoulos, and M. K. Tsatsanis, "Collision resolution in packet radio networks using rotational invariance techniques," *IEEE Trans. on Commun.*, Vol. 50, No. 1, 2002, pp. 146-155.

[4] B. Ozgul and H. Delic, "Wireless access with blind collision-multiplicity detection and retransmission diversity for quasi-static channels," *IEEE Trans. on Commun.*, Vol. 54, No. 5, 2006, pp. 858-867.

[5] G. Dimic, N. D. Sidiropoulos, and L. Tassiulas, "Wireless networks with retransmission diversity access mechanisms: stable throughput and delay properties," *IEEE Trans. on Signal Processing*, Vol. 51, No. 8, 2003, pp. 2019-2030.

[6] R. Samano-Robles and A. Gameiro "Stability properties of network diversity multiple access protocols with multiple antenna reception and imperfect collision multiplicity estimation," *Journal of Computer Networks and Communications*, Vol. 2013, No. 984956, pp. 1 - 10, December, 2013.

[7] R. Samano-Robles, D. C. McLernon, and M. Ghogho "A Random Access Protocol incorporating Retransmission Diversity, Multipacket Reception, and Successive Interference Cancellation," *Workshop on multiple access communications MACOM*, Helsinki, Finland, pp. 70-86, September 2015

[8] F. Ganhao, et al., "Performance Analysis of an Hybrid ARQ Adaptation of NDMA Schemes," *IEEE Transactions on Communications*, Vol. 61, no. 8, pp. 3304-3317, August 2013

APPENDIX

A. Derivation of the first- and second-order moments of the length of an epoch-slot in (3) and (10), respectively, conditional on the number of contending terminals K in the first retransmission scheme (persistent retransmission)

The length of an epoch in NDMA can be regarded as the linear combination of the contribution of the following terms: 1) active terminals correctly detected, 2) idle terminals incorrectly considered as active (due to false alarm), and 3) the contribution of only one time slot when no terminal is detected (either active or idle). The first contribution of active terminals conditional on K contending terminals has a binomial distribution with parameter P_D. Using the properties of the binomial distribution, this component has an average given by KP_D and a variance given by $KP_D(KP_D + \bar{P}_D)$. Similarly, the contribution of the remaining $J - K$ terminals has also binomial distribution with parameter P_F, average $(J-K)P_F$ and variance $(J-K)P_F[(J-K)P_F + \bar{P}_F]$. Finally, the probability that no terminals is detected as active is given by $\bar{P}_D{}^K \bar{P}_F^{J-K}$ with one time slot contribution to the average and the variance of the length of the epoch slot. The expressions for the first order moment is given by the combination of the average lengths:

$$E[l|K] = KP_D + (J-K)P_F + \bar{P}_D{}^K \bar{P}_F^{J-K},$$

while the variance is given by the second-order combination of the three components:

$$E[l^2|K] = KP_D(KP_D+\bar{P}_D)+(J-K)P_F[(J-K)P_F+\bar{P}_F]$$
$$+2KP_D(J-K)P_F + \bar{P}_D^K \bar{P}_F^{J-K}$$

B. Derivation of the first- and second-order moments in (12) and (16), respectively of the length of a relevant epoch-slot in the second retransmission scheme

A relevant epoch is defined as the resolution period where a particular terminal under study is assumed to be always present in the collision event. Since the detection of a persistent terminal has two detection cases, the derivation of the average length of a relevant epoch is split into two cases: when the persistent terminal is correctly detected with probability P_D, and when the terminal is incorrectly detected with probability $\bar{P}_D = 1 - P_D$. When the persistent terminal is correctly detected ($j \in \hat{\mathcal{T}}_d \cap \mathcal{T}$, where $\mathcal{T}$ is the set of colliding terminals and $\mathcal{T}_d$ is the set of terminals detected as active), the Probability Mass Function (PMF) of the length of an epoch is given by a modified binomial distribution with parameter P_A considering one terminal j is always present in the collision set and is always correctly detected:

$$\Pr\{l = m | j \in \hat{\mathcal{T}}_d \cap \mathcal{T}\}$$
$$= \begin{cases} 0, & m = 0 \\ \begin{pmatrix} J-1 \\ m-1 \end{pmatrix} P_A^{m-1} \bar{P}_A^{J-m+1} & 0 < m \leq J \end{cases},$$

and in the case the persistent terminal is not detected as active ($j \notin \hat{\mathcal{T}}_d; j \in \mathcal{T}$) we obtain:

$$\Pr\{l = m | j \notin \hat{\mathcal{T}}_d; j \in \mathcal{T}\} =$$
$$= \begin{pmatrix} J-1 \\ m \end{pmatrix} P_A^m \bar{P}_A^{J-m}, \quad m = 0, \ldots J-1.$$

The unconditional average length of a relevant epoch is obtained by averaging over these previous two PMFs weighted by their probability of occurrence as follows:

$$E[l_r] = P_D E[l | j \in \hat{\mathcal{T}}_d \cap \mathcal{T}] + \bar{P}_D E[l | j \notin \hat{\mathcal{T}}_d; j \in \mathcal{T}],$$

which can be proved, using the properties of binomial distributions, to lead to:

$$E[l_r] = P_D[(J-1)P_A + 1] + \bar{P}_D[(J-1)P_A + \bar{P}_A^{J-1}],$$

which after some algebraic operations yields the desired expression in (12). Similarly the second order moment can be computed as follows:

$$E[l_r^2] = P_D E[l^2 | j \in \hat{\mathcal{T}}_d \cap \mathcal{T}] + \bar{P}_D E[l^2 | j \notin \hat{\mathcal{T}}_d; j \in \mathcal{T}],$$

which yields:

$$E[l_r^2] = P_D\{(J-1)P_A[\bar{P}_A + (J-1)P_A] + 2(J-1)P_A + 1\} +$$
$$\bar{P}_D\{(J-1)P_A[\bar{P}_A + (J-1)P_A] + \bar{P}_A^{J-1}]\},$$

which after some algebraic operations yields the desired expression in (16).

AUTHOR INDEX